Alexander McKenzie

Lectures on the history of the First Church in Cambridge

Alexander McKenzie

Lectures on the history of the First Church in Cambridge

ISBN/EAN: 9783337261825

Printed in Europe, USA, Canada, Australia, Japan

Cover: Foto ©ninafisch / pixelio.de

More available books at **www.hansebooks.com**

Meeting-House erected in 1870-72, with the Washington Elm.

LECTURES

ON

THE HISTORY

OF THE

FIRST CHURCH IN CAMBRIDGE.

BY

ALEXANDER McKENZIE,

PASTOR OF THE FIRST CHURCH IN CAMBRIDGE AND SHEPARD
CONGREGATIONAL SOCIETY.

BOSTON:
CONGREGATIONAL PUBLISHING SOCIETY.
1873.

UNIVERSITY PRESS: WELCH, BIGELOW, & CO.,
CAMBRIDGE.

PREFACE.

THE materials for these lectures have been found in part in various histories which treat of the different periods and events, and in part in the records of the church. I have freely introduced collateral matters whenever they explained the position or action of the church.

The first lecture was delivered December 18, 1870, and the last April 14, 1872. This will account for some repetitions which would have been out of place in an ordinary history.

I am indebted to Rev. John L. Sibley of the University Library for advance sheets of his Memoirs of the Graduates of Harvard College, and for advice from time to time. I wish also to acknowledge the continual encouragement I have received from my own parishioners, and especially from William A. Saunders, Esq., whose interest in our personal and local history has been of the greatest service to me. As this book is now to be given to the public, I desire to dedicate its pages to those who in their turn constitute the First Church in Cambridge and the Shepard Congregational Society.

ALEXANDER McKENZIE.

CAMBRIDGE, 1872.

FIRST CHURCH IN CAMBRIDGE.

LECTURE I.

"WE HAVE HEARD WITH OUR EARS, O GOD, OUR FATHERS HAVE TOLD US, WHAT WORK THOU DIDST IN THEIR DAYS, IN THE TIMES OF OLD." — Psalm xliv. 1.

IT is in the order of nature and Providence, that one generation shall praise the works of the Lord to another, and shall declare his mighty acts. He teaches men by men, using them to illustrate his character and will, to announce his purposes, to glorify his name. Holy men of God, speaking as they were moved by the Holy Ghost, have given much of their teaching to the world by relating the history of men and nations. Inasmuch as the Lord changes not, and men are of one blood, the story of any human life, whenever, wherever its course may have run, is instructive to those who shall hear it. Not those alone who have found mention in sacred history, but others, in every age of the world, can teach us out of their experience, and reveal to us the ways of God with man. If it be true in other lands that the fathers can instruct the children, and that the lives of the fathers deserve the devout study of the children, surely here, in a land sought out in the name of God, and consecrated to his service at the beginning, by men who for love of him and of his truth made themselves homes in the wilderness, and built up churches and schools and the institutions of free government, with his Word for their guide, his commandments for their statutes, his goodness for their comfort and strength, — surely here we must inquire concerning the former times, that we may know our place and duty, may preserve the memories and virtues of those into whose labors we have entered, may honor him who by his right hand and his arm and the light of his countenance gave them the land in possession, because he had a favor unto them.

We are following the Divine method when we trace out the history of this ancient church, remembering the days of old, considering the years of many generations, asking our fathers that they may show us, our elders that they may tell us. From the tale which they have written, which has remained after their hands have become still, we are able to tell again what work the Lord did in their days, and by what men he gave to us the inheritance for which we bless him. The fathers of our land, of our church, were Englishmen. The spirit which compelled them to abandon the land which had given them birth, and the church in which they had been reared, belonged to the manliness of England's better days. They wanted purity and liberty in state and church. Willing to submit to all rightful authority, they could not consent to a tyranny which was both grievous and perilous, to oppression which burdened the conscience and blighted the life. They asked for other things for themselves and their children. They asked in vain. Some went out from the national church to secure by themselves what they must have at any cost. Separation dates from 1567. Scorned, hunted, afflicted in many ways, these little bands of Separatists suffered, and kept the freedom and the faith. One of these new churches, founded after the Apostolic model in the year 1606, in the village of Scrooby, in Nottinghamshire, tarried for twelve years in Holland, then crossed the seas, and at Plymouth became the first church in New England; for nine years the only Protestant Church in the Western World, unless there were some remains of an ecclesiastical organization in the almost forsaken colony of Virginia. But many who were greatly discontented with the Church of England were not willing to become Separatists, but sought to find within its fold the freedom and purity they desired. These were the Puritans, as their enemies called them in derision. It became plain to many of these, at last, that the hope of reformation was vain, and that the liberty sought could only be found in another land. They turned their eyes westward. Colonization in New England was much discussed among the Puritans. A company known as the "Dorchester Adventurers" came over in 1624, and two years later settled down in Naumkeag. In 1629 a royal charter created a corporation under the name of the "Governor and Company of the Massachusetts Bay in New England." Under this charter the colony of Massachusetts conducted its affairs for fifty-five years. The charter said nothing of religious liberty. Great accessions were made to the settlement at Naumkeag, which was changed to Salem, and in this year (1629) the second church on these shores was organized. It is clear that these settlers at Salem had no intention of separating themselves from the English Church when they gave up their home. But the formation of a new church came about naturally, providentially. There was much sickness among the colonists, and Samuel Fuller, the Plymouth physician, was called to their aid. He was a deacon as well as a doctor, and, besides caring for the physical wants of the sick, gave the new-comers information concerning the church at Plymouth. His account of things in the older settlement was instructive to those who had heard a far different report of their Separatist neighbors. Governor Endicott of Salem wrote to Governor Bradford of Plymouth acknowledging his love and care in sending Dr. Fuller, and added, " I rejoice much that I am by him satisfied touching your judgment of the outward form of God's worship." The Salem colonists proceeded to organize a church. There were with them two nonconformist clergymen of the Church of England, both men eminent for virtue and learning, and these were chosen to the chief offices. Mr. Samuel Skelton was chosen pastor, and Mr. Francis Higginson, teacher. Mr. Higginson, at the request of his brethren, drew up a " Confession of Faith and Covenant." On a set day, with preaching and praying and fasting, thirty persons assented to the Declaration which had been prepared ; and, after thus constituting themselves a church, ordained their pastor and teacher with the laying on of hands. In their proceedings they sought the fellowship and counsel of the Plymouth church, which was represented by Governor Bradford and others, who were so long hindered by cross-winds that they came in too late for the earlier services of the day, but were in season to extend the right hand of fellowship, and to give to their brethren their blessing and good wishes. These Salem Puritans builded larger and better than they thought. Accused of being Separatists, the ministers replied, " that they did not separate from the

Church of England, nor from the ordinances of God there, but only from the corruptions and disorders there; and that they came away from the cumbersome prayers and ceremonies, and had suffered much from nonconformity in their native land, and therefore, being in a place where they might have their liberty, they neither could nor would use them, because they judged the imposition of these things to be sinful corruptions in the worship of God. The Governor and Council, and the generality of the people, did well approve of the ministers' answer."

But this was, in fact, separation from the English Church, and their other proceedings were independent of her usage and her authority. The ministers who had received Episcopal ordination were ordained by their own church to the particular care of that church. Elders and deacons were also chosen and ordained by the church.

This was building on the ancient foundation. These men had learned something in their days of trial at home, something in the study and meditation of their long voyage, with the Bible to teach them the ways of the primitive churches. In a new land, filled with a free spirit, glorying in the liberty wherewith they had been made free, encouraged by the example and counsel of the Pilgrims, it is not strange that they went back to the former simplicity, and built upon the foundation of apostles and prophets, with Jesus Christ himself for the chief corner-stone.

I have dwelt upon this procedure, because it was the first instance in which Puritans, not Separatists, formed a Congregational Church. Other churches followed in Charlestown, Dorchester, Boston, Roxbury, Lynn, Watertown. With Congregational churches at the basis of civil society, a Republican form of government for the State was inevitable. These earliest churches were a prophecy of the Nation. We come now to Cambridge. It was at first designed to build here a fortified town, and to make it the capital of the Province. The ground was laid out, the lines of the fortification drawn, the streets arranged at right angles. Some idea of the topography of the place may be derived from such names as Market Square, Creek Street, Water Street, Crooked Street, Spring Street, Long Street, Marsh Lane. Governor Winthrop set up the frame of a dwelling-house on the spot where he first pitched his tent. The Deputy-Governor, Dudley, completed a house and moved his family into it. Other gentlemen of high standing prepared to reside here. The place received the appropriate designation of Newtown.

As the relations with the Indians became more settled, it was thought that the neighboring peninsula offered superior advantages for the capital, and it was accordingly established in Boston. The removal of Winthrop's house to Boston greatly offended Dudley, and "the ministers, for an end of the difference, ordered that the governor should procure them a minister at Newtown, and contribute some toward his maintenance for a time," or else make Dudley a suitable recompense. It was in 1631 that the plan for Newtown was changed. There seems still to have remained some thought that this place might become the metropolis, and it received legislative patronage. In 1632 the Court of Assistants levied an assessment upon the several plantations "towards making a palisade about the new town." A writer who was here at this time thus describes the place: "This is one of the neatest and best-compacted towns in New England, having many fair structures, with many handsome contrived streets. The inhabitants, most of them, are very rich." In some of the earliest years the annual election of the governor and magistrates was held here, when the people assembled under an oak which stood upon the northerly side of our Common. In this year (1632) the town received a considerable addition to its numbers by the arrival of the Braintree Company, as it was called, better known to us as Mr. Hooker's Company. Thomas Hooker was a graduate and Fellow of Emmanuel College, Cambridge, England, where he displayed great ability and fidelity. After leaving college he preached with acceptance and success. In 1630 he was silenced for nonconformity, to the great regret of many of the clergy of the Established Church. He taught school for a time, having John Eliot, afterwards the apostle to the Indians, as an usher. It was while in the family of Hooker that Eliot was converted, and under his influence that he decided to devote himself to the Christian ministry. Besides being silenced, Hooker was put under bonds to appear before the High Commission Court. His bond was paid by a friend, and he remained for a short time in retirement, and then crossed to Holland, where he remained for three years. Meanwhile the emigration of the Puritans to this country was going forward, and many of Hooker's friends came over. There were about two hundred emigrants in one company. Many of these settled in Newtown, where they erected a meeting-house preparatory to the full establishment of the ordinances of religion. Having enjoyed Mr. Hooker's ministry in other days, they desired to have him accompany them, which he was unable to do. But returning to England,

and with great difficulty escaping from his enemies, in the midsummer of 1633 he sailed for New England, in company with John Cotton and Samuel Stone. A passage of six or seven weeks brought them to Boston. The voyage was enlivened with three sermons or expositions on almost every day; and also with the birth of a son to Mr. Cotton, who at his baptism was called Seaborn.

The people could hardly fail to play upon the names of the ministers, and liked to say, merrily, "that their three great necessities would now be supplied; for they had Cotton for their clothing, Hooker for their fishing, and Stone for their building."

A Church was organized at Newtown, and with fasting and prayer Mr. Hooker was chosen pastor, and Mr. Stone teacher. Both had received ordination in England, but were again ordained by their own church to the offices to which they were elected, in the presence of "neighbor ministers," who gave the right hand of fellowship. What their meeting-house was we are not told. In the year of its erection the first house of worship in Boston was built. That had mud walls and a thatched roof. Into that house came John Cotton from St. Botolph's Church in Boston, England, one of the most stately parish churches in the land, and able to contain five thousand people. It was a change, from the lofty cathedral tower to the low door of the New England meeting-house. It was more than balanced by the joy of preaching the gospel, a free man to free men. But to guard against fire, it had been ordered in the previous year that in Newtown no man should "build his chimney of wood, nor cover his house with thatch." It is probable, therefore, that the house here was of logs.

Many years after its erection a vote was passed in Town Meeting that the church should be repaired "with a 4 square roofe, and covered with shingle." This house stood on the west side of Water, now Dunster Street, a little south of Spring, now Mount Auburn Street. It is particularly recorded that the house had a bell upon it. It must have been a small, plain structure. The plainness of the early churches was in part a necessity, and in part an intentional departure from the architecture which had been left. The colonists built for use. They needed a house to meet in, and one which would answer this purpose made them quite content. They gave it a name which clearly explained its use, and called it the meeting-house. It was used for the general gathering of the people. In many cases it was furnished with means of defence against the Indians.

In a few months the people of Newtown complained that they were straitened for want of room. They asked of the General Court leave "to look out either for enlargement or removal," which was granted. At the next meeting they asked leave to remove to Connecticut. They said that there was not land enough, especially meadow, so that they could not maintain their ministers, nor receive more inhabitants. Mr. Hooker said that it was an error that towns were set so near together. By removing, as they proposed, they would get more room, and keep out other settlers from the place they should possess. It has been conjectured that there were certain personal jealousies between the leading men in Boston and Newtown, which made a separation desirable. But this cannot be proved. Strong objection to the removal was made, and the matter was found difficult of adjustment. After the excellent custom of the time, the whole Court agreed to lay the question before the Lord, and a Fast Day was kept in all the congregations. When the Court assembled again Mr. Cotton preached from Haggai ii. 4, upon the relations of the magistracy, the ministry, and the people. The fasting and preaching seemed to have a good effect, as the Newtown congregation "accepted of such enlargement as had formerly been offered them by Boston and Watertown, and so the fear of their removal to Connecticut was removed." But the result was only temporary; the desire to remove continued. At last leave was granted, and in the summer of 1636 Mr. Hooker's church and congregation, a hundred in number, with great difficulty made their journey of above a hundred miles, travelling by the compass, through a trackless wilderness, driving their cattle with them. Mrs. Hooker, being in feeble health, was carried in a horse-litter. The company formed a settlement in Connecticut, where some preparation had already been made, and called the place Hartford, after the birthplace of Mr. Stone. Mr. Hooker was at Newtown less than three years, but he distinguished himself as a preacher and counsellor, and was an efficient man in the affairs of both church and state. After his removal he was connected with many important movements through the New England colonies. He was one of the moderators of the Synod held at Cambridge in regard to Anne Hutchinson. He was invited to be a member of the Westminster Assembly of Divines which formed the famous Catechisms. He left at his death a goodly number of printed works. He died in 1647, at the age of sixty-one. Some one standing in tears by his bedside said, "Sir, you are going to receive the reward of all your labors." He replied, "Brother, I am going to receive mercy." John Cotton honored his memory with elegiac lines of which I give the first two stanzas:

> "To see three things was holy Austin's wish, —
> Rome in her flower, Christ Jesus in the flesh,
> And Paul i' the pulpit : lately men might see
> Two first, and more, in Hooker's ministry.
>
> "Zion in beauty is a fairer sight
> Than Rome in flower, with all her glory dight ;
> Yet Zion's beauty did most clearly shine
> In Hooker's rule and doctrine, both divine."

With this we come to our own church. There were those who had more recently come out from England who stood ready to purchase the meeting-house and dwelling-houses and other immovable property which Hooker's company desired to leave, and these things were accordingly transferred to them. It was not their design to remain here permanently, but here they stayed. Here their successors worship, even in this house. We must read again the story of their leader, whose name is preserved in connection with the church. I shall give you this story somewhat in detail because of its historical value, as showing the position of the Puritans at that time, and the causes which drove them across the seas. Thomas Shepard was more than a founder, for he shaped the beginnings of the church and gave it a character, a strength and beauty, which have endured, and shall stand through the long future. If we study the character of the man, or survey his works, we admire him, and give him praise for that he wrought out. I would that we all were familiar with his life and with his works. His written words should be in every house, that he may still teach in a perpetual pastorate. I have in my care, as his successor, a small book, some five inches long, which contains in his own handwriting the Biography and Diary of Thomas Shepard, and a few pecuniary accounts. He lives, therefore, in his own record of his life. An excellent Memoir of Shepard, with a brief but instructive account of the times in which he lived, was written by the late lamented pastor of this church, and is now in our Sabbath School Library.

The year 1605 was marked in England by the infamous plot to destroy the King and Parliament. On the 5th of November, the day when the plot was discovered, "and that very hour wherein the Parliament should have been blown up," there was born in Towcester, in Northamptonshire, a child who was named Thomas, after the doubting disciple, because the father thought his son would hardly believe that " ever any such wickedness should be attempted by men against so religious and good a Parliament." William Shepard, the father, was a prosperous grocer, a wise and prudent man, and "toward his latter end much blessed of God in his estate and in his soul." So earnest was he in his love of the truth, that he removed from a town where there was no good ministry, that he might be under the stirring preaching which the Puritans offered. The mother died when Thomas was about four years old, when the father married again. He died when the son was about ten years of age. The childhood of the boy was unpromising. He was sent when very young to his grandparents, where he was surrounded with ignorance, and much neglected. He was then sent to his uncle, who lived in " a little blind town," where he was more content, and learned the corrupting sports of the youth of that day. On his return home his stepmother treated him harshly, and his father sent him to a free school in Towcester, kept by a Welshman, who was exceedingly cruel towards him, so that the boy was wholly discouraged from desire of learning, and often wished he was a keeper of beasts instead of a schoolboy. But upon the death of his father he was taken by his brother, who agreed to bring him up for the use of his portion of £100, and who was faithful to his trust, being both father and mother to the orphan boy. He had prayed heartily for his father's life while he was sick, and promised to serve God better if his prayer should be granted. His religious impressions were therefore early. He came under the care of a better teacher, who gave him a desire to be a scholar, and at fourteen he was admitted a pensioner at Emmanuel College, though "very raw and young." He was studious in college, and became proud of his attainments. But he lived in neglect of God and private prayer. There were times when his heart was touched, but he resisted all good influences, and fell into bad company, and even became intoxicated once or twice. Shame and remorse followed his indulgence. The searching preaching of Dr. Preston, Master of the College, gave him knowledge of himself, and he determined to flee from the wrath to come and to lay hold upon eternal life. He found the way hard and long. Doubts and questionings assailed him. His struggle was severe and protracted. But he prevailed, and at last he found rest. "The Lord gave me a heart to receive Christ, with a naked hand even a naked Christ, and so he gave me peace." The God of his father and mother remembered the youth, and he was blessed according to their desire.

The covenant which parental faith had made and sealed brought its blessing to the favored child. He left college with a high reputation for scholarship, and with the usual honors of the University. He was undecided what to do next. In the religious condition of England, his way was much hedged up. He came for a time under the ministry of Thomas Hooker, which he found profitable. There was a plan in those days for supplying with preachers parts of the country which were without a proper ministry. The Puritans raised a fund for this purpose, and the men who were appointed were called Lecturers. They were not to remain in any place, upon this foundation, for more than three years. Thomas Shepard was appointed a Lecturer, and received Deacon's orders in the English Church, "sinfully," he afterwards thought. He was sent to the town of Earles-Colne, where, so far as he could find, there was but one man who had any godliness. But his earnest labors were widely blessed, especially to the chief house of the town, where he won to the Lord and to himself his steadfast friend Roger Harlakenden, whose mortal part now lies in yonder burying-ground. Then "Satan began to rage, and the commissaries, registers, and others to pursue him as thinking he was a nonconformable man, when for the most of that time he was not resolved either way." He stood on the original Puritan ground, loving the Established Church, reluctant to leave it, willing to conform to its rules and customs in many things, unwilling to conform in others. Being such a man as he was, and the temper of the rulers what it was, the result could hardly be other than separation, gradual at first, but complete at last. He was busy at this time with what seemed to him weightier matters than forms and ceremonies. "The course I took in my preaching was, first, to show the people their misery. Second, the remedy, Christ Jesus. Third, how they should walk answerable to his mercy being redeemed by Christ." He finished his three years, and remained about half a year longer, at the request and charge of the people, when Laud, Bishop of London, summoned him to answer for preaching in his diocese. The Bishop was in a rage, and "looked as though blood would have gushed out of his face, and did shake as if he had been haunted with an ague-fit." At the request of Shepard that he would excuse him, the Bishop railed upon him. "You prating coxcomb, do you think all the learning is in your brain?" At last the sentence came. "I charge you that you neither preach, read, marry, bury, or exercise any ministerial functions in any part of my diocese; for if you do, and I hear of it, I'll be upon your back and follow you wherever you go, in any part of this kingdom, and so everlastingly disenable you." Shepard asked mercy for the poor town, and prayed that he might catechise on Sabbath afternoons. The Bishop answered, "Spare your breath; I'll have no such fellows prate in my diocese. Get you gone, and make your complaints to whom you will!" "So away I went, — and blessed be God that I may go to him." The wrath of man praises God: the rage of Laud gave this church of ours its first minister. Not just then. Shepard was silenced there. "I did think it was for my sins the Lord did set him thus against me." Samuel Stone, who preceded him in the ministry here, received, by Shepard's proposal, the Lectureship he relinquished, and was sent with it to Towcester, Shepard's birthplace, where he accomplished much good. It is interesting to find their names, afterwards to be associated here, so early united beyond the seas.

But the oppressed, silenced preacher was not alone. He found friends. The Harlakendens were so many fathers and mothers to him. He remained about six months with them, and "the Lord let him see into the evil of the English ceremonies." Then the Bishop was again upon him, and cited him to appear before his court, when he charged him to depart the place. He was then invited to go to Yorkshire and be chaplain in the family of Sir Richard Darley, at a town called Buttercrambe. He was unwilling to go so far from his present post, unless compelled to do so. "I did not desire to stir till the Bishop fired me out of this place." The Bishop was not long in doing this. A few days after he had ordered Shepard away, he held a visitation in a neighboring town. With a companion, one Mr. Weld, already excommunicated, Shepard travelled to the place, discussing as they went the plan of going to New England. They thought it was better to go to Ireland and preach there. That was not God's plan for Shepard, or for us. They drew near to hear the Bishop's speech, when Weld was recognized by the Bishop, and arrested for being on forbidden ground, and Shepard was saved from the same fate by being seized away by watchful friends while the officers were looking for him. He was again urged to accept the position in Yorkshire, and decided to do so; "the rather because I might be far from the hearing of the malicious Bishop Laud, who had threatened me if I preached anywhere." It was a weary, perilous journey, and late on Saturday night he reached the house where he was to serve. The prospect was dismal enough. He found "divers of them at dice and tables." He was far from all friends, "in a profane house," "in a vile, wicked town and county," with small likelihood of doing any work, and the consciousness of ill-desert burdening his troubled soul. But things were to come out better than this homesick stranger dared to think. Sir Richard treated him kindly, and he found three servants who were friendly. The name of one of these stands upon the list of the members of our church. Another, the knight's kinswoman, with the hearty approval of the family, became Shepard's wife, and came hither with him. The words of the preacher were blessed to those with whom he labored. A sermon, on the occasion of the marriage of one of the daughters of the house, wrought great changes for the better with all the household. But the life of Shepard was not to be spent in that obscurity. His good wife was unwilling to remain there, and another Bishop was on his track. The Lord gave him a call to the town of Heddon, in Northumberland, a place where he "might preach in peace, being far from any Bishops," and thither he went. He found friends, and his labors were blessed, but his tarry was of more importance in that, as he has written it, "I came here to read and know more of the ceremonies, church government and estate, and the unlawful standing of Bishops than in any other place." The poor man had troubles in all their variety. For some reason he removed from Heddon after a year's preaching, and came to a town near by, where he dwelt "in a house which we found haunted with the Devil as we conceived, for when we went into it a known witch went out of it, and being troubled with noises four or five nights together, we sought God by prayer to remove so sore a trial; and the Lord heard and blessed us there, and removed the trouble." But there was no rest, for the Bishop put in a priest who would not suffer him to preach publicly any more, and no efforts could secure him the liberty, so that he preached up and down the country and in a private house. But things were working well. The wrath of man was beginning to praise God more clearly. At this time there came to him a call from divers friends in New England to come over to them, and many in Old England desired him to go, and promised to accompany him. Cotton, Hooker, Stone, and Weld had already come, and to his mind the Lord seemed to have departed from England with them. Shepard resolved to come with his friends, to seek here the liberty and purity which he could not find in England. He has left us the reasons of his decision, which were in all respects honorable and sufficient. He was willing to stay and to suffer, if that was best, but he turned with relief to the door of escape which the Lord had opened. "I saw no reason to spend my time privately, when I might possibly exercise my talent publicly in New England." Let us cherish the memory of Margaret Shepard. "My dear wife did much long to see me settled there in peace, and so put me on to it." He came down from the North with his wife and child, in a ship laden with coals, coming "in a disguised manner," and at length reached his old home at Earles-Colne, where he waited privately at the house of his friend Richard Harlakenden, the brother of Roger. After a prolonged delay, the ship was ready to sail. It was very late in the year, but he would not turn back. Soon after he sailed there came a violent storm, and the heavily laden ship was nearly driven upon the sands, and for a time all hope was gone. Prayer brought help. The wind abated, the anchor held, and boats came from the shore, and the tossed preacher and his little family were again upon the land. God's time was not yet. After a sickness of two weeks his child died, and was buried privately at Yarmouth. The father did not dare to be present at the burial, lest the officers of the church should seize him. His afflictions and disappointment made him more ready to remain in England. He found the reason for his troubles in his own guiltiness, and feared he had gone too far in separation from the "Assemblies in England." He had not gone too far. Why should he stay? Honorable martyrdom is honorable, yet one is not called to throw away his life. This young minister must have bread for his household, must preach the gospel, must preach it in its own freedom and its own simplicity. That seagirt isle, dear as it was, was not all the world. God had his plan, which he was leisurely working out.

Which way should the poor man turn? He was offered a vacant house in Norfolk, owned by an aged, pious woman, and there he passed the winter out of sight of his enemies, with his expenses defrayed by Roger Harlakenden. Though he could not preach publicly, he was busy with his pen, and wrote some things which we can read to-day. Out of this time came his treatise entitled "Certain Select Cases Resolved; specially tending to the right ordering of the heart, that we may comfortably walk with God in our general and particular callings. In a letter to a pious friend in England." Silenced, his words went out to the end of the world. In the spring of 1635 he went up to London with his good friend, to prepare again to leave

England. It was dangerous ground, for his great enemy, Laud, ruled there. He found a very private place, where another son was born to him, who, like the former one, was named Thomas. This was he who was afterwards pastor of the First Church in Charlestown, and was succeeded in that pastorate by his son Thomas. The birth of this child was kept secret, so that he was not baptized till he was brought to New England. The officers found out in some way that Shepard was in London, but he escaped to another house the very night they came to search for him. Then the Lord seemed to make his way plain to come to New England, and in August he embarked with his wife and child, his brother Samuel who had befriended him in his troubles, Mr. Roger Harlakenden, and other precious friends, lamenting the loss of their native country when they took their last view of it. It is supposed that Shepard sailed under the name of his brother, inasmuch as the list of passengers has the name of "John Shepard, husbandman, aged thirty-six." It was exceedingly difficult for ministers to escape from England, and it may have seemed necessary to resort to this disguise. We cannot help regretting his course, while we cannot doubt that he acted conscientiously. It is possible that the register of his name may have been made by some one else. The ship was the "Defence," of London, and she was "very rotten and unfit for such a voyage, and at the first storm began to leak badly, so that the passengers thought they might have to turn back." There were many storms, but after "a longsome voyage" they reached Boston, where they were welcomed by many friends with much love. On the second day after their arrival Shepard came with his family to Mr. Stone's, in Newtown. This was just at the time when the congregation here were preparing to remove to Connecticut. Shepard and his friends, numbering about sixty persons, purchased the houses of the Hooker Company, and decided to remain here until they could find a better place; a few of the former congregation remained with them. On the 1st of February, 1636, O. S., they organized their Church, with the assistance and fellowship of the neighboring churches. Soon after Mr. Shepard was installed as pastor. Here beginneth the present First Church in Cambridge.

Here we must pause. But as we bring the past into the present, shall we not gain an impulse which shall bear us on through all the work which is given us to do? "One generation passeth away and another generation cometh." It is something to have an honorable record for two hundred and thirty-four years. It has been gained by the piety, devotion, and generosity of those who have been before us. This church has been rich in saints, and is blessed still through those who have fallen on sleep. They were thoroughly in earnest, from first to last. Their labors, example, spirit, are our inheritance. Their tears and prayers, — "are they not in thy book?" We have planned well for the generations to come. Should we not, while we glory in those which are passed? Where will you set the name of that first minister? When? In what spirit? It has come to be our turn to build a meeting-house. We shall do it. We shall do it well. It has begun well, on paper and in stone. We should not blush if we saw the phantom "Defence" sail up our river, and yield its burden of men to these seats and this pulpit, and send the former residents of Cambridge beneath the shade of our venerated Elm. A good present is secure thus far! What shall another Sabbath show? O my brethren, join heartily in the good work which comes to you to-day. Let every hand help it forward, every voice speak words of cheer, every treasury yield its treasure. With promptness and decision we will give as it is given to us. Two centuries, and more, speak to us from the ground where our first sanctuary stood, and from the unknown grave of Thomas Shepard. We hear. We will heed. The generous beginning we have already made shall have a grand consummation. And here and in our finished sanctuary the praise shall be to Him of whom are the fathers, unto whom is our homage for ever and ever.

LECTURE II.

"FOR THEY GOT NOT THE LAND IN POSSESSION BY THEIR OWN SWORD, NEITHER DID THEIR OWN ARM SAVE THEM: BUT THY RIGHT HAND, AND THINE ARM, AND THE LIGHT OF THY COUNTENANCE, BECAUSE THOU HADST A FAVOR UNTO THEM." — Psalm xliv. 3.

HISTORY is the record of God's plan. It is easy to trace his working in the deeds of our fathers. We praise the men, yet the honor which we pay them goes beyond, and rests on him. For love of him and his truth, for the freedom of the conscience which he had implanted, for liberty to worship him in simplicity and purity, for the privilege of widening his kingdom and blessing those who should come after them, they deserted a land they loved, and the church in which they had been reared, to found on these open shores a free state and a free church. They accomplished their intent, and wrought out greater things than they imagined. The homage of a continent is their due; the world owes them admiration. But while we honor them, we glorify Him whom they served, whose hand and arm gave them the land in possession, the light of whose countenance in the constancy of his favor made them a people. In tracing the history of a church we follow out the lives of the good men who laid its strong foundation and began the enduring superstructure. Yet all is of God. Unto him be the glory of all we admire, the gratitude for all we enjoy.

It was on the first day of February, in the year of our

Lord 1636, that this First Church in Cambridge was organized. It was the year in which, on a later day, Henry Vane was chosen governor of Massachusetts. A man of twenty-three years, born of an ancient line, son of a Privy Counsellor of England, prizing the pure ordinances of the gospel more than the preferments of Court, sent hither by the command of the King who knew his desire to come, whom Milton has described as

> " Young in years, but in sage counsel old.
> . . . . .
> On thy firm hand Religion leans
> In peace, and reckons thee her eldest son."

Sagacious, vigorous, prompt, restless in any condition which might be improved, eager for reform, willing to lead the way; entering on his office amid the enthusiasm of the people, with John Winthrop for his deputy and successor; after the troubled service of a single year to seek the stirring scenes of his native land to find in them "higher and harsher fortunes"; to die on Tower Hill after the Restoration, speaking for liberty and right, praying calmly and confidently through the blast of trumpets, "Father, glorify thy servant in the sight of man, that he may glorify thee in the discharge of his duty to thee and to his country."

Yet brief and disturbed as were his tarry and service here, there came to him rare honor, in that he was permitted to preside over the first assembly of men " in which the people, by their representatives, ever gave their own money to found a place of education." " The ancient world in all its monarchies or republics," England with its ancient schools and universities, furnished no precedent for the public action out of which rose Harvard College.

That was in September. This was the time when John Hampden, of Buckinghamshire, determined to resist the imposition of a tax for ship money, laid upon people who never saw a ship, by a fiction of government which made a country a hundred miles inland border upon the sea, and refused to pay the assessment of twenty shillings upon his estate. He was defeated in the courts, but out of his defeat grew larger liberties than he sought, and the King who had beaten him went through the window of Whitehall Palace and laid his head upon the block. That was in the year in which the first pastorate of this church came to an end, by the death of a man whom Charles's Primate had driven across the seas. The reforms which were entered upon by the Long Parliament were felt in these colonies, distant but closely allied with the mother-land. Strafford was beheaded, Laud imprisoned to be afterwards beheaded, and many other persons of unhappy notoriety, bishops, judges, officers, were reckoned with for their deeds of oppression. England promised to become a home for freemen. There was less need for men to flee the country. Those who would have come hither waited for a new world in the old land. Emigration stopped. In 1640 some four thousand families, embracing about twenty-one thousand persons, had come to New England. For a century and a quarter after that "it is believed that more had gone from hence to England than had come from thence hither." For two hundred years there was nothing which could be called an immigration. The Puritan ranks abroad were reinforced by New England men. Many of the early graduates of our College sought service in the busy field from which their fathers had turned away in a time when there was less to do and less to hope. It is said that the abler part of the first graduates always returned to England to render there the service of their lives. The effect of this turning of the tide is manifest. New England needed the men whom Old England claimed. But the contest for liberty and right must be waged on both sides of the wide sea. The cause was one. The victory would be the common advantage. Still, the colony, left to itself, would have but a slow growth, and the state would be delayed. Remembering this, the vigor and advance here will seem the more remarkable.

I take up our own history again. It is coming into quiet out of tumult. The field seems narrower. Yet the deeds done upon it were of wide and lasting influence. Our church history blends with the colonial history, which widens into our national career, and takes a large place in the annals of the world. It was a simple thing done on that winter day, but the end is not there, is not yet. Thomas Shepard and his company, about sixty persons in all, had purchased the houses of Thomas Hooker and his company, and were ready to form themselves into a church. Governor Winthrop has described the proceedings at length. The magistrates were informed of the desire of these new-comers and gave their approbation. The neighboring churches sent their elders, by invitation, to give their assistance. A great assembly was convened. It was a grand company, containing as it did the chief men of the churches and of the colony. The two Winthrops we must imagine here, and Dudley, and Haynes, and Vane, and Peters, and Wilson, and Cotton, and Mather, and Hooker, and Stone. It is a fine sight as we look back upon it. Mr. Shepard and two others who were afterwards to be chosen to office sat together in the elders' seat. I think that one of the two was Edmund Frost, who preceded Shepard to these shores, and was made one of the first ruling elders of the church. The other may have been Thomas Marriot, who was one of the first deacons. "The elder of these began with prayer. Mr. Shepard prayed with deep confession of sin, and exercised" out of that glowing passage of St. Paul, "That he might present it to himself a glorious church." The cause of the meeting was declared, and it was asked how many were needful to form a church and how they should proceed. Some of the ancient ministers conferred together, and reported that seven was a fit number. In accordance with their further counsel, those who were to form the church, beginning with Mr. Shepard, made confession of their faith and of their personal religious experience. Then the covenant was read and assented to. Mr. Cotton of Boston, on behalf of the churches, gave the right hand of fellowship. Mr. Shepard made an exhortation, explaining the nature of the covenant and urging his associates to stand firm to it, closing with "a most heavenly prayer." The Elder then announced that the church proposed to choose Mr. Shepard for their pastor, and gave the members of the council thanks for their assistance, "and so left them to the Lord." At a subsequent day, which cannot be precisely determined, Mr. Shepard was installed in the pastoral office.

Let us linger for a moment upon the constitution of this church. At its beginning and during its early years, as at a later time, it numbered among its members various men of influence, whose names are found in other connections. Of Shepard himself I can speak better in another place. We know through what toils and trials he found the repose of this wilderness and liberty to preach the Word. Besides his Autobiography, he left a small book in which he had recorded "the confession of divers propounded to be received, and who were entertained as members." From that and other sources we learn the names of many of the early members of the church, and something of their history. So long as the law required the freeman to be a member of the church, the list of freemen gives us the names of many members. If there were any complete church records prior to 1696 they have disappeared, and we are compelled to gather up the fragments of our early life wherever they can be found. Happily, many of the events in which this church and its ministers bore a part were of sufficient public importance to gain a place in the histories of the times. Among those early members was John Haynes, Governor of Massachusetts when the church was organized, who came over with Thomas Hooker and John Cotton; a man of good family, rich enough to be able, generous enough to be willing, to refuse the salary of his office. "A heavenly man," Roger Williams said. He married Mabel, the sister of Roger Harlakenden, and in 1637 removed to Connecticut, where he was made governor. A man of sterling worth, of courteous manners, of public spirit, who never lost the confidence of those whom he served in his high station, and filled a large place in the rising state. There was Roger Harlakenden, of that house which protected and supported the young Shepard and his family in the days of their persecution, who came with them to this country, and after three years was called up higher. Winthrop says of him, "He was a very godly man, and of good use both in commonwealth and in church. He died in great peace, and left a sweet memorial behind him of his piety and virtue." As he was lieutenant-colonel, he was buried with military honors, but now no man knoweth of his grave. And Richard Champney, ruling elder of the church, descended from Sir Henry Champney, one of the thirty brave warriors who fought in 1066 at the battle of Hastings, under William the Conqueror. There was Samuel Green, who came in 1632, and was for fifty years a printer, whose greatest work was the Indian Bible, which he and Marmaduke Johnson brought out. John Dunton speaks of him in terms of great friendliness, while he lavishes admiration on his wife. And Matthew Day, the first known steward of the College, son of the first printer; who died in 1649, and in his will left 20 s. to his minister, and "a table-cloth and napkins not yet made up" to his minister's wife, and gave tokens of remembrance to little Samuel and Jeremy Shepard. There was Thomas Cheeseholme, the second steward of the College, a tailor by trade, but apparently the first person in Cambridge licensed to keep a house of entertainment and to draw wine. And Edward Winship, for many years honored by his fellow-citizens with election to office, and giving to the town his daughter Joanna, who was long the maiden school-mistress. And Nathaniel Eaton, of whom we do not boast, who was the first head of the embryo College, but who, for beating his tutor and abusing his students, with other misdemeanors, was thrust from his place and fined, and subsequently cast out of the church.

There was the first of the Sparrowhawkes, the house which in different generations gave the church four deacons, and served the community in other offices of trust. And Edward Collins, the deacon, father of famous sons, one of whom, after joining the church, was the chaplain of Monk when, by Cromwell's orders, he brought Scotland into subjection to the Parliament. There was Henry Dunster, the first President of the College, who after fourteen years of service was compelled to resign his place. He went away in sadness, and at his death gave directions that he should be buried here, by the side of the school he loved. So it was, and careful research has discovered his grave; "as true a friend," says Mr. Quincy, "and as faithful a servant, as this College ever possessed." Among the records to which I have alluded is a long statement of his religious belief and character, evidently made by himself when he united with this church. And Thomas Danforth, Treasurer and Steward of the College, Representative, Assistant, Deputy-Governor, President for Maine, and Judge of the Supreme Court for the proceedings against witches. And Daniel Gookin, the "Worshipful Captain," Representative, Speaker, Assistant, Major-General; who had a prominent part in public affairs at home, and an influence which was recognized abroad; the friend of the Indians; the protector of Whalley and Goffe, yet loyal enough to dedicate his Historical Collections to the King. There was Herbert Pelham, who, after befriending the cause of the colonists for ten years as a member of the company in London, came to this country. He was of high rank, matriculated at Magdalen Hall in Oxford, and for a long time engaged in public service. He was the first Treasurer of our College. He married the widow of Roger Harlakenden, and in 1649 returned to England. There was Elijah Corlet, for more than forty years the schoolmaster here, and highly approved for his "abilities, dexterity, and painfulness in teaching." These were all in Shepard's time. These selected names suggest a goodly list for the day of beginnings. Our ecclesiastical ancestry is noble.

What was this organization? It was a Congregational church. Its members were men and women who confessed God as their Creator and Sovereign, and Jesus Christ as their Saviour. They confessed the Bible to be the word of God, and promised to walk by its precepts. They professed to have been born again by the Holy Ghost, and to have entered thus upon a new life, whose inspiration was from heaven, whither its aspirations bore it. They banded themselves together for the worship of God and all the ordinances of religion. They made covenant one with another, and all with God. They claimed the right to order their affairs for themselves, subject only to the Great Head of the Church, and obedient to his revealed will. But they owned the fellowship of the churches, and asked counsel in their important affairs, and held themselves bound by the laws of Christian communion and affection. Their model was in the first Christian churches. They had suffered from human inventions, and found comfort and strength in the simplicity which is in Christ and his Apostles. The infant colony has become a mighty nation; many generations have come and gone; but their church remains, cleaving as fondly and firmly as ever to the faith and order which were once delivered unto the saints. Time testifies to their wisdom.

The form of covenant to which this church assented has not been preserved. But we have the covenant of the First Church in Charlestown, formed a little earlier, and it is probable that the covenant here agreed substantially with that. The Charlestown covenant is in these words: "In the Name of our Lord God, and in obedience to his holy will and divine ordinances. We, whose names are here written, being by his most wise and good providence brought together, and desirous to unite ourselves into one Congregation, or Church, under our Lord Jesus Christ our Head, in such sort as becometh all those whom he hath redeemed and sanctified unto himself, do here solemnly and religiously, as in his most holy presence, promise and bind ourselves to walk in all our ways according to the Rules of the Gospel, and in all sincere conformity to his holy Ordinances, and in mutual love and respect each to other, so near as God shall give us grace." There was another covenant, in almost the same words, with the change of form which was needed, to which those assented who were received to the church after its formation.

There was no written confession of faith besides this. The church at Salem had a fuller confession, framed by Mr. Higginson, but that was not usual. The fathers did not think it needful to make a formal statement of doctrine which should be peculiarly their own. In doctrine they agreed with other reformed churches, and it was not on that matter, but upon the question of worship and discipline, that they separated themselves from the English Church, and came out into a new land They thought it an advantage, and to the honor of their Lord, if many churches could unite in the same confession. In 1648 the Synod composed of the Elders and Messengers of the churches, which met here and framed the Cambridge platform of church discipline, having been requested by the magistrates to draw up a public confession of that faith which was constantly taught and generally professed, thought it good to present to the churches the confession which had been recently issued by the Westminster Assembly of Divines, excepting certain parts which related to discipline. In 1680, by the call and encouragement of the General Court, the elders and messengers met again in council in Boston, and prepared what is known as the Boston Confession. It was a declaration of faith. For matters of discipline they referred to the Cambridge Platform. These two documents have been essentially the constitution of our churches, while it has become almost universal for each church to have an abridgment of their statements for common use. But while our earliest churches had no written confession, they required of their members as full and distinct an avowal of their faith and their personal religious life as has ever been demanded. They had their creed. Every church has. It may be written or unwritten. But a body of men formed for a distinct purpose must believe something in common, and that belief, be it ever so narrow, be it on paper or in the general consent, is a creed. Men may contend against this or that particular statement, but warfare against creeds is simply beating the air; it is warfare against belief, that is, against reason, intelligence, conscience. Our fathers left no one in doubt regarding their views of truth. They knew the men whom they admitted to the establishment and increasing of a church. The covenant itself was no blind confession, as we have seen. The book kept by Thomas Shepard, of which I have spoken, gives us the confession of fifty persons. On the day of the organization here, those who were to be formed into the church made public confession of their faith. These statements agreed in point of doctrine. The preaching of such men as Shepard would keep the people instructed in the truth and prepared to make covenant with God and their brethren. "The matter of a visible church are saints by calling," so they said here. The theory of the fathers was that each church should make its own officers and administer its own affairs. But in doing this they were working in fellowship with others who were seeking the same ends by the same means, owning allegiance to the same Lord and Saviour, following the precepts of the same inspired Word. In their statements they emphasize the freedom of each church. They are the more careful to do this because they have broken away from a consolidated body, with a hierarchial clergy. Their past sufferings, their present exile, their own experience and dread and hope, put the stress upon their independence. Yet they loved the other churches, and lived in fellowship with them. One chapter of the Cambridge Platform is devoted to "the communion of churches one with another." Their common history, position, perils, desires, united them. Advice, assistance, communion, we may call that which the churches gave and took among themselves; but in meaning, in force, in regard, it was law. There are no bands stronger than love throws around us. Silken and soft, they hold when iron breaks. The decrees of the High Commission Court came with more sound of authority, but men resisted them and turned their faces to the wilderness to render willing allegiance to the elders and messengers of the churches. We find freedom at the Mount of the Beatitudes; yet from the lips of our Lord Christ fall commandments as strict, as exacting, as were heard amid the thunders of Sinai.

I dwell on this now, because there is some tendency towards a mere independence among our churches. Congregationalism confers independence under the law of Christian fellowship. For men, for churches, the commandment is one: Love thyself; love thy neighbor as thyself. Under this the Fathers acted; in this is our safety and honor. In the view of the fathers a church should have five officers, — pastor and teacher, who were called elders, ruling elder, deacon, and deaconess. The last I do not find that they ever had in form. These officers were to be chosen and ordained by the church in which they served. The pastor's special work was to "attend to exhortation, and therein to administer a word of wisdom." He was to apply the precepts of Scripture to the lives of men. The teacher was to "attend to doctrine, and therein to administer a word of wisdom." The one, therefore, had what we should term the practical, and the other the doctrinal, part of the present ministerial office. Both were to administer the sacraments of the church. Both were also "to execute the censures." The earliest church here had both pastor and teacher, but in our own church the two offices seem to have been combined from the beginning. The ruling elder was to attend to the discipline of the church, and to take the lead in all matters of business. " To feed the flock of God with a word of admonition, and as they shall be sent for, to visit and pray over their sick brethren." The office was not of long continuance. In fifty years from the settlement of the country it had fallen into comparative disuse, although it was continued here till near the close of the century. The deacon was to be a man proved and found blameless. His work was " to receive the offerings of the church, and to keep the treasury of the church, and therewith to serve the tables which the church is to provide for; as the Lord's table, the table of the ministers, and of such as are in necessity, to whom they are to distribute in simplicity." Some churches had one deacon, some two, some three. The number of elders varied in different churches. In the two hundred and thirty-five years of the history of this church there have been eleven pastors; and I find the names of four ruling elders and thirty-one deacons. Having seen the constitution of the church, shall we look now at its methods, and somewhat at the ordering of the social life about it?

"The public worship," says an early writer, " is in as fair a meeting-house as they can provide, wherein, in most places, they have been at great charges." If we could go within the rude sanctuary which once stood near this spot, we should find a rough room, divided by a central passage, and furnished with benches. On one side of the house the males would sit, on the other the females. Very likely some of the men would have carnal weapons. The pulpit would be found to be a stand or desk, within a railing, and in its plainness in keeping with its surroundings. On the Lord's Day there was a bell here to call the people, but for some reason there was at one time the beating of a drum for the same purpose. In our town records for 1646 is an entry of "fifty shillings paid unto Thomas Langhorne for his service to the town in beating the drum these two years past." It was common to have an hour-glass in the church by which to measure the time of the services. When the people became able to arrange the meeting-house according to their idea of the fitness of things, the ruling elders had a seat below the pulpit, and the deacons a seat a little lower down, where they faced the congregation. The pulpit was an elaborate structure under a sounding-board. The boys had a place by themselves, in one of the galleries, with a tithing-man to maintain order. In 1666 we have this record on the town-book, "Thomas Fox is ordered to look to the youth in time of public worship." In 1669 there was complaint that sundry persons were spending holy time unprofitably without the meeting-house, and the constable was ordered to see "that they do attend upon the public worship of God." In many cases the meeting-house was finished by degrees. At first benches would be put in. A man could obtain a deed of a space on the floor, some six feet square, and erect a pit or pew upon it. He was to keep his pew in repair, and "maintain all the glass against it." Where there was no such private arrangement, the people had seats assigned them by a committee, according to rank or property or age. This was called "dignifying" a house. Here is an order of 1658: "That the elders, deacons, and selectmen for the time being shall be a constant and settled power for regulating the sitting of persons in the meeting-house from time to time as need shall require." Here is the committee's appointment for 1662. I will not read it, but it begins in this way: "Brother Jackson's wife to sit there where Sister Kempster was wont to sit. Mrs. Upham with her mother. Esther Sparhawke in the place where Mrs. Upham is removed from," and so on. In the New England customs the congregation met as early as nine o'clock on Sabbath morning and about two in the afternoon. The services consisted of prayer, singing, reading and expounding the Scriptures, for it was generally accounted improper to read them without exposition, — "dumb reading," they called it. There was a sermon also by the pastor or teacher. As they accounted a man a minister only in his own congregation, when one was in the pulpit of another clergyman it was common for the ruling elders of the place to give him authority to speak in some such form as this: "If this present brother hath any word of exhortation for the people at this time, in the name of God let him say on." His "saying on" was called prophesying. An hour was considered the proper length for a sermon, although upon occasions the preacher might "take another glass," as it was sometimes facetiously described. The sermon was usually preached without notes in the first century. The prayers were, of course, extemporaneous. Children were baptized in the meeting-house, generally on the next Sabbath after their birth, sometimes on the day of their birth. The pastor or teacher stood in the deacons' seat, as that was an "eminent place," and with an address to the church and the parents, and two prayers, administered the sacred ordinance. "No sureties were required." The Lord's Supper was administered once in each month, at the morning service. The form was very much like our own. Persons were received to membership in public, but with more of examination and profession than with us. Cases of discipline were more publicly dealt with than is usual now. It is to be remembered that the whole life of the people was marked by a simplicity and frankness and familiarity which have lessened with the changes which have come upon society. Every Sabbath afternoon there was a contribution. One of the deacons stood up in his place, and said, "Brethren of the congregation, now there is time left for contribution, wherefore, as God hath prospered you, so freely offer." "On some extraordinary occasions," says an old writer, "as building and repairing of churches or meeting-houses, or other necessities, the ministers press a liberal contribution, with effectual exhortation out of Scripture." Then the people passed up to the deacons' seat with their offerings. "The magistrates and chief gentlemen went first, then the elders, then all the congregation of men, and most of them that are not of the church, all single persons, widows, and women in absence of their husbands." Money and papers were dropped into a box; if the offering were "any other chattel," it was set down before the deacons. The writer just quoted says, "I have seen a fair gilt cup with a cover offered there by one, which is still used at the Communion." It was customary for visitors in the congregation to make an offering which was called "the strangers' money," and was often stipulated for by the clergyman as a perquisite of his office. At first the minister's salary was paid from the voluntary contribution made on the Sabbath, but this soon gave way to the system of taxation. In a list of the salaries given to different ministers during the first twenty years of the Massachusetts colony, Mr. Shepard's salary is stated at seventy pounds. This was among the largest salaries of the time. Two are given at ninety pounds, three at eighty pounds, and they decrease gradually to thirty pounds. At almost every point we can see where the fathers were swinging away from the customs of the church in which they had lost and endured so much. Thus, marriage was not a sacrament, but a civil contract, entered into by the parties before a magistrate. This marrying by a magistrate was for the Pilgrims "according to the laudable example of the Low Countries in which they had lived." To perform this ceremony was nowhere found in the gospel to be laid on the ministers as a part of their office. Winthrop mentions a great marriage to be solemnized in Boston, when the bridegroom invited his minister to preach on the occasion. "The magistrates sent to him to forbear. We were not willing to bring in the custom of ministers' performing the solemnity of marriage, which sermons at such times might induce; but if any minister were present, and would bestow a word of exhortation, etc., it was permitted." In like manner funerals were stripped of the ceremonies which had attended them abroad. The dead were no longer buried with imposing rites beneath the floor of the church or in consecrated ground, but were laid in some convenient enclosure, without even a prayer. Lechford, writing in 1641, says, "At burials nothing is read, nor any funeral sermon made, but all the neighborhood, or a good company of them, come together by tolling of the bell, and carry the dead solemnly to his grave, and there stand by him while he is buried. The ministers are most commonly present." No burial was allowed on the Sabbath, except by leave obtained from a justice. It was long the custom when a woman was buried for the women to walk first in the procession; the men when a man was to be interred. Funerals were somewhat expensive, although not in the same direction as at present. This was especially the case when a person of note was buried: wine, cider, gloves, were provided; and in one case, in Ipswich, at the funeral of a minister, in 1768, the bearers were furnished with gold rings, one of which was also given to "a candidate who was preaching for them," and the attending ministers received eighteen pairs of white leather gloves. At length an Act was passed to retrench extraordinary expenses at funerals. They kept none of the former holy days, except the Lord's Day, associating the observance of them with superstition and oppression. But they instituted days of public fasting and thanksgiving. In addition to the Sabbath services there was a weekly lecture. The Thursday lecture in Boston has come down to our own time. They gave great heed to the training of the young in religion and good learning. This town was early divided into districts, which were assigned to certain persons who were to see to the catechizing and educating of the youth. The school which here grew into the College was established the same year with the church, and watched over with interest and generosity. In 1648 is an order that a part of the Common shall be sold "for the gratifying of Mr. Corlet for his pains in keeping a school in the town." In 1644 the General Court granted, on the petition of Cambridge and Charlestown, one thousand acres of land to be forever appropriated to a grammar school; and also made a grant of two hundred acres of land to Mr. Corlet. The instruction in the family and school was simple, compared with that which is now given. There were no spelling-books, no English grammars, little of what is now considered the essential apparatus of instruction. Children learned to read from the Bible, taking in truth with the letters and syllables. An out-of-door life gave the youth object-lessons and teaching in practical mechanics. A grammar school was one where Latin and Greek were taught. Students learned to talk in

Latin, and gained a familiarity with its usages which our present system hardly gives. Our schools are in advance of the old, doubtless. But there was some advantage in having only a few books, and those the best, which were to be read till they were almost known by heart. Printing in this part of America began here. The first printer was Stephen Day, who brought out "The Freeman's Oath" in 1639; an almanac by William Pierce, Mariner, in the same year, and in the following year a psalm-book. The singing in the churches was without instrumental accompaniment. This was thought to be forbidden by the words of Amos, "I will not hear the melody of thy viols." It was compared to the idolatrous performance which Nebuchadnezzar delighted in, "the sound of the cornet, flute, harp, sackbut, psaltery, and dulcimer, and all kinds of music." Through the first century there were not more than ten different tunes, it is said, and few congregations could sing more than five. In the singing it was customary for the ruling elder, or deacon, or some other proper person, to read the hymn line by line and give out the tune. When a line had been read, it could be sung by the people. The amount read at each time was increased in some cases, and after a time the whole hymn was read at once by the minister. In the old Ipswich church in 1763 there were seats assigned the choir, "two back on each side of the front alley." Afterwards the choir went into the gallery. The rude simplicity of our fathers had some things to recommend it in comparison with the services which in some places have of late been thrust into public worship under the guise of sacred song. The version of the Psalms in use here, as far as I can determine, was that made by Sternhold and Hopkins, and printed at the end of the Bible. But there was a desire for a better book. There was complaint that the translation in use had "so many detractions from, additions to, and variations of, not only the text but the very sense of the psalmist, that it was an offence unto them"; so Cotton Mather explains it. A number of prominent divines were appointed to make a new version. Eliot of Roxbury and Mather of Dorchester were among them. Our Thomas Shepard gave them warning in a stanza which makes us submissive to his absence from the committee, and reminds us that great men are not always poets.

> "You Roxb'ry poets, keep clear of the crime
> Of missing to give us very good rhyme.
> And you of Dorchester, your verses lengthen,
> But with the text's own words you will them strengthen."

The book came out in 1640, and was well received. It was revised by Mr. Dunster, and received the addition of "spiritual songs." It passed through seventy editions, and was used extensively in Great Britain, especially in Scotland. It was in use in some of our churches until after the Revolution. It was entitled "The Bay Psalm Book," and afterwards, "The New England Version of the Psalms." In order to compare it with the work which it displaced, I give a part of the Twenty-third Psalm, first in the version of Sternhold and Hopkins: —

> "My Shepheard is the living Lord,
>   Nothing therefore I neede;
> In pastures faire, with waters calme
>   he sets me for to feede.
> He did convert and glad my soule,
>   and brought my mind in frame;
> To walke in paths of righteousnesse,
>   for his most holy name."

This is from the new book: —

> "The Lord to mee a Shepheard is,
>   want therefore shall not I.
> Hee in the folds of tender-grasse,
>   doth cause mee downe to lie:
> To waters calme me gently leads
>   Restore my soule doth hee:
> he doth in paths of righteousnes
>   for his names sake lead mee."

It is pleasant to linger upon the customs of our fathers, but the sands warn me that your patience must be run out. These glimpses will show something of the life that was once going on here where we are living. These usages seem strange, sometimes uncouth to us; but if we had been born into them it would have been different. They may suit our taste now hardly better than the garments of our ancestors; but they were fashionable and natural once. They must be estimated in their surroundings; judged in their relation to those who employed them. Yet it is good to think that if those sturdy men should enter this house to-day, they would find the same simplicity of worship which they left; that the early ministers might resume their place and seem little strange in it. No institution binds us more closely to our past than our congregational churches and modes of worship. In thinking of the ancient times, let us keep it in mind that the ruling spirits here were men, gentlemen, scholars; not boors nor bigots. Newtown had her share of the choice wheat which came from the sifting of a whole nation. We see this in the names we have read to-night, and it will continually appear as we pursue this story. They were men determined in character, in opinion, in conduct. These New England colonists differed from those who had sought other places in that, contrary to the vain experiments of the preceding century, the women came with the men, and homes were established with all their security and influence. It is partly because we see so little of the home life, of the lighter side of the men, that they look to us austere. They had little time or taste for idle sport; but they had comfort in a strange land, and found enjoyment in their rugged path. It is the solid part of their character and work which has remained; their graces and adornments have been lost. We see their face in repose, or in work, after the smile has passed away. But men smiled, children played; they were married and given in marriage; and here and there the wilderness blossomed with the rose. We talk of amusements; some may fancy those were dreary years which lacked the modern improvements for wasting time, and trifling with these years of trial. They might have done differently. The money they put into Harvard College would have furnished public sports for a small portion of the year. Would it have been better spent? These men knew literature. Shakespeare died in 1616, and possibly some of these men had seen him face to face. Lord Bacon died in 1626. Our fathers stood close to them. They believed in learning and goodness. They had confidence in men who had studied, thought, wrought. They had confidence in such men as Thomas Shepard and Henry Dunster and Elijah Corlet and Samuel Green, for the conservators and promoters of intelligence and piety. King James passed the manor-house of Scrooby on one of his hunting days. He thought he should like to buy the place. Every Sabbath, at that time, there gathered a company of plain men and women under that roof. They met to pray and worship God. Who has lived, — James, the royal hunter, or Brewster, the Separatist worshipper? What is a royal palace beside Plymouth Rock? Not the employments of idleness and recklessness, but the pulpit, the school-room, the printing-press, were to make the state. They did make it. We should choose such men, and not others, to make a state again. There was spirit here and life, unrepressed, exuberant. The woods and streams offered recreation to the boys when their tasks were done. The girls had their quiet enjoyment in the safety of their homes, in the companionship of their best friends. Morality was abroad in the earth. "One may live there from year to year, and not see a drunkard, hear an oath, or meet a beggar," wrote the author of "New England's First Fruits." They built houses, churches, schools, colleges. They took pains to get good citizens and to keep them good. In this practical age, it should be some honor that they succeeded in their undertaking. The Congregational Church held the germ of the nation. The devotion, intelligence, religion of these Puritans have given us our glory, which must be preserved through the like virtues in these later days. We go back to them, and they are gathering in their rude meeting-house, they are bending over their Bible, they are bowing the knee at the mercy-seat of God. Behind them is their Father and ours. His is the wisdom, his the might, his the success. For his right hand and arm, and the light of his countenance, gave prosperity, because he had a favor unto them.

LECTURE III.

"THERE IS A RIVER, THE STREAMS WHEREOF SHALL MAKE GLAD THE CITY OF GOD, THE HOLY PLACE OF THE TABERNACLES OF THE MOST HIGH." — Psalm xlvi. 4.

"THE two things in history which preserve the reign of James from contempt are the translation of the Bible and the settlement of America. And I can give no better illustration of the way in which history has been written in the past, than by saying that in the two great English histories of this reign the translation of the Bible is not so much as mentioned, and that Lingard does not give a word to the planting of America. Hume only squeezes out for it a wretched page." These remarks of a recent writer remind us how easy it is to overlook the grand glories of any time, the great causes which are moving quietly forward to the accomplishment of results which shall compel the notice and admiration of the world. That to a mind blinded or prejudiced, the large and small affairs of kings and courts, the changes in material and political interests, are likely to be more attractive, and seem more important, than the deep principles of religion and liberty, the unobtrusive movements which immediately concern the kingdom of God. It is a happy fact in our own national history, that it can never be dissevered from its sources, — from the fear of God, the regard for truth and purity, the determination to have a free church with a free worship. Our history can never be profane, secular. He who writes of the state writes of the church. In idea, in the order of events, the State House is within the meeting-house. Men's motives and deeds are directly related to their religion. "It concerneth New England always to remember," said the venerable Higginson of Salem, "that they are originally a plantation religious, not a plantation of trade. . . . . If any man among us make religion as twelve and the world as thirteen, such an one hath not the spirit of a true New England man."

It is plain, therefore, why it is that he who attempts to follow out the life of our early churches, especially of one which, from its location and the character of its membership, was as influential as this whose narrative we are reading together, is continually led beyond the local church, and compelled to treat of affairs which move in larger circles. Matters of colonial politics, of the higher education, of missionary work, of ecclesiastical government, come before us to-day, even in the brief period of our history which we are to survey. For these to a large extent centred here, and from this place went forth an influence to be long and widely felt. The colonies flourished, passed on into an independent national existence, and have gained the foremost place among the nations. We are at no loss to find the cause of this stability and advancement. There has been a river, — the stream of piety, of devotion, of regard for religious liberty, of zeal for the greatest good of man, — there has been a river, the streams whereof have made glad the city of God. While we rejoice in the verdure and luxuriance which surround us, the streams have been found full of water, and have flowed for the enrichment of the land. We will not forget them. Shall we not deepen and widen their channels, that they may flow over our spreading domain, till the fruitfulness which gladdens us shall make the whole land rejoice?

We have already witnessed the formation of this church and marked the installation of Thomas Shepard, its first minister. That was in 1636. Of the number of those who united in the church we can give only a conjecture. There were about sixty persons in Shepard's company. Our new church manual will give the names of fifty-seven persons who are presumed to have been members of the church during the first year. The original design of the company was to remain here for a time, while they could look about them and find a more favorable place in which to make their permanent settlement. Their desire to tarry was furthered by the opportunity to purchase the buildings of Hooker's company. But it was soon manifest to the majority that it was best to remain here permanently. They found ample means of subsistence; they remembered that their lives were short, and that removals to new plantations were full of troubles; and they prized the fellowship of the churches, a novelty and refreshment in the wilderness. Hence the church was organized. The hand of Providence is seen in bringing them hither at the very time when houses waited for them, and in keeping them here where their influence would be so widely felt.

Mr. Shepard, at the time of his installation, was thirty years old. He is described by a contemporary as a "weak, pale-complexioned man." He was a man of unusual talent, of liberal learning and deep piety. His own character had been matured in the trials and toils of his earlier life. He was well suited to the new labors

4

to which he was called, and well fitted to enjoy the repose and freedom of the new world where he had sought a refuge and a work. We shall find this promise of the beginning abundantly fulfilled. His ministry began with sorrow in his own house. The health of his wife had been failing for some time. The exposure to which she was subjected, and the care of her feeble and froward child, during the long, stormy voyage from England, exhausted her strength, and she soon passed into a consumption, and was taken from the world. But before her departure she had the satisfaction of seeing her husband settled in a safe place, of being herself received to membership in his church, and of having her child baptized. The account which Mr. Shepard gives of her admission to the church upon the day of its formation is one of the most touching passages in the annals of the time. After the public services of the day were ended, "we came," he says, "to her chamber, she being unable to come unto us. And because we feared that her end was not far off, we did solemnly ask her if she was desirous to be a member with us, which she expressing, and so entering into covenant with us, we thereupon all took her by the hand, and received her as became one with us, having had full trial and experience of her faith and life before. At this time and by this means the Lord did not only show us the worth of this ordinance, but gave us a seal of his acceptance of us and of his presence with us that day; for the Lord hereby filled her heart with such unspeakable joy and assurance of God's love, that she said to us she had enough; and we were afraid that her feeble body would have at that time sunk under the weight of her joy." "A fortnight after which," he writes in another place, "my deare wife Margaret dyed." She was "exceedingly cheered and comforted with the sense of God's love, which continued until her last gaspe," and with resignation and hope she entered upon her rest. But though she died so early, she deserves to be held in high esteem. Wherever her husband is praised she shall be tenderly remembered. As we have seen, Mr. Shepard first met her in Yorkshire, at the house of Sir Richard Darley, where he served as chaplain. She was then Margaret Tauteville, the kinswoman of the knight. She befriended the homesick, persecuted young man, in a strange house, in a family where he could expect little sympathy. The labors of Shepard there produced good results. He found favor and friends. "When the Lord had fitted a wife for me he then gave me her, who was a most sweet, humble woman, full of Christ, and a very discerning Christian; a wife who was most incomparably loving to me and every way amiable and holy, and endued with a very sweet spirit of prayer." The family consented to the alliance, and even enlarged the portion of the bride. "Thus did I marry the best and fittest woman in the world unto me." The marriage was in 1632. The wife was unwilling to remain at Buttercrambe, and they set out, not knowing where their home would be. They shared their fears and faced their enemies together. The hunted minister had a true helpmeet. She went with him through his perils and privations on the land and on the sea. Her faith and hope reached out to the land beyond the wide waters. It has already been given as one reason which moved him to come to New England, at the time he made the first attempt, that "my dear wife did much long to see me settled there in peace, and so put me on to it." Within a fortnight after the formation of the church she left him desolate. But her influence for the four years of her wedded life was marked. The distrustful, cautious man needed one who excelled him in courage and enterprise. Wise enough to appreciate her position and be content with it, she was able by her faith and her affection to incite him to bold purposes. She was given to him at the time when he needed her the most for the determining of his career, and when that work was done she had rest. But let her memory be honored. We delight to write the name of our first minister wherever we can. The society to which the church is united is called after him, and many of our works of benevolence have been done under his name. The granite column we have reared bears it to posterity. It will be on the mural tablet in our new sanctuary. It is well. Shall there not be found some conspicuous place on which we can gratefully inscribe " Margaret Shepard"?

From this domestic life we pass among more exciting scenes. At the time of the organization of the church, trouble had already begun in connection with that restless and resolute woman whose name is "dismally conspicuous in the early history of New England." Mrs. Ann Hutchinson had been attracted from England by her desire to continue to enjoy the preaching of Mr. Cotton. Her husband, who had left a good estate in Lincolnshire, is described as "a man of a very mild temper and weak parts, and wholly guided by his wife." She was destined to encounter some who would be less submissive to her control. They came in the fall of 1634, and she soon showed herself a kind neighbor, especially to the sick, and won the esteem of the people, over whom her attentions and talents gave her influence. She became connected with the Boston Church, and soon avowed doctrines at variance with those commonly held here. Winthrop mentions two dangerous errors which she brought with her: "first, that the person of the Holy Ghost dwells in a justified person; second, that no sanctification can help to evidence to us our justification. From these errors grew many branches." Her fundamental idea was, that a person is not to find evidence of his being a Christian in any changes in himself, or any grace or holiness he may possess, or in the conditional promises made to such as believe, but in an immediate revelation made to his own soul. To receive this doctrine was to be under a "covenant of grace." To depend upon other evidence was to be under a "covenant of works." Under these two designations Christians became divided. The party which she headed were known as "Familists," from a short-lived sect which sprang up in Leyden in the preceding century, and held that the essence of religion consists in the sense of Divine love. They were also called "Antinomians," which was likewise a borrowed name taken from a sect formed a hundred years before, which denied the obligation to observe the law under the gospel dispensation.

Error is commonly some perversion of truth. We are, indeed, not under the law, but under grace; yet grace has its law. "These things I command you," said our Saviour, Christ. His service is perfect freedom; but even in that "the love of Christ constraineth us." We are not freed from the obedience of the moral law; but we are not left to the consequences of our neglect, seeing that the grace of Christ comes in to atone for our sin; so that, hopelessly lost through our works, we are saved through his grace. We are, truly, not justified by works, and virtue is not proof of piety, manliness of godliness. Still, a man's works are a testimony to his character, and will always be held as witnesses to the sincerity of his profession. "By their fruits ye shall know them." The children of God have the witness in themselves, his Spirit working in their spirits, and the last witness to one's piety must be sought in his consciousness; but consciousness will take account of his grace and growth and life. It will be fatal to our hope of salvation to rest upon that which we can do or that which we feel. It is the free choice of God which saves us; his independent, sovereign working. Yet we are called upon to work out our own salvation, to behold the Lamb of God, to believe the gospel which is preached. "He that believeth and is baptized shall be saved." There is a beautiful harmony between the grace of God and the faith of man. Always will the Christian render the full praise of his redemption unto God, who loved the world and gave his Son. It will be the rejoicing of heaven.

To her imperfect, perverted views of great truths Mrs. Hutchinson attached great importance. Gathering weekly assemblies of women, she expounded her views and denounced the ministers, with the exception of her brother-in-law, Wheelwright, and Cotton, who seemed for a time to favor her, being impressed with her piety and ability, but afterwards came to see the false ground upon which she was standing. Her opinions spread with amazing rapidity. Dr. Albro has characterized them as "absurd, licentious, and destructive"; adding, "wherever they took root they produced the bitter fruits of alienation, hatred, and slander." The ministers were openly ridiculed, and ignorant men and women were put forward as preachers, with the boast that they could excel the "black coats" who had been trained at the "Ninneversity." Churches and families became divided. Old friends were separated and made enemies. Many Christians wavered, uncertain with which party to side. All the associations of common life became infected with the disputes. Even the marching of troops, which had been raised to assist Connecticut against the Indians, was opposed on " the ground that the officers and soldiers were too much under a covenant of works." To understand how so great a commotion could come from so small a cause, it is only needful to remember how intimately religious ideas were connected with all affairs. The churches, the clergy, the doctrines, were the most substantial interests of men. To question a man's orthodoxy was to question his character. As well call him a knave outright as pronounce him under a "covenant of works." The dissension was really fearful. English congregations in Holland had fairly gone to pieces by falling upon similar contentions. There was the greatest peril that the colony would be wrecked in this war of the elements, among these frowning rocks. The churches and towns in the country, for the most part, were opposed to this troublesome woman. The church in Boston was in her favor, with the exception of a few members, among whom were the pastor, Wilson, and Winthrop, who in 1636 was deputy-governor under Vane, who was a partisan of Mrs. Hutchinson. A meeting of magistrates and elders was held to devise a way of quieting the disturbance. Wilson laid the blame where it belonged, for which he was reproved by his church. At length a fast was appointed on account of these and other troubles, but this evil was not put down. Wheelwright and one Greensmith were reckoned with for their seditious language, and this enraged their friends and provoked resistance. Boston was in so great confusion that the General Court met here. An election was held on our Common, and Winthrop was chosen governor. There were many fierce speeches and some threatening deeds. The venerable Wilson is said to have spoken from a tree into which he had climbed. Vane soon after returned to England, and one element of the strife was removed. There was warm discussion which tended towards a settlement. The real points of difference among the people were found to be small. The preaching of Mr. Shepard on the day of election contributed to this result. Matters seemed in so promising condition, that the ministers, with the consent of the magistrates, called an ecclesiastical synod. It was composed of the ministers and messengers of all the churches, with a few who had recently arrived in the country. It was the first synod held in America, and it met with this church of ours. The General Court adjourned on account of this convention. This was in 1637.

I must leave it to your imagination to reproduce that grave and reverend assembly which convened in the humble meeting-house in Dunster Street. It is fitting to mark this beginning of such assemblies, and to connect it with our own church. It was not the last great and good thing which began here, as we shall have occasion to see. Mr. Shepard opened the first session with a "heavenly prayer." Mr. Hooker of Hartford and Mr. Bulkeley of Concord were the moderators. The sessions continued for three weeks, with freedom of speech, but with due regard for propriety and order. Eighty-two opinions were condemned with great unanimity. The peculiar views of Mrs. Hutchinson and her adherents were among them. Certain questions of church discipline which had arisen were decided, and matters were carried on peaceably and "concluded comfortably in all love." Mr. Shepard says, "These errors, through the grace and power of Christ, were discovered, the defenders of them convinced and ashamed, the truth established, and the consciences of the saints settled, there being a most wonderful presence of Christ's spirit in that assembly held at Cambridge." He mentions as one result of the synod the discomfiture of the Pequot Indians. For, as the internal dissensions flourished, wars from without had opportunity to arise, and these were quelled by the restoration of harmony among the people. It was found necessary to send away a very few persons who had been prominent in the disturbances. Mrs. Hutchinson herself was tried before the General Court, for railing at the ministers and continuing her lectures in defiance of the synod. A sentence of banishment was passed, but as it was winter she was committed to a private house in Roxbury. Her conversation there was so offensive, that the church in Boston cited her to appear and answer to the charge of holding gross errors. The result was her retraction of a part of her declaration, and an admonition by the church, inasmuch as she persisted in holding others. She was then allowed to be at Mr. Cotton's house, that he and Mr. Davenport might reason with her. She retracted all the opinions imputed to her, and went so far as to say she had never held them. A question of veracity was raised and decided against her, and she was excommunicated for having "impudently persisted in untruth." This was the end of her power and her party here. She was ordered by the governor to depart from this jurisdiction, which she did. Some of her adherents dispersed in different directions. It is not necessary to trace her fortunes farther. Her afterlife was troubled and troublesome. She became a widow, and finally moved to a place within or near the Dutch border, where the whole family, except a daughter of eight years, were murdered by the Indians. Her stormy life had a stormy close. But after her departure from Massachusetts a long period of tranquillity was enjoyed here.

Thus early were this church and its minister brought to contend earnestly for the faith, for the purity and quiet which they had sought in exile and privation. The prayers and thoughts and conversation of the people who walked our ancient streets, the preaching of the youthful but experienced minister, must have had large reference to the scenes we have been hurrying through. But Mr. Shepard gratefully acknowledges that this town "was kept spotless from the contagion of the opinions." A course of lectures which he preached during and after these times, based upon the Parable of the Ten Virgins, we are permitted to read, adding to their intrinsic interest by transferring them to the days which called them forth.

It is pleasant to turn from these conflicts to more peaceful events. The early settlers of New England were men who knew the value of education. Many of them were graduates of the English universities, and were possessed of the best learning of their day. They knew that the well-being of the state, and the purity and stability of the church, demanded that the people should be educated, and that learned men should be raised up to take the place of those who were passing away. Hence, in 1636, later in the year of our church organization, the General Court adopted this order: "The Court agree to give four hundred pounds towards a school or college, whereof two hundred pounds shall be paid the next year, and two hundred pounds when the work is finished, and the next Court to appoint where and what building." Four hundred pounds was "equal to a year's rate of the whole colony." It was a grant of fifty cents from each of the four thousand inhabitants. A like assessment now would yield more than seven hundred thousand dollars. The next year it was ordered that the College should be at Newtown. Why did they choose to come here? Two reasons led to this choice: this was "a place very pleasant and accommodate," and it was "under the orthodox and soul-flourishing ministry of Mr. Thomas Shepheard." Twelve of the leading men of the colony were appointed to take orders for the College. Among these were Shepard, Cotton, Wilson, Harlakenden, Stoughton, Dudley, Winthrop. Thus did the College come at once under the fostering care of this church and its minister. Side by side have they come down the years; side by side are they going into the future. In the following year the Rev. John Harvard died, bequeathing one half of his whole property and his entire library to the youthful institution. The amount of his gifts was a little less than eight hundred pounds. His library consisted of three hundred and twenty volumes of theological, classical, and general literature. Others followed with gifts of money and books and various articles, according to their ability. In this year, 1638, the regular course of studies began. In the same year the name of Cambridge was given to the town, after the literary home of many of the chief men of the colony. In the following spring it was ordered that the College should bear the name of Harvard. In the next year, by order of the Court, " the ferry between Boston and Charlestown is granted to the College."

The institution was first placed under the charge of Nathaniel Eaton, who managed both the instruction and the finances. He made so good a beginning that in 1639 he received a grant of five hundred acres of land, upon condition that he would continue his employment for life. Then, for his fame's sake, he should have died. He was a scholar, doubtless, but had no other qualification for his office. He seems to have been extravagant in his use of the funds. Besides that, he abused his scholars and his usher, Briscoe, and in connection with his wife brought college commons to their lowest state. He was tried by the Court, and convicted of passion and negligence and cruelty; was fined and dismissed from his place; was excommunicated from the church, and compelled to leave the colony. He returned to England, became the persecutor of Nonconformists, and finally died while in prison for debt. Mr. Shepard was charitably inclined towards his parishioner, but before long was convinced of his real character, and approved of his sentence. It is characteristic of the good minister that he mourned not only over the sin of Eaton, but also on account of his own ignorance and want of wisdom and watchfulness over him. Upon Eaton's discharge, the business affairs of the College were put into the hands of Samuel Shepard, who attended to them until the arrival of Henry Dunster, who became President in 1640. Eaton had been known only as Master or Professor. From that time the College steadily advanced. In 1642 the Board of Overseers was established. Besides the governor, deputy-governor, and magistrates, it consisted of the teaching elders of the six next adjoining towns, Cambridge, Watertown, Charlestown, Boston, Roxbury, and Dorchester. The influence of our minister, both from his official connection with the College and his personal character, must have been considerable. We find him at one time addressing a memorial to the Commissioners of the United Colonies, asking a general contribution for the maintenance of poor scholars, to the end "that the Commonwealth may be furnished with knowing and understanding men, and the churches with an able ministry." He begs that it may be recommended to every family throughout the plantations, able and willing to give, to contribute a fourth part of a bushel of corn, or something equivalent to this, as "a blessed means of comfortable provision for the diet of such students as stand in need of support." The plan was approved and adopted. This may illustrate his interest in the College and his efforts to promote its high objects. It was the first charitable provision made in New England for the benefit of indigent scholars. It is good to connect the beginning of so good a work with the name of one we venerate.

Our church had another point of connection with the College in its earliest days, through our brother, Elijah Corlet, of whom mention has already been made. The grammar school appears to have begun soon after the town, and it was supported with great care. Mr. Corlet was master for more than forty years. The author of "New England's First Fruits," in 1643, writes: "By the side of the College is a fair grammar school, for the training up of young scholars and fitting of them for academical learning, that still as they are judged ripe they may be received into the College of this school." He speaks of our brother as one who had well approved himself for his abilities and dexterity. Mather calls him "that memorable old schoolmaster in Cambridge, from whose education our College and country has received so many of its worthy men that he is himself worthy to have his name celebrated in our church history."

I cannot close this notice of the College without repeating the familiar words which embody the thoughts of Shepard and his associates, — words which deserve to be written in letters of gold on the front of the University, that the youth of this generation may know the purpose of the fathers, and may gratefully execute it in their lives. "After God had carried us safe to New England, and we had builded our houses, provided necessaries for our livelihood, reared convenient places for God's worship, and settled the civil government, one of the next things we longed for and looked after was to advance learning and perpetuate it to posterity; dreading to leave an illiterate ministry to the churches, when our present ministers shall lie in the dust." The College seal of 1643 bore the motto "Veritas," which was inscribed on three open books. This was soon exchanged for "In Christi gloriam." After a time this was changed to "Christo et Ecclesiae." Let the spirit of the College and the lives of its graduates exhibit the three legends, — standing upon the truth, seeking the glory of Christ, rendering good service to his church.

It may not seem to be in close connection with the purpose of this discourse, but I am unwilling to bring these remarks upon education to an end without a few words of affection and respect for the memory of that great teacher who one week ago entered into his rest.* He deserves to be honored wherever sound learning is revered. We honor him for his wide learning, his patient research, his faithful instruction; for his "imperial memory," his "massive judgment," his "resolute will"; for his devotion to his work, his love for the institution he adorned, his kindness to all who came under his care; for his great heart, his unostentatious goodness, his unsparing charities. He died at the height of his fame; "his eye was not dim, nor his natural force abated." He died in the academy his toils had reared. His old boys took up his stalworth form and bore it to its repose among the honored, sainted dead. His boys of many years will mark the spot with the monumental column. But his memory will be green in the hearts of his six-thousand scholars. There are those here this morning who will join me in laying this simple tribute of love and respect upon his bier.

In the formation period we are surveying there were naturally differences of opinion regarding various matters of ecclesiastical usage. In the year in which Shepard was installed, some of the Puritan ministers of England, hearing that the churches here had adopted a new mode of discipline of questionable expediency, addressed to them a letter of inquiry upon this matter. The questions were concerning a form of prayer and set Liturgy; concerning proper subjects for infant baptism and admission to the Lord's Table; concerning the rights

---

* Samuel H. Taylor, LL.D., of Andover.

of the majority with regard to excommunication; concerning the removal of church members; the relation of a minister to his own church and neighboring churches, and the relation of the members of one congregation to another. A full discussion ensued, in which Mr. Shepard bore a part, joining with Mr. Allen of Dedham in the publication of a book explaining and defending the usages here. The work had a good effect. It solved various perplexing matters, and gave satisfaction to the English brethren. Upon the principles it expounded the churches conducted their affairs until a more formal constitution was adopted. Before many years had gone by, it became evident that a general declaration of faith and a plan of church government were desirable. I have alluded to these before, but they should be mentioned in this connection. In 1646 the General Court took up the matter of calling a synod. It was seen at once that it would be unwise for the Court to do anything which looked like imposing upon the churches a form of government, or even to call a synod for the preparation of a system which might seem to be commanded by authority. The point was important and delicate. The result was a recommendation that such an assembly be convened. The advice was acted upon, and the synod met in Cambridge in the autumn of that year, but, owing to the lateness of the season, adjourned after a short session, and on its reassembling again adjourned on account of a great sickness which prevailed in the country. It finally met in the autumn of 1648. It was a grand gathering. There were men who had won fame in the mother-land. There were scholars, patriots, statesmen, men of prayer, wisdom, patience. An old writer has truly said, "They were Timothys in their houses; Chrysostoms in their pulpits; Augustines in their disputations." They gave their assent to the Westminster Confession for substance of doctrine. For church polity they issued a plan of their own, which is thus entitled: "The Cambridge platform of church discipline, gathered out of the Word of God, and agreed upon by the elders and messengers of the churches assembled in synod, 1648." It is a clear, comprehensive, sagacious document, and upon its broad principles our churches have stood and become established in beauty and strength. The experience of two centuries has taught us some new things, and changed times may demand some incidental modification of the arrangements of our fathers. Possibly another synod at Cambridge may perfect and adapt the ancient work. In the mean time, to borrow the words of the late lamented pastor of this church, "the more closely we adhere to the scheme of polity set forth by that venerable assembly, the more confidently may we expect that Congregationalism will maintain its ascendency in New England, and commend itself to the consciences and the hearts of intelligent Christians throughout our country."

But while this church and its minister were engaged with others who held the same faith with the same purpose in establishing the churches in purity and order, they were also regardful of those around them who needed to learn the first principles of the gospel. Our national connection with the Indians is far from satisfactory. It is well to relieve the picture with brighter shades. The early government and churches of this State were perhaps as zealous in their missionary work as their successors. Foreign missions do not of necessity involve the crossing of the sea. Preaching was, sustained among the Indians by legal provision. Their rights were protected by a special court. The people sought to be just in their dealings with them. The wars against them were for defence. The College turned its attention to their education. A building of brick was erected for their accommodation by the "Society for propagating the Gospel," and was known as the Indian College. Although several students entered on a course of study, but one attained to academic honors. The catalogue for 1665 shows one Indian graduate. The effort to train up a native ministry for the aborigines was a noble one, but it proved ineffectual. In 1644 the General Court ordered that the county courts should take care that the Indians residing in the several shires be civilized, and should have power to take order from time to time that they be instructed in the knowledge and worship of God. John Eliot has won immortality by his labors for their spiritual good. In his efforts he had the counsel and assistance of Thomas Shepard. The first fixed missionary station of Eliot was in Cambridge, at Nonantum, now Newton. Shepard watched over the church gathered there. He wrote tracts which were translated into the Indian tongue. A long letter written by him to a friend in England bears the title, "The clear Sunshine of the Gospel breaking forth upon the Indians in New England." "An Indian sermon," he called it.

Eliot had also a faithful co-laborer in our brother Daniel Gookin. He removed from Virginia in 1644, and settled here, "being drawn hither by having his affection strongly set on the truths of Christ and his pure ordinances." He became the "constant, pious, and persevering companion of Eliot." He attained to political and military honors; was made superintendent of all the Indians who had submitted to the government of Massachusetts; was one of the licensers of the printing-press; in 1681 was appointed major-general of the colony. He was a man of integrity and ability, and died poor in this world's goods, but having the affection of those over whose interests he had watched, and the esteem of all the people. A monument was erected over his grave in the neighboring churchyard. His son was the fourth pastor of this church.

Eliot's translation of the Bible was printed here by our brother Samuel Green, in connection with Marmaduke Johnson. A copy handsomely bound was sent to Charles II. Baxter says, "Such a work and fruit of a plantation was never presented unto a king." This was the first Bible printed in America, — another of the good things which began here. It was followed by the publication of numerous works in the Indian language. Let it be remembered to the honor of our fathers, that the first Protestant mission to the heathen in modern times began in Cambridge; the first Protestant sermon in a heathen tongue was preached here; the first translation of the Bible by an Englishman into a heathen tongue was printed here; the first Protestant tract in a heathen language was written and printed here. In all these missionary works we may be sure that the minister and the members of our church took a lively interest and had an active part.

I have dwelt, perhaps overlong, upon matters of public interest with which our church was concerned. It may help to increase our honest pride in our religious ancestry, and stimulate us to the good works which are required of this generation. But while these large interests were engaging the attention of the people the more regular work of the church was going on. The word of God was faithfully preached on the Lord's Day. A weekly lecture was carefully prepared and delivered. The ordinances of the church were administered. The training of the youth was regarded. Our records of all these private doings are painfully scant. But the value of the work is inestimable.

I am compelled to reserve my remarks upon the personal character and the teaching of our first minister. It is interesting to find his name and the affairs of the church entering into our public records. The General Court which met here in 1636 made a grant of £50 to Mr. Thomas Shepard. In our town records you may find a vote in 1638 granting to him two and two thirds acres of land on the road to Charlestown. In 1647 there is a grant of six acres of meadow land. In 1650 there is a record stating that three hundred acres of land beyond Watertown Mill had been formerly given to Mr. Shepard, and also two hundred acres more near Mr. Samuel Shepard's farm. I find no other record of provision directly for his maintenance. But we know that in 1640 he was brought into great embarrassment through the depression in the financial condition of the colonists. It was a time of public extremity, threatening the very existence of the church. There was no money. Mr. Shepard's salary was then £70, payable in corn, which in this year was made a legal tender for new debts. The emergency was so pressing that a removal to Connecticut was discussed, and Shepard was urged to this step by Hooker. He bore his trial with patience and faith, submitting to the will of the Lord, and waiting for better times. We are thus permitted to know something of the things our fathers talked about and suffered in the days which are gone. To show further the regard of the town for the church, there is the vote in 1648, at a general town-meeting, "that there should be a farm laid out of a thousand acres, and improved for the good of the church, and that part of the church that shall here continue." This was in that portion of Cambridge known as Shawshine. The census of 1647 gives as the number of ratable persons in the town one hundred and thirty-five, with ninety houses.

In 1642 there is this record: "It is ordered that according to an order of Court made the last General Court for the townsmen to see to the educating children, that John Bridge shall take care of all the families of that side the highway his own house stands on to My Bro. Winship's," and so on, dividing the town into six parts, which were assigned to different persons.

The house of worship seems to have fallen in need of attention. It was a house humble in appearance, but comparing well with other houses in the town, and famous for some things done within its rude walls. There this church had its beginning. There, it appears, was held the first College Commencement in 1642. There the Cambridge Platform was framed in 1648. Other events which related to the interest of the community and the churches around it found a place within its courts. It was a building famous for beginnings. But the years would not spare it. In February, 1649, at a general meeting of the whole town, "it was voted and agreed by a general consent, that the meeting-house shall be repaired with a 4-square roofe and covered with shingle, and the charge thereof levied upon the Inhabitants of the Towne by equale rate." Either because it was found cheaper to build a new house than to repair the old one, or a better house could be afforded, or a better site procured, three weeks later "it was voted and agreed that the five men chosen by the Town to repair the meeting-house shall desist from the same and agree with workmen for the building of a new House about 40 foote square, and covered as was formerly agreed for the other." It was also agreed that the new house should stand on "Watch-house Hill." The site selected was near the place where Dane Hall now stands, and near the dwelling-house occupied by Mr. Shepard, which stood also in the present College yard, nearly opposite to Holyoke Street. But it was not to be given to Thomas Shepard to fill the new sanctuary with the sound of the "silver trumpet from whence the people of God had often heard the joyful sound of the gospel." His constitution had never been vigorous, and his labors and trials must have impaired his health. He says of himself that he was "very weak and unfit to be tossed up and down and to bear persecution." We find him at one time brought near to the gate of death, but graciously restored through God's good providence. One child had died in England. Two children died here. His wife died soon after his arrival here. In 1637 he married Joanna, the eldest daughter of his friend and predecessor, Thomas Hooker. She was a woman of remarkable loveliness and piety and wisdom. But after less than nine years of married life she, too, was taken from him. In 1638 his old and dear friend Roger Harlakenden died, and was buried with military honors. Mr. Shepard afterwards married Margaret Boradel, who survived him, and became the wife of his successor. There were four sons remaining to him when he died.

Among his honored descendants were John Quincy Adams and the remainder of that illustrious line.

The 25th of August, 1649, was a day long to be remembered by this church. With perfect memory and clear understanding Mr. Shepard made his will, making a brief but explicit statement of his faith and then giving small bequests to his sons and a few friends, — among whom was the faithful Ruth Mitchenson, the Yorkshire servant who followed him to this country, — and leaving the rest of his temporal estate to his wife. The inventory of his estate amounted to £810. Some of his last sayings are preserved. To his weeping friends he said, " I love the Lord Jesus Christ very much ; that little part which I have in him is no small comfort to me now." To several young ministers who visited him a little before his decease he said, " Your work is great, and calls for great seriousness. As to myself I can say three things: that the study of every sermon cost me tears ; that before I preached a sermon, I got good by it myself ; and that I always went up into the pulpit as if I were to give up my account to my Master." He was solicitous concerning his successor, and when he found that the man of his choice had commended himself to his people, he was content to depart. So he died, in the forty-fourth year of a large life, after a career of singular diligence and usefulness, leaving upon many hearts and lives the impress of his character and work. No man knoweth of his grave ; but he is with his Lord. He died, but the stream flowed on, making glad the city of God. It flows still to clothe in living green the holy place of the tabernacles of the Most High.

> " His name and office sweetly did agree ;
> Shepard, by name, and in his ministry.'

LECTURE IV.

"THERE SHALL BE AN HANDFUL OF CORN IN THE EARTH UPON THE TOP OF THE MOUNTAINS; THE FRUIT THEREOF SHALL SHAKE LIKE LEBANON: AND THEY OF THE CITY SHALL FLOURISH LIKE GRASS OF THE EARTH." — Psalm lxxii. 16.

IT is a question whether the word translated *handful* should not be rendered *plenty* or *abundance*. The rabbinical tradition favors the rendering of our version, while modern lexicographers prefer the other. It is a question of etymology. The psalm portrays the glories of the Messiah's reign, taking its imagery from the peaceful, prosperous reign of Solomon. There shall be an abundance of all blessings; the fruits of the earth shall grow in luxuriance, and man shall be full of all vigor and honor. Either rendering of the verse now before us will be true of that happy time. Its promise of plenty will be fulfilled. From the beginning there will be an abundance. Yet to the eyes of men the beginning of the Messiah's career, the earthly life of our Lord, promised little of stability or grandeur. Few dreamed that Jesus of Nazareth would show himself Lord of Hosts; that he who was nailed to the cross would sit upon a throne which should be for ever and ever. There was enough of power, of rule, of majesty, for the work of his earthly years; more of marvels, of wisdom and mercy, more of divine revelation, of the close presence of God, than the centuries had ever known. Men might call it a handful; it was abundance. Even they who saw the most would see yet more and more as the kingdom of the Great King widened. Christianity now has possession of the earth, and moves on to bring all lands, all men, under the beneficent sway of Christ, the King.

The New England Pilgrims and Puritans sought to establish upon these open shores a kingdom within the kingdom of God, and subject unto it. Their attempt won a small place in the annals of their own and later times. Few in number, persecuted and contemned, engaged in an undertaking resembling others which had failed, the world, so far as it cared anything for them, had slight expectation of their success. They were as a handful of corn; a handful in the earth upon the top of the mountains, a place so rocky and bleak that there was little prospect of a generous harvest. Yet it was more than a handful. Those men and women, with the spirit which had brought them across the seas, with a purpose as noble as could be cherished, with a courage and persistency which no storm of elements or enemies could break, with learning and virtue and piety, with God's Word in their hands and in their hearts, and God himself within and on every side of them, they were an abundance, the plentiful seed of a great harvest, a harvest which began at once in the liberty and purity and usefulness which made the wilderness to smile. Call it a handful, call it an abundance, — either will be true, — to-day the green and golden stalks shake like the trees upon Mount Lebanon, and the world hears the rustling, and men out of all lands are glad to sit in the pleasant shade and feed upon the exuberant fruitage.

Of this plentiful handful a goodly portion was here

where we are dwelling. They of this city are now flourishing like grass of the earth, while they are widely scattered who have been raised up and nourished here for high service and grand accomplishment.

We are to look more carefully at the beginning of these large things. Once again we are with that little company gathered about Thomas Shepard, receiving form and impulse from his hands. What was there in him, in his ministry, productive of abiding results? The personal history of the man we have already examined. We come now to his work. He was a preacher. His influence was largely through his preaching. Of the doctrines which he held, and of his manner of presenting them, we are able to judge intelligently from his printed works and from the testimony of men of his own time. What did the first minister of the First Church in Cambridge preach to our predecessors? There is still to be seen a Bible, containing the Old Testament in Hebrew and the New in Greek, and having at the bottom of the title-page this inscription: "Thomas Shepard. ἐν τούτοις ἴσθε. Immanuel." That book holds the truth which he taught. Its teachings he received for himself and carefully inculcated. Whatever of good he wrought out was accomplished by one resting upon the Divine Word. He was a faithful student, and brought to his study of the truth a deep knowledge of himself, a wide experience of others, and the varied helps which a university training affords. The scheme of doctrine which he learned from the Holy Scriptures is easily discovered in his writings. He framed a system for himself, which was published under the title of "The Sum of Christian Religion, in way of Question and Answer." It is a catechism, and could be studied now with profit. The beginning gives the key-note of his whole system of theology: "What is the best and last end of man? To live to God." An answer which seems better than the corresponding one in the Catechism of the Westminster Assembly, which adds our own enjoyment of God to the glory which it is our chief end to pay to him. As we advance from this beginning, we find these teachings: God is a spirit living of himself, infinite and eternal, understanding at once all truth, and purely willing all good. There is one God, yet he has three subsistencies or persons, who are "coequal, coeternal, subsisting in, not separating from each other, and therefore delighting in each other, glorifying each other." God has his decree, that is, "his eternal and determinate purpose, concerning the effecting of all things by his mighty power, according to his counsel." Man was made by him, in his image, and was placed in the garden of Eden to live unto God. He apostatized, or fell, by eating of the forbidden fruit; and because "we were in him as the members in the head, as children in his loins, as debtors in their surety, as branches in their roots," in his falling we all fell, by the imputation of his sin, as, if he had stood, we all had stood, by the imputation of his righteousness. There are two kinds of sin: original sin, which is "the contrariety of the whole nature of man to the law of God"; and actual sin, which is "the continual jarring of the actions of man from the law of God, by reason of original sin." The recovery of man is his return "to the favor of God, merely out of favor and the exceeding riches of his free grace." The Redeemer is Jesus Christ, God and man, who by his perfect obedience, and his death in bitter sufferings, both of body and soul, hath paid the price which justice demands, and delivered man out of captivity to sin, Satan, and death. Christ rose from the dead and ascended into heaven, whence he will return to judgment, " to the confusion of all them that would not have him rule over them, and to the unspeakable good of his people." The Holy Spirit applies this redemption to men, cutting off the soul from the old Adam and ingrafting it into the second Adam, Christ Jesus. He produces contrition and humiliation in the soul, so that the whole soul hears the call of Christ and the offer of his rich grace, and " comes out of itself unto Christ, for Christ, by virtue of the irresistible power of the Spirit in the call : and this is faith. . . . . The soul possessed with Christ, and right unto him, hath by the same Spirit fruition of him, and all his benefits"; hath justification, reconciliation, adoption, sanctification, glorification. The law still remains as a rule of life, but while the eternal curse of God falls upon the unregenerate for their disobedience, God does not withdraw his loving-kindness from the regenerate, but accepts their imperfect obedience when they observe the will of Christ by confessing and lamenting their sin, by desiring mercy in the blood of Christ and more of his spirit, by returning to him the praise of the least ability to do his will. The church is " the number of God's elect. . . . . None are to be members of the church but such as are members of Christ by faith." The members are bound to cleave to Christ by faith, and to one another also by brotherly love. By uniting with a particular church the believer receives special benefits and promises. The ceremonial observances are the two sacraments, Baptism and the Lord's Supper.

I have taken these statements from the Catechism, nearly in the words of the author. These doctrines are more clearly unfolded in his larger treatises, and to those I must refer any one who wishes to know more fully what Shepard taught. His views of sin were deep and painful. His consciousness of sin tormented him. He was ready to refer his own troubles, and the sorrows of those connected with him, to his wickedness. He has left a record of certain "Meditations and Spiritual Experiences," concerning which David Brainerd says in the Preface, that whoever reads attentively "must own that he finds a greater appearance of true humility, self-emptiness, self-loathing, sense of great unfruitfulness, selfishness, exceeding vileness of heart and smallness of attainments in grace, than some are willing to admit of." He dealt severely with himself; yet his heart rested on God, and from his despondency he sprang back upon the Divine mercy and promises. He closes the record, "I saw also how exceeding precious Christ was, by whom I came to have all favors, and how precious his blood was, so as I desired to rejoice in nothing but in Christ." His portrayal of the punishment of the wicked is frightful. But this is matched by his portrayal of redemption. "Christ is a redeemer by strong hand," he cries. "Here is encouragement to the vilest sinner, and comfort to the self-succorless and lost sinner. O, look up here to the Lord Jesus, who can do that cure for thee in a moment which all creatures cannot do in many years. . . . . God, as a creator, having made a law, will not forgive one sin without the blood of Christ; nay, Christ's blood will not do it neither, if thou dost join never so little that thou hast or dost unto Jesus Christ, and makest thyself or any of thy duties copartners with Christ in that great work of saving thee. Cry out, therefore, as that blessed martyr did, 'None but Christ, none but Christ.'"

It is interesting to mark the place which his teaching gave to children. This is made clear by a treatise sent to a friend as a letter, and afterwards published with the title, "The Church Membership of Children and their Right to Baptism, according to the holy and everlasting covenant of God, established between himself and the faithful, and their seed after them, in their generations." This was "published at the earnest request of many, for the consolation and encouragement both of parents and children in the Lord." Dr. Albro says of this, "Of all the works upon Infant Baptism which have been written in New England, this letter of Shepard's may be regarded as one of the most able and satisfactory." His main positions are that "the children of professing believers are in the same covenant God made with Abraham: that baptism is a seal of our first entrance and admission into covenant, and therefore is to be immediately applied to children of believing parents as soon as ever they be in covenant, and that is as soon as they become the visible seed of the faithful. . . . . The children of godly parents, though they do not manifest faith in the gospel, yet they are to be accounted of God's Church until they positively reject the gospel, either in themselves or in their parents." He cherished "high thoughts of faith" concerning them, as children and sons of God by promise. "For want of faith in God's promise about our children, certainly God smites and forsakes many of our children." I commend this work to the reading of all with whom God graciously offers to make covenant for their children's sake. It is most touching to see the anxiety of this young father to have his son baptized. Hunted and watched as he was in England, he was not able safely to obtain for him this Christian ordinance in its purity until he had found a new home. Most tenderly does he admonish that son afterwards: "God gave thee the ordinance of baptism, whereby God is become thy God, and is beforehand with thee, that whenever you shall return to God, he will undoubtedly receive you; and this is a most high and happy privilege: and therefore bless God for it." We are loyal to this beginning, for this Divine ordinance of our holy religion is held in high honor; and few are the children born into this church who are not blessed with its sacred advantage.

We are able to learn from the published writings of Shepard his views regarding the Sabbath. In a long treatise he discusses the Lord's Day in all its bearings. It contains the substance of several sermons, and was thrown into the form of theses at the earnest request of the students in the College for their use. In these days, when the Sabbath is so much misunderstood, and when the Puritan idea of the day is thought austere and formal to the last extreme, these masterly pages will be found profitable reading. The question of the Sabbath had been considered and settled in the minds of the Puritans before they left England. The English reformers accounted the day holy. Elizabeth took much lower ground, and by her precept encouraged her people to engage in active labors on the Lord's Day, and by her example to devote a part of the day to merry-making. The people went farther than the Queen designed. Fairs, markets, festivals, work of all kinds, games, theatrical performances, profaned the consecrated time. At length a frightful accident at a bear-baiting on the Sabbath alarmed the people, and aroused the public conscience. A bill passed Parliament "for the better and more reverent observing of the Sabbath day." The Queen refused her signature, because "she would suffer nothing to be altered in a matter of religion or ecclesiastical government."

The leaders of the movement would not rest there. The appeal to law had failed. There was another tribunal, — the popular heart. This was not addressed in vain. A reformation followed, in which the Puritans took the foremost part. Many who believed with the Puritans in the sacredness of the day, and favored its scrupulous observance, became alienated from the Established Church, whose influence was thrown on the other side. It came to pass after a time that "a rigid or lax observance of the Lord's Day was the sign by which, above all others, the two parties were distinguished." Out of this contest, from this reformation and these divisions, from this settlement of the question, our fathers came here to begin a state, to whose well-being the keeping of the Sabbath was essential. But one who reads the work of Shepard will be convinced that, however rigid may have been their domestic and public Sabbath laws, they kept the day as a sacred, precious time, finding its advantage not in austerities or formalities, but in real spiritual benefits, which no man, no house, could gain save by remembering the Sabbath day to keep it holy. With these exalted ideas of the worth of the day, Mr. Shepard urged upon men a faithful regard for its duties and privileges. He rested for authority upon the Fourth Commandment, and recognized the first day of the week as the Christian Sabbath. In regard to the beginning of this holy period he says, "At evening, after the setting of the light of the body of the sun, wherein darkness begins to be predominant over the light, the Sabbath begins." It was to be a day of rest: not of common, but of sacred or holy rest. He says, "The Lord enjoins this rest from labor upon this day, not so much for the rest's sake, but because it is a medium or means of that holiness which the Lord requires upon this day. . . . . Works of necessity, not only for preservation of life, but also for comfort and comeliness of life, are not unlawful. . . . . We are to abstain from all servile work, not so much in regard of the bare abstinence from work, but that, having no work of our own to mind or do, we might be wholly taken up with God's work, being wholly taken off from our own that he may speak with us, and reveal himself more fully and familiarly to us (as friends do when they get alone), having called and carried us out of the noise and crowd of all worldly occasions and things. . . . . Upon every Sabbath we should be in a holy manner drowned in the cares and thoughts and affections of the things of God. . . . . Such is the overflowing and abundant love of a blessed God that it will have some special times of special fellowship and sweetest mutual embracings. . . . . Herein God's great love appears to weary, sinful, restless man; all the treasures of his most rich and precious love are set open." I make these extended quotations that you may see what views of the Sabbath were cherished by one of the chiefest Puritan ministers. To keep the day according to his principles would make the Sabbath a delight for old and young. He regarded the Sabbath as a day to be kept in spirit and in truth.

His idea of heaven was spiritual. It was not simply a place full of delight for any one who might get through a gate; it was a place where the time is passed in the enjoyment of God and holiness, in love for Christ the Saviour. If one had shown no interest in these things here, there was little for him to anticipate with joy as he looked on to a future life.

It will be obvious, from all that has been said, that Thomas Shepard was a man of an eminently spiritual temper. He was thoroughly sincere. Against self-deception he continually admonished his hearers. His lectures upon the Parable of the Ten Virgins are full of warnings against having vessels without oil, and lamps whose light would go out. This hurried survey of his teachings should convince us that the Puritans were men of heart, of feeling, of affection; earnest in religion, even up to exile for its sake, but able to know the sweetness of religion and to enjoy the choicest of its benefits.

To preach the truth Shepard made careful preparation. His manner and matter agreed well. He learned before he taught. He made thorough work of a subject. His style is condensed, almost devoid of ornament, rich in comparisons and similes, clear and nervous. He was much in prayer. He lived deeply and thought deeply. Hence his works have not grown old. They are grand reading still. Some one has made the computation that in the "Treatise concerning the Religious Affections," by Jonathan Edwards, of the one hundred and thirty-two quotations more than one half are from Thomas Shepard. His writings are rich in pithy sentences, condensations of truth. I wish I could read many of them to you, but must be content with two or three. "The body may as well subsist without the soul, as the soul can without a promise. Do not flutter up and down from one promise to another, but lie a great while on some one, and wring and squeeze it, by meditation upon it."

"A woman that is matched to a prince may have never a penny in her purse, and yet she rejoiceth in that her husband hath it." Thus he illustrates the wealth of the poor man who is one with Christ. "Mariners long to be on shore; but before they come there they would not venture in a mist, but see land first; so should we desire the Lord in the land of the living. It is the honor of a Christian to be ripe for death betimes, yet still before he is ripe he is not to desire it. Children that will be up before it is day must be whipped; a rod is most fit for them; stay till it is day."

He took time to prepare himself for preaching. It is said that he always finished his preparation for the pulpit by two o'clock on Saturday afternoon, accounting "that God would curse that man's labors who goes lumbering up and down in the world all the week, and then upon Saturday afternoon goes into his study, when, as God knows, that time were little enough to pray in and weep in and get his heart into a frame fit for the approaching Sabbath." Thus tearfully, prayerfully, did he make ready for the house of God, taking to his own heart the truth he preached to others, and declaring the counsel of God as one who is to give account. He dealt honestly with his hearers. He sought no smooth things to please those who needed to be aroused, but spoke the truth with great plainness, always in love. With firmness and kindness he guarded his people against their own delusive hopes, promoted the interests of the church committed to his care, and advised others which sought his counsel. He was a shrewd man and a skilful casuist, as is shown by his treatise called "Certain Select Cases resolved; especially tending to the right ordering of the heart." In controversy he was fair, candid, charitable, striving for the upholding of the truth. So successfully did he watch over his own flock, that it was largely saved from the errors and commotions which disturbed many churches around him. Conscious of his faults, convicted of sin, he trusted so implicitly in the Saviour Christ, and his revealed truth, that he could preach the gospel with such unction that others, sinners like himself, heard to believe and obey. A tradition has come down that he " scarce ever preached a sermon but some one or other of his congregation were struck with great distress, and cried out in agony, What shall I do to be saved?" There is a glow and fervor in his sermons, even as we see them on the cold page, which accounts for their power. He pleads with men. His earnestness yet lingers in his sentences. In the frequent repetition of the "O," with which he appealed to his hearers, we have a glimpse of his longing desire to have men heed his message of life and live. He is described as "a poor, weak, pale-complectioned man," but his words had a marvellous power. This is evident from the epithets which different persons have applied to him. He is called "the holy, heavenly, sweet-affecting and soul-ravishing minister"; "this soul-melting preacher"; his was an "orthodox and soul-flourishing ministry." He was "that gracious, sweet, heavenly-minded, and soul-ravishing minister, in whose soul the Lord shed abroad his love so abundantly that thousands of souls have cause to bless God for him." "A man of a thousand, endued with abundance of true, saving knowledge for himself and others; yet his natural parts were weak, but spent to the full."

"Shepheard's sweet sermons from thy blessing came" —
"Oh Christ why dost thou Shepheard take away,
 In erring times when sheepe most apt to stray ?"

It will naturally be asked, What was the influence of such a man upon society? It was healthful in every way. He was a good overseer of the College. In 1636 he was entreated by the General Court to join with the governor and others in making a draft of laws agreeable to the Word of God, to be the "fundamentals of this commonwealth." Without limiting ourselves to Cambridge, we can learn from many sources what the community was which Puritans, Puritan preaching, Puritan influences, formed. It was a community which reverenced God, his Word, his Sabbath, his church. The Bible was the supreme law, but this was no sealed book; it was to be read by all, that every man might know his duty. They gave their interpretation to it, and were careful whom they made teachers; but it was an interpretation founded on the book itself and sustained by argument; and on the strength of that interpretation they had forsaken the land and church they loved, and in its application their success and hope were bound up. It was a community which endowed a college with a liberality which should excite this generation; and founded schools, and set good men over them, — men who feared God and knew his truth; which provided that children should be trained to some useful employment; which preserved its own morality and exalted the Christian virtues; which dealt so kindly by criminals, that, when English law punished more than thirty offences with death, here the extreme penalty was reserved for ten crimes; which loved freedom so well, that, with slavery sent upon it, there has not been a slave born in Massachusetts since 1641; which cherished kindly feelings towards the Indians around it, and sought their present and eternal well-being; which prospered in adversity, and kept its place and name till colonies could become a nation; which made its own time memorable for its valor and devotion, and wrote the first lines in the nation's heroic annals. It was a community of men with human limitations and infirmities; but of strong men, bent upon the right, instructed in all good learning. They were firm, but they were not bigots. They kept to their original purpose, and would not brook destructive interference. But the world was not so narrow that all men must live here. Any who disliked Puritan ways could follow their own ways on sunnier shores. They were not morose, sour, tyrannical. There were some such, it may be; there are now. Men of bigoted temper, long visaged, sullen, are to be seen any day in our streets. They are not puritanic, they are badly human; not a reproach to the fathers, but a sorrow to us. That snarling remark of Macaulay that "the Puritan hated bear-baiting, not because it gave pain to the bear, but because it gave pleasure to the spectators," is simply a blunder, or a falsehood, certainly so far as it relates to those who consented to expatriation in devotion to liberty and truth, in love for God and man. One of our own countrymen, who will not be suspected of any undue admiration of the early settlers of New England, has frankly said, — according to the public report, — that the only intolerance they indulged in was the "noble sort which belongs to those who are absolutely confident that they are the servants of almighty truth. They were not intolerant of things that meddled with their private interests; they were intolerant of those who hated God and loved sin and worked in iniquity, and that is the sort of intolerance," continues Mr. Emerson, " I should be glad to see a great deal more of to-day, here and everywhere." We have been reading the story of one Puritan minister; in him we may see how the two parts of a vigorous, manful character were united, the strength and gentleness, the firmness and affection, the courage which made a nation in a wilderness and laid its hand of blessing on the heads of children.

We are permitted to recognize the influence of Thomas Shepard upon certain individuals, and from their experience to infer his influence upon others. The narrative of the famous Edward Johnson has become familiar. He came hither for the second time in 1636, a zealous Puritan. It seems probable that he had known Shepard in England, possibly had been instructed by him. He arrived here at the height of the Antinomian controversy, and was nearly beside himself with the commotion and strife. He wandered out from Charlestown till he came to a large plain, where he heard the sound of a drum, and he moved towards it along a broad, beaten way. Meeting a man, he asked what the drum meant, and was told that it was to call people to the meeting-house where Mr. Shepard preached. He found his way to the house, where he stayed till the glass was turned up twice, and he was "metamorphosed, and was fain to hang down his head lest his watery eyes should blab abroad the secret conjunction of his affections." The words of the preacher impressed him, so aptly did he apply the truth, as if he had been Christ's privy councillor. The result was that he resolved to live and die with the ministers of New England. He was a man of learning and property, and had a leading part in the erecting of a church and town at Woburn, and in the administration of public affairs.

We have another illustration of Mr. Shepard's influence. In 1638 there came from England one Thomas Fuller. He proposed to make a tour of observation, and, when he had gratified his curiosity, to return home. But while in Massachusetts he heard the preaching of Thomas Shepard. Through his influence he became interested in the religion of the Puritans, in their methods and purposes, so that he decided to remain here, and bought a large tract of land in New Salem and settled down upon it. He married here, and died sixty years after his coming to the country. He founded a large and eminent family, and his descendants now worship with us in this house of the Lord.

Mr. Shepard's own sons, in their after-career, praise him for his wisdom and fidelity. Thomas graduated in 1653 and became pastor of the church in Charlestown, to be succeeded in the pastoral office by his son. Samuel graduated in 1658, and became pastor of the church at Rowley. Jeremiah graduated in 1669, and was ordained as pastor at Lyme, Conn., and enjoyed a ministry of forty-one years. "These all died in faith."

As we read the names of those who were in college during Mr. Shepard's ministry, we have another indication of his influence. His sympathies must have gone out to the youth who came to his humble sanctuary to learn the greatest lessons. Out of this happy seminary, says Cotton Mather, "there proceeded many notable preachers, who were made such very much by their sitting under Mr. Shepard's enlightening and powerful ministry." Among the young men who listened to him and were to a greater or less degree influenced by him, was William Hubbard, long the most eminent minister in the county of Essex; a man of learning, a superior writer, a good historian; of a catholic spirit, greatly interested in the Indians, and diligent in his efforts for their good. And Samuel Mather, of that house whose name and deeds are intertwined with our early ecclesiastical history, who was himself one of the first Fellows of Harvard College, afterward a chaplain at Oxford, and Senior Fellow at Dublin, where he was pastor of a church. And Samuel Danforth, Tutor and Fellow of the College, colleague of John Eliot, accounted among the first ministers of his day. And William Ames, son of the famous William Ames, the acute controversialist who fled from England to the Continent, where he was Professor of Theology, and for a time was the opponent of John Robinson. The father designed to come to New England, and after his death the mother came with the son, who graduated in the class of 1645, and returned to England, where he preached till he was ejected for nonconformity, and still preached on, filling up a ministry of forty-nine years. And John Brock, the laborious pastor, the shrewd fisher of men, mighty in prayer, full of faith and of the Holy Ghost, toiling with success until, "as the ancients expressed it, he took his journey a little before his body into another country." And John Rogers, president. And Urian Oakes, pastor and president. And Leonard Hoar, president. And Samuel Phillips, the eldest son of the first minister of Watertown, "an incomparable man, had he not been the father of Samuel"; a man so much respected and beloved by his people that they made provision for the education of his son, who for a long term of years was the minister of Rowley; who was the ancestor of men able and willing to make the house illustrious by founding the academies at Andover and Exeter, and writing the family name upon them. There are still extant notes of the sermons of Mr. Shepard in the handwriting of Samuel Phillips.

This glance at some of the men who came within the range of Shepard's preaching and personal influence will convince us how effective and enduring his work was. It is worthy of our boasting, that, from the beginning to our own time, so goodly a portion of our congregation is always enrolled in the catalogue of Harvard College.

There was one other student of whom special mention must be made. This carries forward the history we are reading. At the head of the names of the class of 1647 stands Jonathan Mitchel, Mr., Socius. Once again the history of our church springs from Yorkshire, England, where Mitchel was born in 1624. He was the son of pious and wealthy parents, who sought " to make him learned by a proper education." When he was about eleven years of age, in feebleness of body because of a recent illness, his parents were compelled to leave England on account of the persecutions there, and they sailed for this country in company with many other Puritans. After a perilous voyage they reached Boston in the summer of 1635. The family soon settled in Connecticut. Because of the feeble health of the son, troubles with the Indians, contentions in the community, and severe domestic misfortunes, the studies of young Mitchel were suspended for seven years, and he was employed in secular affairs. But his studies were resumed at his own desire, and the earnest advice and entreaty of friends who marked his great capacity for learning. He seems to have been mature even in his youth. "He had a clear head, a copious fancy, a solid judgment, a tenacious memory, and a certain discretion without any childish levity in his behavior, which commanded respect from all that viewed him; so that it might be said of him, they that knew him from a child never knew him any other than a man." His severe sickness seems to have made him serious. The sudden death of a servant, who "instead of going to the lecture at Hartford, as he had been allowed and advised, would needs go fell a tree for himself," and was killed by the falling of a bough, did much stir the heart of the youth, and set him upon repentance. He entered college in 1645, and came at once under the influence of Mr. Shepard. Concerning the impression made upon him during his student life by that godly minister, Mitchel testified, " Unless it had been four years living in heaven, I know not how I could have more cause to bless God with wonder, than for those four years." While in college, and afterwards, he kept a brief diary in Latin, from which Mather makes copious extracts. These reveal a close watch of his spiritual state, a deep humility and abasement of soul, and a strong desire to walk with God. Sometimes on Saturday he would retire into the neighboring woods and there spend a great part of the day in self-examination and mourning and praying. He had done this even when a school-boy. After graduating, he was made one of the Fellows of the College, and for a time was Tutor. His learning, gravity, and piety commended him to all. He used his offices well, and to the customary instruction of his scholars added diligent efforts for their spiritual good. While residing at college he wrote to his brother, who sought the counsel, what Mather calls "that golden letter," wherein he showed how well fitted he was, both by study and experience, for the ministry of the gospel.

Several churches sought to make him their pastor. "The Church of Hartford sent a man and horse above an hundred miles to obtain a visit from him, in expectation to make him the successor of their ever-famous Hooker." With much shrinking he went to Hartford and preached his first sermon from the text, "He endured, as seeing Him who is invisible." He was greatly dissatisfied with himself, but the church on the next day "concluded to give him an invitation to settle among them." They offered to allow him to remain at the College another year, and to advance him money to procure a library. But Mr. Shepard and the principal persons here had been before them, and had prayed him to come back as free as he went up, "insomuch as he did upon divers accounts most belong to Cambridge, and Cambridge did hope that he would yet more belong unto them." When this was first mentioned to him by Mr. Shepard, he wrote in his diary, "I wondered at this matter! What is it that the people of God sees in me? I left the whole business to the Divine management." On the 12th of August, 1649, he preached here. In the evening Mr. Shepard told him "this was the place where he should, by right, be all the rest of his days." Mr. Shepard inquired of some good people "how Mr. Mitchel's first sermon was approved among them. They told him, very well. Then, said he, my work is done." In less than a fortnight, Shepard was called to his rest; "so that the unanimous desire of Cambridge for Mr. Mitchel to be their pastor was hastened, with several circumstances of necessity for him to comply with their desire." On the 21st of August, 1650, he became the minister of this church. The neighboring pastors ordained him. John Cotton gave him the right hand of fellowship. Thenceforth he filled the office in which he had been set by Christ and the Church. Of this ministry I must speak more particularly at another time. But the great reputation which he acquired, and the high estimate set upon his talent and success, are abundantly proved by the testimonies published after his decease. Morton pronounces it an eminent favor of God to this church to have had the vacancy made by Shepard's death filled " with a man of so much of the spirit and principles of the former pastor, and so excellently qualified with respect to the College." " For," he continues, " reason and prudence requireth that the minister of that place be more than ordinarily endowed with learning, gravity, wisdom, orthodoxness, ability, sweet and excellent gifts in preaching; that so the scholars which are devoted and set apart, in order to be preachers of the gospel, might be seasoned with the spirit of such an Elijah; in which regard this holy man of God was eminently furnished, and his labors wonderfully blessed; for very many of the scholars, bred up in his time, do savor of his spirit, for grace and manner of preaching, which was most attractive." It is pleasant to see how important this position was considered, and how well fitted to occupy it Shepard and Mitchel were found.

This second pastor, like the first, was a student; " an over-hard student," one says, imperilling his health by sparing no time for recreation; yet "from a principle of godliness he used himself to bodily exercise." His advice to another illustrates his own feeling in regard to his work. " My serious advice to you is, that you keep out of company, as far as Christianity and civility will give you leave ; take it from me! the time spent in your study you will generally find spent the most profitably, comfortably, and accountably." His sermons cost him pains. "He ordinarily meddled with no points," says Cotton Mather, "but what he managed with such an extraordinary invention, curious disposition, and copious application, as if he would leave no material thing to be said of it by any that should come after him." He took a prominent part in the concerns of the College. "The College was nearer unto his heart than it was to his house, though next adjoining to it." "He loved a scholar dearly; but his heart was fervently set upon having the land all over illuminated with the spirit of a learned education. To this end he became a father to the College which had been his mother." He was actively engaged in the general ecclesiastical affairs. In all places he acquitted himself well. President Chauncy said, "I know no man in this world that I could envy so much as worthy Mr. Mitchel, for the great holiness, learning, wisdom, and meekness, and other qualities of an excellent spirit, with which the Lord Jesus Christ hath adorned him." Richard Baxter said of him, "that if there could be convened an Œcumenical council of the whole Christian world, that man would be worthy to be the Moderator of it."

In person Mitchel was at first slender, but afterwards grew corpulent. Or, in the words of an old biographer, "of extream Lean, he soon grew extream Fat." The fever in his tenth year settled in his arm, so that as it grew it kept a little bent, and he could never stretch it out right. His manner of preaching was peculiarly effective and pleasing. His fame was in all the region. From the neighboring towns people flocked to his monthly lecture, and listened to his exposition of the grandest truths of duty and destiny. It is said that "his utterance had such a becoming tunableness and vivacity to set it off as was indeed inimitable; though many of our eminent preachers, that were in his time students at the College, did essay to imitate him. And though he were all along in his preaching as a very lovely song of one that hath a pleasant voice, yet, as he drew near to the close of his exercises, his comely fervency would rise to a marvellous measure of energy. He would speak with such a transcendent majesty and liveliness, that the people would often shake under his dispensations, as if they had heard the sound of the trumpet from the burning mountain, and yet they would mourn to think that they were going presently to be dismissed from such an heaven upon earth." "He wrote his sermons very largely, and then used with enlargements to commit all to his memory, without once looking into his Bible after he had named his text, and yet his sermons were scriptural." He had "a very clear style," and was careful in his use of words. "Though he preached long sermons, the people were never weary of hearing them." From these descriptions of the man, we can see with what reason President Mather exhorted the members of the College, "Say each of you, Mitchel shall be the example whom I will imitate."

Mitchel was to have married Sarah, the daughter of John Cotton. When he "addressed himself unto the venerable old Mr. Cotton for leave to become his son-in-law," Mr. Cotton, "prognosticating the eminency which he would arrive unto, gave leave unto it." "But the immature death of that hopeful young gentlewoman" prevented "so desirable a match." In November, 1650, he married Margaret Shepard, second of that name, the young gentlewoman whom his predecessor had wedded near the close of his life. The students celebrated the marriage with epithalamiums, expressing the satisfaction of all the good people in the vicinity at the union of the minister whom they loved with one whom, for her own excellences and the honor of her name, they held in high regard. Upon the ancient Steward's book is an entry in Mitchel's account whereby he is debtor " by commones and sisinges and a super on his weedinge night." Upon the records of the General Court is the confirmation of a deed " wherein is conveyed to Mr. Jonathan Mitchel, now husband of Margaret, the relict of the said Mr. Shepard, a dwelling-house, yards, orcharde, and seven acres of land adjoining thereunto, in behalf of his said wife." The inventory of Mitchel's estate was nearly £ 800. Two sons, Samuel and Jonathan, both of whom graduated at the College, and one daughter, Margaret, gladdened his home.

In the summer of 1668, " in an extream hot season," after he had been preaching from the words, " I know that thou wilt bring me to death, and to the house appointed for all living," a putrid fever arrested him with a mortal malignity, and on the 9th of July " it pleased God to take him to rest and glory," in the eighteenth year of his ministry, and the forty-fourth year of his age. His departure caused a great mourning and lamentation here among his own people, and throughout the churches. " The chief remaining pillar of our ministry," as Hull ventured to designate him, had fallen. Only one sentence has come down to us from his last hours. To a young man standing by his bed he said, " My friend, as a dying man, I now charge you that you don't meet me out of Christ in the day of Christ." In our ancient church records is an entry of £8 13s. 6d., paid in silver, by the appointment of the committee for the minister's house, unto the Deputy-Governor, Mr. Francis Willoughby, for the discharge of Mr. Mitchel's funeral.

There are a few expressive lines, signed "J. S.," which stands, probably, for the Rev. John Sherman of Watertown. They are entitled, "An Epitaph upon the deplored Death of that Super-eminent Minister of the Gospel, Mr. Jonathan Mitchel."

> "Here lyes the Darling of his time,
> Mitchell, Expired in his prime;
> Who four years short of Forty seven
> Was found full Ripe and pluck'd for Heaven.
> Was full of prudent Zeal and Love,
> Faith, Patience, Wisdome from above:
> New England's stay, next Ages Story;
> The churches Gemme; the Colledge Glory.
> Angels may speak him! Ah! not I,
> (Whose worth 's above Hyperbole)
> But for our Loss, wer 't in my power,
> I'de weep an Everlasting Shower."

LECTURE V.

"SO HE FED THEM ACCORDING TO THE INTEGRITY OF HIS HEART; AND GUIDED THEM BY THE SKILFULNESS OF HIS HANDS." — Psalm lxxviii. 72.

THE Lord "chose the tribe of Judah, the Mount Zion which he loved. He chose David also his servant, and took him from the sheepfolds. From following the ewes great with young he brought him to feed Jacob his people, and Israel his inheritance. So he fed them according to the integrity of his heart; and guided them by the skilfulness of his hands." The singular favor with which God regarded his ancient people, his continual care for their interests, and the prosperity they enjoyed under his rule, have a parallel in the early history of our own land, in the Divine watchfulness and guidance granted to our fathers, in the abundant success which crowned an enterprise undertaken in his name, through love of his truth, with the hope of extending his kingdom. We may well confess that a generous portion of God's favor has been given to this church, if our study of its history shall confirm and extend the judgment of President Mather, that "there have been few churches in the world so lifted up to heaven, in respect of a succession of super-eminent ministers of the gospel." The line of my predecessors in this office, long in years, yet compassing few names, is one of which we may gratefully boast ourselves a little. When we read what men thought of Thomas Shepard, and repeat the sounding epithets with which the minister and his ministry were described, we are hardly prepared to turn from his early grave to find another standing in his place, carrying forward his work, winning as lofty admiration, wielding as wide an influence, seeming again to impoverish the language in the demand for laudation made by his character and work in his own and later times. The sketch of the life of Jonathan Mitchel in the Magnalia, under the title "Ecclesiastes," begins in this way: " It is reported concerning the ancient Phrygians, that, when a priest expired among them, they honored him with a pillar ten fathom high, whereon they placed his dead body, as if he were to continue, after his death, from thence instructing the people. Nor can a minister of the gospel have any more honorable funeral than that by which his instruction of the people may be most continued unto the people after his expiration. But I may, without any danger of mistake, venture to affirm, that there cannot easily be found a minister of the gospel in our days more worthy to have the story of his life employed for the instruction of mankind after his decease than our excellent Mitchel. And therefore I shall now endeavor to set him on as high a pillar as the best history that I can give of his exemplary life can erect for that worthy man; for whom statues of Corinthian brass were but inadequate acknowledgments." It is both honorable and profitable for us to cherish the memory and influence of one to whom we are so closely related, to whom is assigned a position so conspicuous. To some extent we have already surveyed his personal history and character. It remains for us now to examine his ministry with this church. We have seen that he was a Yorkshire boy who, at eleven years of age, came to this country with his parents, who are described as pious and wealthy persons; that he graduated at our College in 1647, and three years later was ordained and installed as pastor of this church. It was greatly to the joy of the church that he consented to become their minister, and it comforted the last hours of Mr. Shepard that he was to leave his beloved flock in so good hands. Mr. Mitchel's own feelings, as he entered upon his work, were those most becoming a man in his position. For his predecessor he cherished the utmost reverence. I have already repeated his words in which he expressed his estimate of Mr. Shepard's influence. Speaking of the time he spent at the College, he said, " Unless it had been four years living in heaven, I know not how I could have more cause to bless God with wonder than for those four years." It is well that a pastor should highly esteem his people. Of those committed to his charge, Mitchel testifies "that they were a gracious, savoury-spirited people, principled by Mr. Shepard, liking an humbling, mourning, heart-breaking ministry and spirit; living in religion, praying men and women. Here I might have occasion of many sweet heart-breakings before God, which I have so much need of." The new minister was a man of great talent, of deep and various learning, a diligent student, an eloquent preacher, a " most intense and faithful" pastor. He was of a very humble spirit. He wondered what the people of God saw in him, that they so much desired his labors among them. He meditated much upon his own character and the ways of God with him. He wrote in his diary, " O that I could remember this rule, never to go to bed until I have had some renewed, special communion with God." He sought to improve his trials. He would say, "When God personally afflicts a man, it is as if he called unto the man by name, and jogged him, and said, 'O, repent, be humbled, be serious, be awakened.'" Like his predecessor, he traced a connection between his faults and his trials. Kept from preaching by a hoarse cold, he made this record: "My sin is legible in the chastisement; cold duties, cold prayers (my voice in prayer, i.e. my spirit of prayer, fearfully gone), my coldness in my whole conversation, — chastisement with a cold; I fear that I have not improved my voice for God formerly as I might have done, and therefore he now takes it from me." "He wrote whole pages of lamentations" at the death of several lovely children in their infancy; but he humbled himself under the mighty hand of God, and was exalted in due time. When death summoned him, he was ready to abide or to depart, as it should be appointed for him. In near view of dying, he "fell to admiring the manifold grace of God unto him, and exclaimed, 'Lord, thou callest me away to thee; I know not why, if I look to myself; but at thy bidding I come.'" When he died, there was general mourning throughout all the churches. "It was feared there would be few more such rich grapes to be seen growing in this unthankful wilderness."

With great promise of success, he entered upon what was to form an eventful ministry. To attempt to state the truth as he preached it would be to restate the views of his predecessor. The truth which Thomas Shepard preached has been the staple of the preaching in this pastorate for almost two centuries and a half, and there is no likelihood that it will cease to be preached and heard until our Lord Christ cometh in the clouds of heaven. How close was the agreement between your first two ministers is indicated by the publication of Shepard's largest treatise, based upon the "Parable of the Ten Virgins," under the direction of Mitchel, with a Preface by him, in which he earnestly commended it to his own people, as a choice and precious treasure for their hearts to feed upon. Mitchel's preaching appears to have been very systematic. "He preached over a great part of the body of Divinity." "He made a most entertaining exposition of the book of Genesis and part of Exodus; he made many incomparable discourses on the first four chapters of John; occasional subjects he also handled with much variety; he likewise kept a monthly lecture, where he largely handled man's misery by sin and salvation by Christ, and entered on the doctrine of obedience due thereupon, and vast assemblies of people from all the neighboring towns reckoned it highly worth their pains to repair unto that lecture."

His ordinary labors were quite enough for him. But he was obliged to engage in others, less to his taste, yet needing to be done. Singularly his first public trial came from one from whom he could have expected only comfort and support. Henry Dunster, President of the College, and a member of this church, was, to use the language of Cotton Mather, "unaccountably fallen into the briars of antipædo-baptism; and being briar'd in the scruples of that persuasion, he not only forbore to present an infant of his own unto the Baptism of our Lord, but also thought himself under some obligation to bear his testimony in some sermons against the administration of baptism to any infant whatsoever." This seems to have been in 1653; of course this made a great excitement in the church and the community.

The brethren of the church were somewhat vehement and violent in the expression of their dissatisfaction with the position taken by one so eminent. They thought that for the good of the congregation, and to preserve abroad the good name of the church, he should cease preaching until he "had better satisfied himself in the point doubted by him." The Divine ordinance which he opposed was held in the highest veneration by our fathers. It had come to them from the earliest days of the church, and was sanctified before them by all the saintly associations of life. It connected them with God by his ancient covenant. It was a heavenly boon to the child upon whom parental faith and fidelity bestowed it. Its meaning and value and authority had been carefully taught by their first minister, of blessed memory. With the boldness and decision with which they set themselves against all wrong, all encroachment upon religious ordinances, they lifted up their voice against one who presumed to contradict what the church had always held, and to deny where Shepard affirmed; and not even his sacred calling, nor his lofty official position, could shield him from censure. If Dunster might claim any consideration by virtue of his character and office, it was to be remembered, on the other hand, that it was especially important that such a man should be right, and should be held to "the faith which was once delivered unto the saints." But it was not merely because it swerved from the faith of the church, and opposed what was deemed an important duty and an inestimable privilege, that this new doctrine was so greatly dreaded and opposed. For a hundred years the name Anabaptist, denoting primarily one who held that the adult believer, though he had been baptized in infancy, should receive the rite again, had been associated with fanaticism and extravagance. In Germany this sect denied the authority of magistrates, opposed all laws, made war against governments, rejected nearly all the Christian doctrines, and were guilty of the most seditious and vicious practices. There is no necessary connection between their views regarding baptism and the enormities into which they hurried. But the historic connection was enough to alarm the colonists here in the critical period of their infancy. The dreaded name was promptly applied to Dunster and those of like judgment, who could accept the religious doctrine implied in it, but could never have done the deeds which had attended it in the Old World. It is not to our present purpose to trace the conflicts of the Puritans with those who opposed their religious opinions and usages. But it is due to the Puritans that it should never be forgotten that their active proceedings were not against persons who simply differed from them in points of doctrine, but against those who added to such differences a hostility and opposition to the order of things which the first settlers had secured at the cost of expatriation. To have tolerated them, and let them have their way, would have endangered the liberty and peace which had been purchased at a heavy cost. Very likely they went farther than was necessary in their opposition to some who came among them. They may have exaggerated their peril. But they are not entirely without excuse. It is hard to transfer ourselves to their place. We do not claim for them perfection either in judgment or practice. They were men. But they were grand men, of heroic virtue; an ancestry of whom we have yet to prove ourselves worthy. Mr.

Peirce, in his excellent history of the University, commenting upon the case of Dunster, makes these distinctions, which deserve notice: "Facts like these exhibit our worthy ancestors to some advantage, even with respect to a virtue in which they have been supposed not to abound, — charity for those who differed from the orthodox standard of faith. . . . . They were rigid, rather than cruel; intolerant, but not inquisitorial; and they seem even to have been willing that men should enjoy their peculiar sentiments without molestation, so long as they refrained from obtruding them upon the public, and conformed to those regulations which were deemed necessary for the good order of society." Let not our sympathy for those who claim to be persecuted blind us to the fact that our Pilgrim and Puritan fathers had some rights. They had paid dearly enough for liberty to do as they pleased under the law of God. For those who differed from them the world was wide, and there were more genial spots than this New England coast.

Keeping in mind the inestimable value of the ordinance in question, and the practical significance of the term Anabaptist, it is not surprising that we find in 1644 a decree of the Court that any persons who should openly condemn or oppose the baptizing of infants, or should go about secretly to draw others from the approbation or use of the ordinance, or should purposely depart from the congregation when it was administered, or deny the lawful authority of the magistracy, and should obstinately continue in this opposition after due time and means of conviction, should be sentenced to banishment. This was not a decree against mere errorists, but against fanatics and seditious persons. It was prompted by the prudence of men themselves banished for conscience' sake, and for liberty and quiet in the truth; who dreaded to see here the turbulent scenes which had been witnessed abroad, and who were compelled to mark the beginning of similar causes here, which would "bring guilt upon us, infection and trouble to the churches, and hazard to the whole commonwealth." Of this law Winslow wrote that it was designed always to remain a dead letter, unless there should arise some extraordinary necessity for enforcing it. Two years after the passage of the law the Court itself declared, "For such as differ from us only in judgment, ... and live peaceably amongst us, without occasioning disturbance, &c., such have no cause to complain; for it hath never been as yet put in execution against any of them, although such are known to live amongst us." Another law was passed "for banishing such as continued obstinate after due conviction." The preamble asserts that "experience hath often proved, that since the first rising of the Anabaptists, about one hundred years since, they have been the incendiaries of commonwealths, and the infecters of persons in main matters of religion, and the troublers of churches in all places where they have been, and that they who have held the baptizing of infants unlawful have usually held other errors or heresies together therewith."

Both on religious and political grounds it was no small thing which Dunster did when, in so sacred a matter, he set himself against the sentiment of the churches and the rulers. There was no danger that he would be led into the excesses which were so much dreaded. But even the ideas which he advanced upon the simple matter of baptism would work incalculable mischief. It must have been with reluctance that this church resisted his influence and rebuked his conduct, for, besides his official station, he had been to them, after Shepard's death, in the place of a pastor. But he was of their own brotherhood, and with that inflexible adherence to right and duty which characterized them they moved against him. It was a trying position which Mitchel was placed in, — called to oppose his own President, a man greatly revered and beloved. He was slow to proceed against him. He thought the church too much excited, and said "that more light and less heat would do better." But the matter sorely oppressed him. He felt his own weakness to grapple with the difficulties: "This business did lie down and rise up, sleep and wake with me." A personal interview with Dunster even brought the young minister into doubts and scruples whether he was himself in the right. Yet he thought it was not hard to discern that such thoughts were from the Evil One. They interrupted his study for the Sabbath, so that it was with difficulty he prepared his sermon. "After the Sabbath was over," he writes, "and I had time to reflect upon the thoughts of those things, those thoughts of doubt departed, and I returned unto my former frame." He fasted and prayed; he sought help from the neighboring ministers; then publicly and formally opposed the new teachings of the venerated President. He is said to have "preached more than half a score of ungainsayable sermons" upon the subject thus brought before the church, and to have rendered good service to other churches in the same cause. The steadfastness with which his church still clings to the blessed ordinance of infant baptism is a witness to his fidelity and success.

It appears that Dunster was indicted by the grand jury for disturbing the ordinance of baptism in this church. The records of the County Court contain the presentment against him. "Severall witnesses tendered to attest uppon their oathes respectively, that uppon the Lord's daye, July the 30th, 1654, Mr. Henry Dunster spake to the congregation in the time of the publique ordinance to the interruption thereof without leave, which was also aggravated in that he, being desired by the Elder to forbeare, and not to interrupt an ordinance of Christ, yet notwithstanding he proceeded in way of complaint, to the congregation, saying, I am forbidden to speake that in Christ's name which I would have testified." Dunster afterwards acknowledged that for the manner, he had not spoken seasonably, but for the matter, "I conceived then, and so do still, that I spake the truth in the fear of God, and dare not deny the same or go from it untill the Lord otherwise teach me." The Court ordered that Dunster, "at the next lecture at Cambridge, should (by such magistrate as should then be present) be publiquely admonished and give bond for his good behavior." Dunster kept his place in the College till 1654, when the General Court passed a vote commending it to the pious care of the officers of the College and the selectmen of the several towns, not to permit any persons to be continued in the office of instructing the youth in the College or schools, that have manifested themselves unsound in the faith. As the views of Dunster were well known, it is probable that he considered this vote as directed against himself; and after five months he resigned his office, and his resignation was accepted. It is reported that the great mass of ministers and magistrates would have retained him in the office he had filled so well, if he could have been persuaded to indulge in his peculiar opinions in silence. This could not be effected. Some ground for the report, which in itself is reasonable enough, is afforded by the fact that his successor, Chauncy, was known to believe that the Lord's Supper should be administered in the evening of every Lord's Day, and that baptism should be administered to infants and adults only by the dipping or plunging of the whole body under water. He was inducted into office upon his agreeing not to disseminate or publish such tenets, or to oppose the received doctrines therein. He doubtless adhered to his agreement, for when he had been in town above a year or two the "church kept a whole day of thanksgiving to God for the mercy which they enjoyed in his being here."

In a petition of touching pathos, Dunster begged the privilege of remaining in the President's house through the winter, to which the General Court agreed. He afterwards removed to Scituate, where he ministered to the congregation which Chauncy had left, and where he died in 1659. He was a man of a remarkable spirit. He bore himself with dignity and meekness through his trials. He would not censure the conduct or motives of those who had been influential in bringing about his removal. In his last will he called Chauncy and Mitchel his reverend, trusty, and judicious friends, and appointed them appraisers of his library. He directed that his body should be brought to Cambridge, that he might lie near the College he had loved so fondly and served so faithfully. He was laid in the old churchyard, but the stone which marked the place disappeared. His grave was, however, quite clearly identified some twenty-five years ago, when a new tablet was placed over it. The esteem in which Mitchel held this great, good man, is evinced by an elegy which he wrote after Dunster's death, a portion of which I copy, as a tribute to his own catholic spirit: —

> "Where faith in Jesus is sincere,
> That soul, he saving, pardoneth;
> What wants or errors else be there,
> That may and do consist therewith.
> And though we be imperfect here,
> And in one mind can't often meet,
> Who know in part, in part may err,
> Though faith be one all do not see 't.

> "Yet may we once the rest obtain,
> In everlasting bliss above,
> Where Christ with perfect saints doth reign,
> In perfect light and perfect love:
> Then shall we all like-minded be,
> Faith's unity is there full-grown;
> There one truth all both love and see,
> And thence are perfect made in one."

Mitchel was called to bear a part in another important public matter, and this also had reference to the baptism of children. The first settlers of this country were, for the most part, members of the church, and their children were duly baptized. But in the course of time there sprang up another generation of children, many of whose parents had not renewed the baptismal vows and become church-members, and who, therefore, were not entitled to receive baptism according to the rules then in force. It was felt that the children of baptized persons should have a different position from Indians or other pagans who might hear the word of God. It was held by many, that if baptized parents, even if not regenerate, were willing to renew the baptismal covenant, and become subject to church discipline, their children could properly be baptized. This feeling and practice were growing up in the churches, when a synod of the elders and messengers of the churches was called. This was held in Boston in the spring of 1662. Mr. Mitchel was a member of this synod. The result was, the declaration of the independence of each church, and of the duty of the communion of churches, — that is, Congregationalism. It was a frequent saying of Mitchel's, that "the spirit of Christ is the spirit of communion." In regard to the matter of baptism, the result was, substantially, that the members of the visible church are subjects of baptism, and that children are members of the same church with their parents, and when grown up are under the care of that church. But this does not of itself admit them to full communion. Yet when they understand and publicly profess the faith, and are upright in life, and own the covenant, and give themselves and their children to the Lord, and submit themselves to the government of the church, their children are to be baptized.

This result was chiefly composed by Mitchel, and when it was opposed, its defence fell largely upon him. Thus did he have an important part in shaping the early policy of our churches. This decision in regard to baptism is known as the "Half-way Covenant," inasmuch as it granted baptism to the children of certain persons who were not considered qualified for admission to the Lord's Table. There arose in connection with this the practice of administering baptism to adults who were not esteemed regenerate, but who owned the covenant and submitted themselves to the care of the church, and were of proper moral character. This gave such persons a certain standing in the community, and was of especial value as long as suffrage was confined to church-members, and there were many persons born here, or who had immigrated hither, who otherwise would be denied the full privileges of citizens, for which they were fitted by age and character. Our own church records, besides the list of members in full communion, contain two lists, both beginning in 1696, the earliest date to which our present complete records reach. Of these two subordinate lists, one is headed, "Persons who owned the covenant in order to their children's being baptized." This extends to 1828. The other is headed, "Persons adult who owned the covenant and were baptized." This extends to 1782, and is quite largely made up of the names of negro servants. The use of the "Half-way Covenant" for children seems to have continued in this church until the division of the parish, although during the later years but few persons availed themselves of its provisions.

There must always have been, as there are now, those who esteemed it a hardship to be denied the sacraments of the church because they did not profess a personal faith in the Saviour, and give evidence to themselves and others that they had been born of the Spirit of God. To these we may answer, in the words of an old writer, "that Christianity is to be begun with repentance, and not with the sacraments"; that the promise is, he that believeth and is baptized shall be saved; and that for the penitent, trustful, obedient friends of Christ the doors of the church stand open wide.

Mitchel was accounted a man wise in council, and of great acuteness, so that the churches far and near sought his assistance in difficult matters. His brethren relied much upon his judgment. Yet he felt his own inadequacy to the work thus put upon him. Once, after he had acquitted himself admirably in an important matter, we find him writing, "How do I mar God's work, and mar what he gives me therein, by my own folly! Sometimes I am ready to resolve to put forth myself no more in public work, but keep myself silent, and unengaged, as I see others do." Then follows a prayer for wisdom. He seems to have been happiest in his study and among his own people. Yet he would not refuse a wider service. A few of his published writings still remain to instruct us.

From this more public ministerial life of Mitchel we come to consider events more confined to our own town and church. What was Cambridge in Mitchel's day? He became the minister in 1650. We have an estimate of the number of persons and of their estate, made by the selectmen in 1647, from which it appears that there were then here one hundred and thirty-five ratable persons, ninety houses, about twenty-six hundred acres of land, two hundred and eight cows, one hundred and thirty-one oxen, twenty horses, with other property of different kinds, making up a total valuation of £9,765 16 s. 1 d., — less than $50,000. Johnson describes Cambridge in 1652 as "compact closely within itself, till of late years some few straggling houses have been built. It hath well-ordered streets and comely, completed with the fair building of Harvard College. The people are at this day in a thriving condition in outward things." He confirms what others have said, that they "have hitherto had the ministry of the word by more than ordinary instruments."

Attention was given to the cultivation of orchards,

The orchard of the College is mentioned in the town records. The first license for an inn appears to have been given in 1652. In 1656 a committee was appointed to execute the order of the General Court for the improvement of all the families in spinning and clothing. About 1660 "The Great Bridge" was built, at the end of what is now Brighton Street. A house of correction was erected about the same time. In 1662 Mr. Mitchel and Captain Daniel Gookin were appointed by the General Court "licensers of the press."

About the time of Mitchel's ordination the second meeting-house was completed, which was a house about "forty foot square, and covered with shingle." It stood on Watch-house Hill, very near the spot where Dane Hall now stands. The town records furnish many little incidents which are of interest as illustrating the ways of our fathers in the church. In 1652 the church agreed to divide the farm in Shawshine, and assigned five hundred acres to Mr. Mitchel. The meeting-house and school-house were cared for, that they might be kept in good order. In 1656 the people on the south side of the river requested that they might have "the ordinances of Christ amongst them, distinct from the town." But the town did not think it expedient to grant their request, and thus divide the church. A few years later the inhabitants of Cambridge village had become so numerous that they formed a distinct congregation for worship, and they were granted an abatement of "one half of their proportion of the minister's allowance, during the time they were provided of an able minister according to law." In 1664 a new church was organized in Cambridge village, which afterwards took the name of Newton, from the original name of this place. This new church was composed principally of a colony from our church. John Eliot, son of the Apostle Eliot, a graduate here in 1656, under Mitchel's ministry, was the first pastor. In 1658 the elders and deacons and selectmen were appointed " a constant and settled power for regulating the seating of persons in the meeting-house." In 1660 sundry young men received permission " to build a gallery on the south beam," but the new seats were to be under the control of the seating authorities. In 1661 Mitchel received a further grant of twenty acres of land. In 1662 Mr. Corlet's scholars were so few that the town made him an allowance of £10. The town afterwards voted him an annual grant of £20. There are votes from time to time regarding the pastor's maintenance. In 1665 the constables were ordered " to make a convenient horse-block at the meeting-house, and causeway to the door, and to get the windows and roof repaired by the first opportunity." In the same year we find the selectmen calling upon several single men and inmates of this town " to give an account of their abode and orderly carriage," and they were required to give satisfaction of their orderly submission to family government, or otherwise they must expect the selectmen would order their abode as the law enjoined. In 1666 Thomas Fox was ordered " to look to the youth in time of public worship, and to inform against such as he find disorderly." In 1661 the town was districted for the catechising of the youth. Elder Champney and Mr. Oakes were appointed for the families south of the bridge, Elder Wiswall and John Jackson for those at the new church, and so on.

We are indebted to Mr. Mitchel for a list of the members in his day, the only church list which we have reaching farther back than 1696, if we except one recently made up from many sources. The original manuscript, in Mitchel's handwriting, is now in the possession of the First Parish. We have a copy of the original. The list was printed a few years since by the Rev. Dr. Newell. It is entitled "The Church of Christ at Cambridge, in N. E., or, the Names of all the Members thereof that are in Full Communion; together with their children who were either baptized in this Church, or (coming from other churches) were in their minority at their present joyning; taken and registered in the 11 month, 1658." The catalogue was continued through Mitchel's ministry. The first names are Thomas Shepard, Jonathan Mitchel, Richard Champney, Edmund Frost, Captain Daniel Gookin, Mr. Charles Chauncy. There are the names of other persons who took an active part in public affairs in their time. Our Triennial Catalogue gives us the names of many persons who during their stay here must have been connected with this congregation. Among the students of this time were William Stoughton, Leonard Hoar, Michael Wigglesworth, Thomas Shepard, Increase Mather, Samuel Willard, Solomon Stoddard, Abraham Pierson, and others who became men of influence. The minister endeavored to aid the young men in acquiring such knowledge and principles as would always be of service to them. A scholar himself, he was in sympathy with all sound learning. His influence extended thus to all the churches. Many were the men who were better preachers because they had been under his teaching. In this way his life repeated itself. President Mather said that in his day there were not above two or three of our churches but that were supplied with ministers from this College, which was thus faithful to the pious design of its founders. Mitchel formed plans for the prosperity of the College, of which one was "A Model for the Education of Hopeful Students at the College in Cambridge." He proposed to have septennial subscriptions by the more worthy and wealthy persons, to be disposed of by trustees for the benefit of promising students. "But through the discouragement of poverty and selfishness the proposals came to nothing." There is another little glimpse at Mitchel's influence in the case of one Singletary, a young man of twenty-three, who was in prison at Ipswich on a charge of slander in calling one Godfrey a witch. There, as he testified, he heard strange noises, and a crackling and shaking as if the house would have fallen. He was naturally frightened. "Yet, considering," he says, "what I had lately heard made out by Mr. Mitchel at Cambridge, that there is more good in God than there is evil in sin; and that although God is the greatest good, and sin the greatest evil, yet the first Being of evil cannot weane the scales or overpower the first Being of good; so, considering that the author of good was of greater power than the author of evil, God was pleased of his goodness to keep me from being out of measure frighted."

These times which we have been reviewing were eventful days for England. Thomas Shepard died in 1649, the year in which Charles I. was beheaded, and the Commonwealth declared. It was a period which called for all the prudence of these colonies, lest they should in some way become involved in the affairs of the mother country. They admired the valor of Cromwell, who was the champion of their own theories. But they refrained from soliciting any favors from the Puritan Parliament. Massachusetts kept silence when Cromwell was made a monarch. Her public records do not even allude to his death. She took advantage of the time when England was busy, and proceeded to coin money, which might be construed as a pretension of independence. She suffered at the Restoration in the persons of Hugh Peter and Henry Vane, and saw herself dishonored in George Downing. But she was able to shelter three men who had signed the death-warrant of the King and fled from the vengeance of Charles II. Of these Whalley and Goffe came immediately to Cambridge, where they intended to reside. The Act of Indemnity, from whose mercy they were excepted, did not reach this country for several months. Meanwhile, and for three months afterwards, they were treated with consideration, though at last there was a division of feeling among the magistrates regarding their duty. They were admitted into the best society here. They attended public worship and lectures, and took part in private devotional meetings, and were received to the Lord's Table. In showing them such favor, Mitchel was not aware of their exact relation to their government. He wrote afterwards in his own vindication, " Since I have had opportunity, by reading and discourse, to look into that action for which these men suffer, I could never see that it was justifiable."

It is evident that the people had enough to talk about during the ministry of Mitchel. We know what subjects occupied their thoughts. With what sadness must Elder Frost and Elder Champney have conferred upon Dunster's sad defection and the church's duty! How earnestly must Deacon Bridge and Deacon Marriot have discussed the Half-way Covenant; while every ship which brought news from England must have brought commotion into the whole community. They were stirring times. It was a good day to live in. The men were equal to their place. It is interesting to mark what was taking place in the world while this church was thus moving on its way. The Waldenses were persecuted by the Piedmontese; Quakers were suffering in Massachusetts; Pascal died, and Jeremy Taylor; the first idea of a steam-engine was suggested; "The Pilgrim's Progress" was published; Eliot's Bible was printed; London was smitten with the great plague, and devastated by the great fire; the Triple Alliance was formed for the protection of the Netherlands, — and there were many other events of general importance.

This second pastorate ended with the death of Mitchel, July 9, 1668, after a ministry of eighteen years. It was more than three years before the church had another pastor. The pulpit in the interim was occupied by President Chauncy and others, as appears from an appropriation made for their payment. The President was voted £ 50 and thirty loads of wood. At the same time £ 30 was voted to Mistress Mitchel. In this interval there is an order that the constable see that certain persons who keep without the meeting-house during the services on the Sabbath, spending their time unprofitably and dishonoring God, do attend upon public worship. Steps were taken, also, to build a house for the entertainment of the minister whom the Lord should send "to make up the breach that his afflicting providence hath made in this place." There is this memorandum in the year 1669 : —

"At a publick meeting of the church and towne to

consider of suply for the ministry (the Lord having taken away that reverant and holy man from among us, Mr. Jonathan Micthell, by death). It was agreed upon at the saide meeting that theare should be a house eyther bought or built for that ende, to entertayne a minister, and a commity was chose for that purpose which tooke care for the same, and to that ende bought fower akers of land of widdow Beale, to set the house upon, and in the year 1670 theare was a house carected upon the sayd land of 36 foote long and 30 foote broad, this house to remaine the churches, and to be the dwelling place of such a minister and officer as the Lord shall be pleased to supply us withall during the time hee shall supply that place amongst us."

The house was built in the present College grounds, on a glebe of four acres, nearly opposite the end of Holyoke Street. In 1726 a new front was put upon the house. Another order directed that the school-house should be taken down and set up again, and an allowance of 40s. was made to Mr. Corlet "for repairing of his house where he kept school." The town was again districted for the catechising of the children. Thus the parish work went on. After Mr. Mitchel's death, an attempt was made to secure Mr. William Stoughton, of the class of 1650, for pastor. This was unsuccessful, and he is afterwards found in the law and holding office in the State. The remembrance of his benevolence is preserved among us in the name of one of our College Halls, which was erected at his expense. An effort was then begun to recall Mr. Urian Oakes from England. He was born in England about 1631, and brought to this country by his pious parents in his childhood. He was a lad of small as he never was of great stature. He possessed a sweet

THE OLD PARSONAGE: BUILT IN 1670.

nature, which he retained, and observers said that if good-nature could ever carry one to heaven, this youth had enough to carry him thither. He was a precocious boy. At the age of nineteen "he published a little parcel of Astronomical Calculations," or an Almanac for 1650. He graduated here in 1649, but continued to reside in College and board in commons until 1653. We get a little insight into the state of things here, in finding among the articles with which he paid his expenses, a calf, a sheep, wheat, sugar, etc. He received from the College an allowance for his scholarship. He preached his first sermon at Roxbury, but "about the time of the Rump" returned to his native country, where he became chaplain to one of the most noted persons in the realm. He was then settled at Titchfield, where, as the historian narrates, after the manner of the silk-worm he wove his own spirit into " garments of righteousness for his hearers." In 1662 he was silenced, with all the nonconformist ministers. For a time he taught school. He then ventured to resume preaching. In one season he received a letter from this church, with a messenger, Mr. William Manning, and a letter from several magistrates and ministers, inviting him to come over and become the pastor here. He accepted the invitation. But the sickness and death of his wife hindered his coming. It does not appear when he was married, but his wife is thought to have been the daughter of the famous William Ames. The call was renewed, but a long sickness of his own delayed his acceding to the wishes of the church, so that there came to be doubt whether the church should longer wait for him. After debating the matter, the church was found willing to wait until the spring of

1671, and in July of that year he arrived; or, as the Magnalia expresses it, "The good Stork flew over the Atlantic Ocean to feed his dam." John Taylor went to accompany the chosen pastor to New England, and we have an account of the disbursement of money for the travelling expenses of the party. There seems to have been one of those unfortunate misunderstandings which will arise to mar the best intentions, for there is this memorandum: "Let it bee taken notice of that Mr. Prout does demand £13 more due to him." Let us hope that Mr. Prout was satisfied. In the town records is a report of a meeting of the church and town, July 16, 1671, at which it was voted: "1st, To acknowledge thankfulness to Mr. Oakes for his great love and self-denial in parting with his friends and concerns in England to come over to us. 2d, To manifest unto him the continuance of the earnest and affectionate desires of the church and people, that, as soon as well may be, he would please to join in fellowship here in order to his settlement and becoming a pastor to this church. 3d, To entreat him forthwith to consent to remove himself and family into the house prepared for the ministry. 4th, That the deacons be furnished and enabled to provide for his accommodation at the charge of the church and town, and distribute the same seasonably for the comfort of him and his family. 5th, That half a year's payment forthwith be made by every one according to their yearly payment to the ministry; and the one half of it to be paid in money, and the other half in such pay as is suitable to the end intended."

That in these changes the old pastor was not forgotten is evident from the next record which concerns us: "Voted, that there be a rate made of £20 and paid to Mistress Mitchell for her supply." Mr. Oakes became a member of this church, and was ordained pastor, November 8, 1671. The church had so deep a sense of the Divine favor in giving them such a minister, that they kept a day of public thanksgiving, when Mr. Oakes preached from St. Paul's words, "I be nothing," in which he sought to turn the thoughts of men from himself to the Lord whom he served. The new minister resided in the new parsonage, which continued to be occupied by the pastors until Dr. Holmes removed from it to a house of his own. The account of disbursements for the ordination is a relic of the olden time, containing, as it does, "3 bushells of wheate, 2 bushels $\frac{1}{2}$ of malt, 4 gallons of wine, beefe, mutton, sugar, spice and frute, and other small things," with similar items, amounting in the aggregate nearly to £10. In 1672 Oakes was made a Freeman. In 1673 he preached the annual Election sermon, in which he declared himself in favor of all moderation, and as compassionate towards the infirmities of others, but as regarding "an unbounded toleration as the first-born of all abominations." He asserts, what must always be remembered, that New England was "originally a plantation not for trade but for religion."

After the death of President Chauncy, Leonard Hoar, a graduate of 1650, a clergyman and physician, was chosen President. From his day the office has uniformly been filled by one of the sons of the College. Mr. Hoar's administration was an unfortunate one. There soon came to be "uncomfortable motions and debates." The students took a strong dislike to him, and did all they could to ruin his reputation. Cotton Mather says, they "turned cudweeds and set themselves to travestie whatever he did and said, with a design to make him odious." He says also, "I can scarce tell how," but he fell "under the displeasure of some that made a figure in the neighborhood. . . . . In a day of temptation, which was now upon them, several very good men did unhappily countenance the ungoverned youths in their ungovernableness."

Quincy thinks that Oakes was one of these injudicious good men, and intimates that he was moved to this opposition out of disappointment because he was not himself chosen to the place. But this is mere conjecture. With others, he resigned his seat as a member of the Corporation, and would not return when re-elected.

Dr. Hoar was a man of learning and of great moral worth, and was considerate and diligent, but he could not overcome the opposition and bring the College out of its low estate. The Court passed a vote in 1674, " that, if the College be found in the same languishing condition at the next session, the President is concluded to be dismissed without further hearing." There was no improvement, and in the ensuing spring the President resigned. On the day of his resignation, Oakes resumed his seat in the Corporation. He was urged to accept the Presidency, but refused, and was appointed superintendent of the College, with the rank and duties of president. He held this office four years. After unsuccessful attempts to fill the vacancy, in 1679 Oakes was again unanimously elected president, and he then accepted the office, retaining the pastoral care of the church. The House of Representatives made a grant of £90 per annum in country pay, in addition to the regular salary, to provide such assistance in the work of the church as should be found necessary. The church extended to Mr. Nathaniel Gookin "a call to be helpful in the ministry, in order to call him to office in time convenient." Mr. Gookin accordingly came to the assistance of the pastor. President Oakes proved himself "faithful, learned, and indefatigable in all the services" belonging to his new station. Small and poor as the College was, hard as were those early times, it was a station accounted worthy of any man's acceptance. He who held it ranked as head of the clergy, which was really as the head of everything. It was a part of the bold foresight and adventurous hope of the fathers that their college would be a power and blessing in the land. It was the solitary seat of advanced learning, and this made the position of president one of high honor.

I find little in the town records during Oakes's ministry which it is interesting to notice. In 1673 there is an order for a gallery in the meeting-house, "from the east beam to the west beam, so far as the roof do not hinder, like that on the other side." In 1675 there was a committee appointed by the selectmen "to have inspection into families, that there be no by-drinking, or any misdemeanor, whereby sin is committed, and persons from their houses unseasonably." The next year Daniel Cheaver was appointed "to sit amongst the little boys at the northeast end of the meeting-house, to see there be no disorder amongst them." In 1678 there was a feeling that the pastor was not sufficiently provided for, and the town made him a gratuity. In the same year leave was given to three men " to lengthen the south gallery to supply them for a seat on the Sabbath Day." This would indicate that the house was full. Among the students were Nathaniel Gookin,

Thomas Shepard, Cotton Mather, John Leverett, William Brattle, and others who served their generation well.

Mr. Oakes was eminent for his knowledge and his piety, and was a very engaging and useful preacher. He is described as "an uncomfortable preacher," because he drove men to despair of seeing such another." President Mather says, " If we consider him as a divine, as a scholar, as a Christian, it is hard to say in which he did most excel." Another, regretting that more of his works were not given to the press, remarks, " Four or five of his published composures are carried about among us, like Paul's handkerchiefs, for the healing of our sick land." He was for many years subject to a quartan ague, which frequently made him unable to discharge his duties, and at last he was seized with a malignant fever. He had been sick but a day or two when his church, having assembled on the Lord's Day expecting to have the Lord's Supper administered to them, " to their horror found the pangs of death seizing their pastor, that should have broken to them the Bread of Life." He died on the 25th of July, 1681, in the fiftieth year of his age, and the tenth year of his ministry here, having been for six years also the head of the College. He was buried in our ancient God's-acre. Some years since the slab which had marked the spot was found in use in the covering of a culvert in one of our streets, and was converted into a step for a neighboring church. It was discharged from that service with the design of building it into our new church. But through some mistake it slipped from our hands, and is now supposed to form part of the foundation of the house of a member of this parish. Another stone, with an elaborate inscription in Latin, now covers the place where his dust reposes.

We have one memento of his burial in a charge upon the College book of £16 16s. 6d., for scarfs and gloves, and £8 14s. for twelve rings, at Mr. Oakes's funeral. Thus passed away another man who had ministered to our church, who "fed them according to the integrity of his heart, and guided them by the skilfulness of his hands." I have given very brief illustrations of the poetical gifts of our first two ministers, and will now read to you a small portion of an elegy composed by Mr. Oakes upon one whom he describes as "that reverent, learned, eminently pious, and singularly accomplished divine, my ever honored brother, Mr. Thomas Shepard, the late faithful and worthy teacher of the church of Christ, at Charlestown, in New England."

> "Oh! that I were a poet now in grain!
> How would I invocate the muses all
> To deign their presence, lend their flowing vein,
> And help to grace dear Shepard's funeral!
> How would I paint our griefs, and succors borrow
> From art and fancy, to limn out our sorrow!

> "Cambridge groans under this so heavy cross,
> And sympathizes with her sister dear —
> Renews her griefs afresh for her old loss
> Of her own Shepard, and drops many a tear.
> Cambridge and Charlestown now joint mourners are,
> And this tremendous loss between them share.

> "Farewell, dear Shepard! thou art gone before,
> Made free of Heaven, where thou shalt sing loud hymns
> Of high triumphant praises evermore,
> In the sweet choir of saints and seraphims.
> Lord! look on us here, clogged with sin and clay!
> And we, through grace, shall be as happy as they.

> "My dearest, inmost bosom-friend is gone!
> Gone is my sweet companion, soul's delight!
> Now in a huddling crowd I'm all alone —
> Almost could bid all the world good-night.
> Blest be my Rock! — God lives — Oh! let Him be
> As He is all, so All in all to me!"

LECTURE VI.

"MY COVENANT WILL I NOT BREAK, NOR ALTER THE THING THAT IS GONE OUT OF MY LIPS." — Psalm lxxxix. 34.

IT was in the interest of liberty and piety that our fathers separated themselves from the church and the land in which they were born and nurtured, and made a new nation and established new churches on these open shores. They planned, endured, achieved, with a faith which no hardship could break, no toil exhaust. They had confidence in themselves and their undertaking; and beneath this, for its support and life, was their confidence in God. They accounted themselves in covenant with him, and they followed whither his hand pointed them. Their confidence has proved well founded. Success, more ample than they sought or saw, has crowned their work. Their monument is on every side of us. While we read the annals of this ancient church, we recognize the great goodness of God. Through all changes he has been its friend. We gratefully acknowledge that his assurance has been fulfilled: "My covenant will I not break, nor alter the thing that is gone out of my lips."

We have already traced the history of this church from its beginning in 1636 to the death of its third pastor, the Rev. Urian Oakes, in 1681. When Mr. Oakes accepted the Presidency of the College, in 1679, the church gave "a call to Mr. Gookin to be helpful in the ministry, in order to call him to office in time convenient." In 1680 it was voted by the town, that, of the maintenance annually allowed to the ministry, Mr. Nathaniel Gookin should have £ 100, and the remainder be paid to Mr. Oakes. After the death of President Oakes, his assistant was invited to the pastorate, and was ordained on the 15th of November, 1682. On the same day Deacon John Stone and Mr. Jonas Clark were ordained ruling elders of the church. The record of the charges of Mr. Gookin's ordination is preserved, and affords a glimpse of the usages on such occasions. The whole amount of the charges is £ 13 14s. 2d., and the account includes "provision for 80 persons," with "burnt wine," sugar, "flower," "porke," "hay for the horses," and similar items. In this year, 1682, it was voted by the town "that 500 acres of the remote lands, lying between Woburn, Concord, and our head line, shall be laid out for the use and benefit of the ministry of this town and place, and to remain for that use forever." Such was the "provident and pious attention" of the people to the wants of those who served them in holy things.

The Rev. Nathaniel Gookin was a son of Major-General Daniel Gookin, of whom mention has been made in another place, the friend of the Apostle Eliot in his labors among the Indians, and a man distinguished for his integrity, benevolence, and piety. Of this son and his ministry we know less than of either of the other ministers of the church. The records are very incomplete, and in the history of his times he seems to have had less part than most of those who have filled this pastorate. He was born in Cambridge, October 22, 1658, graduated in 1675, and died in 1692, in the thirty-fourth year of his age, and the tenth of his ministry. It is good testimony to his character and ability that he was called to be the associate of President Oakes, and that, after his service in that capacity, he was intrusted with the care of the church. The prominent facts of his life praise him, even while we are not able to follow him from year to year. His son and grandson were successively ministers at Hampton, N. H., and are highly commended for their worth and works. Of the latter it is said that he was "both ways descended from those who have been stars of the first magnitude."

There are a few traces of our Mr. Gookin's ministry yet to be seen. We have an account of the money paid him from time to time for his services. The amounts are small, sometimes less than a pound, at other times £10 and more. There is a record of the contributions on the Sabbath day. The sum collected in this way was usually about one pound. Of the pastor's salary some £50 appears to have been collected in the church. It is interesting to notice the care of the poor by the church in those days. Contributions for their relief, and frequently for a single person, were made on the Sabbath. We have the minute record of the sums raised and the method in which they were employed. There were also collections from time to time for the redemption of captives. The laudable custom of a contribution on every Lord's Day prevailed here in early times. At one time the scholars made their contribution, which was entered by itself, and appropriated according to their wish for the benefit of the minister. I find the students' contribution only in the interval after Mr. Gookin's death.

I have a small, oblong, leather-covered book which

has in it the name of Joseph Baxter of the class of 1693, and also of Benjamin Colman of the class of 1692, and afterwards the first minister of the Brattle Street Church, in Boston. It contains reports of sermons preached by Mr. Gookin in 1690, when both of these young men were students here. Occasionally there is the report of a sermon by some other preacher. Judging from these notes, which were carefully written, the sermons were thoughtful, thorough, practical, vigorous, and fitted to awaken and retain the interest of the hearers. Mr. Gookin was a Fellow of the College, and no doubt gave to his public duties and to his private relations with the students his best care and thought.

In our old records I find this entry: "Mr. Nathaniel Gookin, our pastor, departed this life 7th day of August, 1692, being the Sabbath day at night, about nine or ten o'clock at night. Elder Clark departed this life 14th January 1699 or 1700, being the Sabbath day. Our Pastor Mr. Nathaniel Gookin's wife, Hannah, died 14th day of May, 1702, and was buried 16th day of May at the town's charge." Mrs. Gookin was the daughter of Captain Habijah Savage, who was the grandson of the noted Ann Hutchinson. Her grave is in our old burying-ground, and is plainly marked; the grave of Mr. Gookin is not now marked, but a monument by the side of hers, whose inscription has crumbled away, is supposed to cover the spot where our fourth minister was buried. In the November following his death, at a public meeting of the inhabitants of the town, it was voted that "the selectmen should make a money-rate to pay the expense and defray the charges, which amounted to about £18 in money, of our Pastor Gookin's funeral charges." Thus the written record of his life closes.

Nothing of special importance seems to have been done in the town during the ten years of his ministry. It is pleasant to see that Mr. Mitchel was still kindly remembered, for there is an entry in 1687 of a grant of £10 to "Mistress Mitchel." The College records have an entry under date of December 24, 1691, as follows: "At a corporation meeting of Harvard College. It is ordered, 1., That £5 be allowed towards the repairing of the meeting-house in Cambridge. Provided that this present allowance shall not be drawn into a precedent for the future, and that the selectmen shall renounce all expectation of such a thing for the future."

In 1682 the residents of "Cambridge Farms," now Lexington, petitioned to be set off from Cambridge, but the people here opposed the measure, and it was defeated. In 1684 it was renewed, and one reason given for pressing it was that they were five miles from the meeting-house here, where they had worshipped. The request was again denied. In 1691 the petition was once more presented, and was granted by the General Court so far as to constitute the "The Farms" a separate Precinct, with the right to conduct their own parochial concerns. The church at Lexington was gathered from this church in 1696. In 1712 a full act of incorporation was bestowed. A satisfactory arrangement was made of the affairs in which the new parish and the old had a common interest.

We know some things upon which those who were before us here must have conversed in this period. For in this time James II. ascended the throne of England, and entered on his troubled and bloody reign, to be thrust down and driven out when William of Orange and Mary assumed the crown at the hands of the willing people, and brought in a new era with new liberties for these colonies. The "Glorious Revolution" must have stirred the subjects of the English throne whose home was beyond the seas, and entered into the talking and praying heard along these streets and in the homes of the people and the house of God. In 1689 William and Mary were proclaimed in Boston with great ceremony. Then followed the war with the French and the Indians, with its evils and perils, in which the people here bore their part. In Massachusetts, in connection with the expedition against Canada in 1690, the first paper money was issued by the colonies.

After the death of Mr. Gookin the pulpit was filled by various preachers. We have a long list of their names and the sums paid to each. Among the names are Mr. Mather and Mr. Brattle. The amount paid for a single sermon was 10 s.; for a whole day's service £ 1 was the regular stipend. This sum seems, however, to have been increased by the gifts of the students. There is a pleasant record which tells us that during this interval Mr. Increase Mather preached much, and gave his pay to Mrs. Hannah Gookin, widow, and it was paid her. She was also paid for entertaining the ministers who preached at this time. The Rev. Increase Mather was unanimously invited to assume the pastoral charge of the church; but the people among whom he had labored for thirty-six years were not willing to release him, and this, with other obstacles to his removal, led him to decline the proposal.

After the office had been vacant for some four years, the Rev. William Brattle was invited to the pastorate, and he accepted the call. He was of a wealthy family, prominent in colonial days, whose name will always be associated with Cambridge. Mr. Brattle was born in Boston, November 22, 1662, and graduated here in 1680. He was soon chosen Tutor in the College. Dr. Colman, who was an undergraduate at that time, says, "He was an able and faithful tutor. He countenanced virtue and proficiency in us, and every good disposition he discerned with the most fatherly goodness, and searched out and punished vice with the authority of a master. He did his utmost to form us to virtue and the fear of God, and to do well in the world; and dismissed his pupils, when he took leave of them, with pious charges and with tears." We have one instance of his heroism and devotion. When the small-pox prevailed in the College, although he had not had that fearful malady, and inoculation was unknown, he stood at his post, visited the sick scholars, ministering to their bodies and their souls, venturing his life for them. He was himself taken ill, but his sickness was of a mild type, and he soon recovered. He received the degree of Bachelor of Divinity in 1692, when this was conferred for the first time. He was a Fellow of the Corporation from 1696 to 1700, when he was removed, to be reinstated in 1703 to hold the office until his death. At the decease of his brother Thomas, in 1713, he assumed the duties of the Treasurer of the College, and discharged them for two years with intelligence and fidelity. When he retired from this position, the College stock amounted to £3,767, and its revenue from rents and annuities to £114. The only publication of Mr. Brattle now known is a system of Logic, which was long used as a text-book in college, and is even now of value, although rarely to be found. He was a generous patron of learning, and a warm friend to the College while he lived, and at his death bequeathed to it £ 250, the income of which was to be used for the benefit of some student or students. It is evidence of his scientific attainments that he was made a Fellow of the Royal Society of London.

Mr. Brattle was ordained on the 25th of November, 1696. We have the old record of the services. Mr. Brattle preached his own ordination sermon from 1 Corinthians iii. 6: "I have planted, Apollos watered; but God gave the increase." The charge was by Rev. Increase Mather, who had become president of the College, and the right hand of fellowship by Rev. Samuel Willard, of the Third Church in Boston; Mr. Morton of Charlestown and Mr. Allen of Boston also took part in the exercises. A sermon was preached on the same occasion by Mr. Mather, from Revelation i. 16: "And he had in his right hand seven stars." Mr. Brattle's independence is shown in his refusal to have an elder, who was a layman, join in the laying on of hands at his ordination. The charges of his ordination are entered as about £ 20. There was "laid out about the repairing of the ministerial house for Mr. Brattle £ 10 18 s. 8 d."

From the beginning of this pastorate we have complete church records. These give us "a form for the ordaining of a minister of the gospel, used by the Reverend President when Mr. Brattle was ordained at Cambridge." It is as follows. "Whereas you on whom we impose our hands are this day separated to the gospel of God and to the office of a pastor to the Church of Christ in this place, we do in his name ordain you thereunto. And we charge you before God and the Lord Jesus Christ and the elect angels, that you do the work of a minister of Christ: that you take the oversight of this flock of God, not for filthy lucre, but of a ready mind; that you feed all the flock over which the Holy Ghost hath made you an overseer; in doctrine showing uncorruptness, gravity, sincerity, sound speech, which cannot be condemned. That you give yourself to reading, to exhortation, to doctrine, that you be an example of the believers in word, in conversation, in charity, in faith, in purity. And if you keep this charge, it will not be long before God shall give you a place in heaven among his angels who stand by, and are witnesses of the solemnity. And when Jesus Christ, the Chief Shepherd, shall appear, you shall receive a crown of glory which fadeth not away, and shall then shine as the stars for ever and ever."

This is the covenant to which those assented who desired baptism for themselves. "You, and each of you for yourselves respectively, do now give up yourselves to God in Jesus Christ, in an everlasting covenant never to be broken. You do humbly and penitently ask of God forgiveness for your original sin, as also for all your actual transgressions, and you desire with all your hearts to accept of Jesus Christ for your alone Redeemer and Saviour. Solemnly promising that by the help of God's holy spirit you will endeavor to live henceforward more to his honor and glory than heretofore you have done; abstaining from the vain delights and pleasures of this evil world; keeping under the passions and evil lustings which are within you; doing what in you lies at all times to carry it both towards God and towards man as becomes the disciples of Jesus Christ. And particularly you all promise to submit yourselves to the government which Jesus Christ hath instituted and appointed in and over his church."

This is the covenant to which certain persons agreed "in order to their children's being baptized." "You do each of you now acknowledge the God of your fathers to be your God; you do humbly beg of God, through Jesus Christ, forgiveness for your sins original and actual. You do solemnly promise, by the help of the Divine Spirit, to walk with God according to the rules of his holy Word, and to submit yourselves to all the institutions and appointments of Jesus Christ in his gospel, and to bring up your children in the nurture and admonition of the Lord."

In 1722, "Mr. Judah Monis, a Jew by birth and education, being converted to the Christian faith, owned the covenant, and was baptized and declared a member in full communion with the church of Christ, after a prayer and discourse made by Mr. Colman from John v. 46, and a discourse of his own from Psalm cxvi. 10, answering the common objections of the Jews against Christ's being already come, and giving a confession of his faith in the close. Sang part of the 110th Psalm, which solemnity was performed in the College Hall. Soli Deo Gloria."

Mr. Monis was a useful member of the church, and a fund left by him is still used for the benefit of the widows and children of Congregational ministers. He was instructor in Hebrew in the College from 1722 to 1760.

In 1696 – 97 there was important action concerning the reception of members to the church. It is evident that the matter was the subject of much discussion. The result was, in brief, that persons desiring to unite with the church should privately give satisfaction unto the elders regarding their religious character, and should be excused, if they so desired, from giving a public relation of their religious experience. The minister was to state to the church the grounds of his satisfaction with the candidates some time before they were admitted, and they were to be propounded publicly, that if any one knew any reason which should justly bar them from communion, he could privately inform the elders. The vote of the church upon receiving persons thus propounded was to be taken by "handy vote, or silence, or any other indifferent sign," at the discretion of the elders. Those who were accepted by the church were publicly to make "profession of their faith and repentance in their covenanting with God." This is essentially the method still pursued in the church. The consent to dispense with the formal, public relation of experience marked a change from the ways of the past which certainly commends itself to our judgment. The church has a right to know whom it is receiving to its fellowship, both for their sake and its own. Having learned this to its satisfaction, in some simple and pleasant manner, the entrance to the church should be as plain as the nature of the act will allow. To confess Christ before men and make covenant with his people, and to receive those who come confessing their faith and love, should enlist the best feelings of all hearts, and be the occasion of sincere, sacred joy.

The church-book gives the account of the provision made for Mr. Brattle's support. He writes, "My salary from the town is ninety pounds per annum, and the overplus money." For a few years before his death he received £100. The salary seems to have been raised chiefly by a collection every Sabbath. From his receipts I do not find that he received any overplus in money. But there are long lists of the donors of wood. In 1697 he received twenty-two loads. He usually received more than that number till 1712, when the custom seems to have been discontinued for a few years. As this discontinuance of the wood comes at the same time as the advance in his salary, I presume that the two events were connected. We have also accounts of wood which he paid for from time to time. There is a long list in 1697 headed, "Sent in since Nov. 3, the day that I was married. From my good neighbors in town." The list extends through more than a year, and is composed of articles for his table, with the names of the givers and the value of their gifts. The beginning of the list is as follows:—

"Goody Gove, 1 pd. Fresh Butter, 8 d.; Mrs. Bordman, 1 pd. Fr. Butter, 8 d.; Doct^r. Oliver, a line Pork, 2 s.; Sarah Ferguson, 1 pig, 1 s. 9 d." There are accounts of similar donations afterwards. His private affairs were blended in his mind with his office, for another account in the church-book is headed, "Housekeeping, D^r. since we were married, Nov. 3, '97." The list begins with "2 powthering Tubs, 9 s.; 1 Tub of Beef 154 pds. salted Oct. 29, £1 18 s. 6 d.; Wine w^n married and since to ye day, £3; Bear, 19 s. 6 d."; and the list continues after this sort.

At the end of the church-book of this period are various statements regarding Mr. Brattle's gardening, the weather, etc. Of 1697 we read: "The winter this year was a very severe winter for cold and snow. The ground was covered with snow from the beginning of December to the middle of March; many snows, one upon another; in February it was judged to be three foot and a half deep on a level." "Charlestown ferry was frozen up, so that the boat did not go over once from January 17 to February 28, in which time I rode over upon the ice." The summer following this hard winter was a very fruitful summer. In February and March, 1700, he was planting his garden. On Sabbath day, February 11, 1700, he was "taken sick of a feaver; he was "very ill, near to death." In about a fortnight he was able to go out. "Deo sit gloria. Amen." He was often interrupted during his ministry by "pains and languishments."

February 15, 171$\frac{6}{7}$, "The Rev^d. Mr. Brattle, Pastor of the Church of Christ in Cambridge, departed this life." He bore his sufferings "with great patience and resignation, and died with peace and an extraordinary serenity of mind." On the 20th of February he was interred in a tomb on the southeast side of the old burying-ground. They laid him down in hope of a blessed resurrection. "He was greatly honored at his interment." It was on the day of "The Great Snow," and the principal magistrates and ministers of Boston were detained here for several days. Mr. Brattle died in the fifty-fifth year of his age, and the twenty-first of his ministry. During his pastorate seven hundred and twenty-four children were baptized, and three hundred and sixty-four persons were admitted to the church.

In regard to the amount of his pastoral work, we are left to such conjecture as we can base upon the character of the man. We trust he knew all his people and where they lived. Yet we find Dr. Colman saying of his own congregation that he knew not where their habitations were, and should be glad to know them, that he and his associate might do their duty to them. At the funeral of Mr. Cooper, he is extolled for "knowing where to find the poor and sick of the flock, when they sent their notes."

Mr. Brattle was a man of marked politeness and courtesy, of compassion and charity. He had a very large estate, and he scattered his gifts with a liberal hand, yet without ostentation. He was patient and pacific in his temper, and "seemed to have equal respect to good men of all denominations." "With humility he united magnanimity; and was neither bribed by the favor nor overawed by the displeasure of any man." He was of "an austere and mortified life, yet candid and tolerant towards others." He had great learning and ability, and bore a high reputation as a preacher. His manner in the pulpit was "calm and soft and melting." His manuscript sermons show that he was thoroughly of the Puritan school in theology; yet in ecclesiastical usages he was liberal. When the Brattle Street Church was formed by men who sought larger liberties in the ordering of their ecclesiastical offices than the other churches afforded, the movement enlisted his sympathy. The undertakers of the Manifesto Church, as they were called, adhered to the Westminster Confession, but desired to have the Holy Scriptures read in public worship, which was contrary to the New England usage, and also to give a voice in the choice of a minister to every baptized adult person who was to contribute to his maintenance. They somewhat enlarged the range of infant baptism, and made the public relation of religious experience optional with the candidate for church membership. When Mr. Colman, who was then in England, was invited to the pastoral charge of the new church, Mr. Brattle wrote to him, and encouraged his acceptance of the call. "As for my own part," he wrote, "I shall account it a smile from Heaven upon the good design of these gentlemen, if you can send them answer of peace." In an old account-book still in existence are some records of his private thoughts. Under date of 1715, it is written: "I can't but look upon myself as a standing instance of the infinite power and infinite goodness of God. While I consider my unexpressible emptiness and insufficiencies, my heart can't but admire and adore the power of God and the goodness of God in helping me through the duties and difficulties which in his Providence He has call'd me to. O Lord, to thy name be the praise; O Lord, my hope is in thee; Lord, keep me forever humble. Amen, Amen."

Dr. Colman's testimony to his friend is hearty and strong. "They that had the happiness to know Mr. Brattle knew a very religious, good man, an able divine, a laborious, faithful minister, an excellent scholar, a great benefactor, a wise and prudent man, and one of the best of friends. The promotion of religion, learning, virtue, and peace everywhere within reach was his very life and soul; the great business in which he was constantly employed, and in which he principally delighted. Like his great Lord and Master, he went (or sent) about doing good. His principles were sober, sound, moderate, being of a catholic and pacific spirit."

The fifth minister of the church ranks worthily with those who preceded him. He bore the church upon his heart. In his last testament we read, "As a close to this part of my will, it is my desire to consecrate, and with humility I bequeath and present to the church of Christ in Cambridge (my dearly beloved flock) for a Baptismal Basin, my great silver basin, an inscription upon which I leave to the prudence of the Reverend President, and the Rev. Mr. Simon Bradstreet." The basin he designed for our use has passed from our hands. But we may gratefully cherish his thought for those who were to inherit his faith and to be baptized into the name of his Divine Lord and Saviour, and honor the memory of the good pastor who so long ago was " translated from his charge to his crown."

The town records during the period of Mr. Brattle's ministry have some items of more or less interest. Here is a vote that a pew be made and set up on the southwest corner of the meeting-house for the family of the minister. Mr. John Leverett and Dr. John Oliver have convenient places provided for their families in the meeting-house. Here is a tax ordered, payable in money, for repairing the meeting-house, ringing the bell, and sweeping. The little meeting-house bell was given to the Farmers, and a new one was received with thanks from Captain Andrew Belcher. The schoolhouse was ordered to be rebuilt. A public contribution was taken for the relief of sufferers by a late fire. Such charity, it seems, is not all of our day, and even the Puritans had something of kindness. A grant was made to Mrs. Hannah Gookin to pay her house-rent for the year 1701. The selectmen, with the consent of the pastor, were " empowered to rent about five hundred acres of land laid out for the ministry, so that it shall become profitable to the ministry." And here, February 28, 1703, at a town meeting, it is ordered " that the inhabitants apprehend it necessary at this time to proceed to the building a new meeting-house, and in order thereunto there was chosen then" a committee of seven, "to consider of the model and charge of building said meeting-house, and report of the same to the inhabitants." In 1706 the third meeting-house was erected on or near the site of the second, and the first service in it was held on the 13th of October in that year. The Corporation of the College voted £60 towards the building of this house, and instructed Mr. Leverett and the treasurer to "take care for the building of a pew for the president's family," and about the students' seats; "the charge of the pew to be defrayed out of the College treasury." Thus we come to the close: "6th February, 171$\frac{6}{7}$. At a meeting of the Inhabitants orderly convened, voted, that the charges for wines, scarfs, and gloves for the bearers at the funeral of our late pastor, Rev. Mr. William Brattle, be defrayed by the town under the direction of the deacons and selectmen."

The period we are now reviewing presented many matters of interest to those who were then here. We are able to recall their thoughts in some good measure. Queen Mary died in 1694, and eight years afterwards King William III. 1697 brought the peace of Ryswick, closing the war between England and France. The reign of Queen Anne was chiefly occupied by the "War of the Spanish Succession." Thus even this country was for twenty-five years preceding the peace of Utrecht kept in the commotion of war. A large part of the men were in actual service, while those at home were compelled to guard their houses and families against treacherous foes. It is estimated that during these wars not less than eight thousand of the young men of New England and New York fell by the sword, or by disease contracted in the service. Most of the families mourned for friends dead, or carried into cruel captivity. It was a gloomy time; the resources of the country were greatly reduced, fields were untilled, towns lay in ashes. Truly, through scenes of fire and blood has our inheritance come down to us. In 1693 the second college in the United States was founded in Virginia, taking the name of the new sovereigns; and seven years later Yale College came into being. 1702 was a year of great sickness in Boston and New York. In 1704 "The Boston News-Letter" was started, the first newspaper published in America. In 1708 the Saybrook Platform was adopted in Connecticut. The reign of Queen Anne, the last sovereign of the House of Stuart, was marked also by the constitutional union of England and Scotland, which ended the prolonged contest between those countries. This reign was distinguished not only for its military and political achievements, but also for its progress in science and literature. It was the time of Addison, Steele, Pope, Swift, Locke, and Newton, and has now the name of "The Augustan Age of England."

But we must return to our own history. After the death of Mr. Brattle, his place was filled by the Rev. Nathaniel Appleton. Mr. Appleton was born at Ipswich, December 9, 1693, and was the son of the Hon. John Appleton, one of the King's Council, and for twenty years a Judge of Probate in Essex County. His mother was the daughter of the Rev. President Rogers. He graduated in 1712, and, although receiving generous offers to establish him in business, adhered to his previous purpose to prepare himself for the ministry. He preached here for a short time, when, by the concurrent vote of the church and the town, he received an invitation to become the pastor of the church. He entered upon that office on the 9th of October, 1717. At his ordination Dr. Increase Mather preached from Ephesians, iv. 12: "For the perfecting of the saints, for the work of the ministry, for the edifying of the body of Christ." He also gave the charge. Dr. Cotton Mather gave the right hand of fellowship. The Rev. Mr. Angier of Watertown and the Rev. Mr. Rogers of Ipswich joined with the Mathers in the laying on of hands. The town records show an addition of £15 to the taxes of the year, toward defraying the expenses of this ordination. President Leverett presided over the deliberations of the church and congregation with regard to the settlement of a pastor, and when Mr. Appleton had been chosen by a large majority, he closed the entry of the fact in his diary with "Laus Deo." This election gave great pleasure to the Corporation of the College, who at once chose the new minister as a Fellow in Mr. Brattle's place, not even waiting for his ordination. He filled this office with great fidelity and discretion, essentially promoting the interests of this "important seminary." At the Commencement in 1771 the College conferred upon him the degree of Doctor of Divinity, in consideration of his "having been long an ornament to the pastoral character, and eminently distinguished for his knowledge, wisdom, sanctity of manners, and usefulness to the churches, and having for more than fifty years exerted himself in promoting the interests of piety and learning in this society, both as a minister and as a Fellow of the Corporation." This honor was the more marked, in that this degree had only once been conferred since the founding of the College, and that was seventy-eight years before, when Increase Mather was the recipient. President Wadsworth wrote of Mr. Appleton, ten years after his establishment here, " I have often thought it is a great favor, not only to the church and town of Cambridge, but also to the College, and therein to the whole Province, that he is fixed in that public post and station, assigned by Providence to him. I pray God long to continue his life and health, and make him more and more a blessing to all he's concerned with. Tho' he's but young, yet his labors are very instructive and profitable!" His connection with the College continued until 1779, a period of more than sixty years. His pastorate was the longest the church has ever known. The written record of his labors as pastor comprises little more than long lists of persons received to the church, of adults and children who were baptized, and of persons married. The summing up is as follows: Children baptized, 2,048; adults, 90. Admissions to the fellowship of the church, 784.

All through this long ministry the pastor was busy in the duties of his office, preaching the word, striving for the salvation of those under his care, and for the edifying of the body of Christ. Traces of his vigilance still remain. We have the record of church discipline in 1731 and afterwards, when certain individuals had fallen into open sin. At length, on the 26th of February, $173\frac{4}{5}$, the church and whole congregation met in solemn assembly, and spent the forenoon in prayer and preaching. The sermon was from Ezra ix. 5, 6: "And at the evening sacrifice I arose up from my heaviness; and having rent my garment and my mantle, I fell upon my knees, and spread out my hands unto the Lord my God, and said, O my God, I am ashamed, and blush to lift up my face to thee, my God; for our iniquities are increased over our head, and our trespass is grown up unto the heavens." In the afternoon several votes were passed, expressing the apprehension of a general decay of piety, in that many had fallen into evil ways who had been baptized and were reckoned the children of the church, and those who had publicly owned the covenant; and some who were in full communion did neglect their business, frequent taverns and public houses, follow unlawful gaming, and indulge in excessive drinking of strong drinks, and were profane in their conversation, whereby they greatly dishonored the Christian name and profession, broke the good and wholesome laws of the land, misspent their precious time, impoverished their families, blasted their reputation, injured their health, unfitted themselves for business, ran into innumerable snares and temptations, and extremely hazarded their immortal souls.

The assembly apprehended, further, that these evils resulted from a neglect to watch over one another, according to their covenant obligations. With contrition before God, they promised to amend their lives, to discountenance and discourage such sinful practices, and to deny themselves even their lawful liberty to prevent others from stumbling thereat. They promised to exercise the mutual watchfulness and helpfulness which the gospel enjoins. And they voted, finally, that a suitable letter should be prepared by the pastor, and sent to the innholders and retailers of ardent spirits, exhorting them to do what in them lay to prevent intemperance, gaming, or any disorder at their houses. The record closes with this petition: "And now, O Lord God of our fathers, keep these things forever in the imaginations of the thoughts of the heart of this people, and prepare their heart unto thee."

These general measures do not seem to have been sufficiently effective; for two years later, at a meeting of the church, a committee was appointed to consult with the pastor "about such measures as shall be thought most likely, under the Divine blessing, to reform the growing disorders that are among us." The committee in its report advised that nine of the brethren be appointed "to inspect and observe the manners of professing Christians, and such as are under the care and watch of this church." They were to inquire into any sinful and disorderly behavior of which they might hear, and administer appropriate admonition, with faithfulness, but yet with all meekness and tenderness; and if such private treatment did not succeed, they were to advise with the pastor about more public action. In case of such open and scandalous offences as required the public notice of the church, they were to take such steps as were necessary to bring the matter before the church. But the appointment of this committee was not to be construed as excusing private Christians from that watch over the good name and good character of the church to which they were pledged. The committee was appointed, and entered upon its work. Year by year, after that, we have a record like this: "The brethren voted to choose a committee to inspect the manners of professing Christians, etc., according to the method agreed upon April 13, 1737." From time to time we have the record of the work. It is plain that the church meant to deal faithfully with those under its care, but there is a spirit of forbearance which shows that they did not mean to encroach on the Christian liberty of any one. The offences which were brought under the consideration of the church were all such as no church could overlook, and retain its self-respect and preserve its character.

Another matter which enters largely into the records concerns the lands belonging to the church. There is a catalogue signed " N. A." and entitled, " Lands belonging to the Church and Congregation in Cambridge for the Use of the Ministry." The list includes three small lots of four, eight, and three acres, and a lot of forty acres in Menotomy, called Bare Hill. Besides these, there was a lot of twenty acres in Newton, " the gift of Mr. Thomas Beale to the church of Christ in this place and town of Cambridge, whereof he was a member." And a farm of five hundred acres at the farther end of Lexington, towards Bedford, given in former time by the proprietors of the town for the use of the ministry. It was found expedient and convenient, in Mr. Appleton's day, to sell this land in Newton and Lexington. The proceeds of the former were invested in bonds, and the income was to be used as the church should direct. Of the money received from the sale of the Lexington lands, £130 was reserved for the erection of a new parsonage. The rest was applied to the purposes of the original donation. Inasmuch as the proceeds of the Lexington farm were to be for the minister's benefit, the minister made an arrangement with the town whereby he was to receive two thirds of the interest which accrued by the investment of the money received by the sale of the land. The remaining third was to be added, by the minister's own proposal, to the principal. The fund was to be in the hands of a treasurer nominated by the minister and approved by the town. Mr. Appleton solemnly charges the people of the parish to abide strictly by the arrangement which had been made, and never suffer their third of the interest to be applied to any other use than the increasing of the fund. He expresses the hope that no successor of his in the ministry will ever desire or demand more than two thirds of the interest of this money. "Nay, let me add, what some of you may easily compute, that by keeping this vote and agreement, of adding one third of the interest to the principal, sacred and inviolable, that by the 3d or 4th generation it will of itself afford a comfortable and decent support for a minister, without any tax upon the people."

The result which the prudent pastor anticipated could hardly prove desirable. It is best that the institutions of religion should be sustained by the voluntary offerings of those who enjoy them. Our church has been entirely saved from any perils which might have attended the course which he proposed. But the minister of 1800 writes that this fund, by its own accumulation, and by the addition of the product of ministerial lands sold in 1795, has become greatly auxiliary to the support of the ministry. From time to time a committee was appointed to examine into the state of the church stock of moneys, bonds, or notes, in the hands of the deacons. In 1773 such a committee make a long report, in which they recommend that, after allowing the funds to increase by interest for fourteen years, for the next fifteen years one third of the interest shall be used for the support of the minister, and that after that time two thirds of the fund shall be thus employed, and the remainder be added to the principal. In order that the fund may be increased, the committee also recommend to the members of the church that whenever they come together "to commemorate the death and sufferings of Him who spared not to shed his precious blood for us, they would express their thankful remembrance of the benefit they have received, by cheerfully contributing a small part of the substance with which God has blessed them for the important purposes of continuing and spreading amongst mankind that pure and undefiled religion which Christ appeared on earth to propagate." They enter into an elaborate statement "to show that a very small part of our substance, properly applied, would produce a very considerable effect" in enlarging the resources of the church.

As we turn the pages of the church-records, we come upon various matters which were of importance in their day, and are still of interest. Here is Mr. Appleton's wood-account, beginning in 1729: "My good friends and neighbors have for several years past, in the fall of the year, brought me a considerable quantity of wood gratis, some years between thirty and forty loads, sometimes above forty loads, which good and laudable custom, that had been dead for some years before the Reverend Mr. Brattle's death, was revived by good Father Pattin about ten years ago, and continued by the friendship of the people." Then follow the names of the donors year by year, with the quantity of their gifts.

In 1732 the people of the northwesterly part of the town were formed into a separate Precinct, and in 1739 a church was gathered there, and to this second church our church gave £25, "to furnish their communion-table in a decent manner." This was a partial realization of the communion of saints. In 1731 and 1734 additions were made to the communion-service of our own church by private gifts. In 1740 "the Hon. Jacob Wendell, Esq., from his regard to this place," presented "to the minister of the first church, for the time being, a large, handsome Bible for the use of the church," and the gift was acknowledged with thanks.

Here, in 1757, is the account of a church-meeting, at which "some of the honorable brethren of the church moved that for the future it might not be insisted upon with such who should be admitted into the church to come forth and stand in the front alley or aisle at the time of their admission; alleging that it was disagreeable and surprising to some persons, and had been offered by way of objection by some persons, and had been such a stumbling-block to them as to prevent their offering themselves for admission; and considering it was but a mere circumstantial thing, and a matter of indifference, and considering also that the practice of other churches allowed persons to stand in their own proper places all the time of admission. Therefore the brethren agreed to leave the matter to the discretion of the pastor, at the same time manifesting that they did not insist upon the standing in the aisle or alley, and that they should be well satisfied if they appeared in any of the seats or pews that joined upon the front alley, so as to be fairly before the pastor and in view of the assembly; and to this no one of the brethren offered the least objection, although they were desired to do it if they had any objection to offer." Good, honest men, sound but not stiff, and sure that God would have mercy and not sacrifice.

The Revolution was drawing on. As early as 1765 the people of the town had formally instructed their representatives to give no aid to the operation of the Stamp Act, but to do all they could for its repeal. And they ordered that their action should be recorded in the town-books, "that the children yet unborn may see the desire that their ancestors had for their freedom and happiness." We do see it after a hundred years, and give thanks at every thought of their daring and devotion. I need not tell again what Cambridge did in the beginning and consummation of the long struggle which gave being to our nation. Cambridge was long the headquarters of the American army, and the old meetinghouse stood in the midst of stirring scenes, and opened its doors and extended its ministrations to the citizen soldiers. There Washington and his companions in arms came to worship. There the delegates from the towns of the State met in 1779, and framed the Constitution of the Commonwealth, which the next year was ratified by the people. We may be sure that the preaching of the venerable pastor glowed with patriotic fire, and that his prayers were the intercession of a man who believed in God and loved liberty; who was in the spirit of Lexington and Bunker Hill, and taught his people the worth of life, and the honor of a death for one's country; who cheered them in the day of darkness and defeat, and rejoiced with them when victory revived their hope and crowned their toils and trials. Of all this they said little; but we know the men. Here, in 1774, when public and political affairs wear a dark and gloomy aspect, they are keeping, with other towns, a day of humiliation and prayer. Yet they are watchful of the church while solicitous for the country, for on this very Fast Day they choose two deacons.

We have a glimpse of the times in some of the receipts for his salary which the minister gave during the Revolution. Here is one in which he acknowledges the receipt of £3 2s. to complete the payment of his salary in Continental bills, which, "although they are exceedingly depreciated, yet, considering the contributions and subscriptions they have afforded for my relief, and considering the additional grant they have made to my salary for 1778, I accept of this in full for my salary for the year 1777." His salary had been £100, and was probably but little changed; yet the next year he receipts for £600, and the next for £750, and in 1783 for £2,000 paper currency, and £25 silver currency. There is a touching pathos in the simple statement of the good man as he took his bills and called them money, "although they are greatly depreciated."

He was close upon ninety years old. We find this fact of his advancing years creeping into the records. 1777, April 25. "Whereas our Rev. and very aged Pastor is at present under such bodily infirmities as to render it doubtful whether he will be able to administer the sacraments on the approaching Sabbath, voted, in such case, it is agreeable and is the desire of this church that the Hon. and Rev. President Langdon should administer the same, and at any other times when necessary occasion calls for it."

The following Thursday was to have been a day of "Public Fasting and Prayer"; but "the aged pastor, through bodily disorders, was unable to carry on the services of the Fast, neither could any help be obtained, so that there was no public service on the Fast." By 1782 the people had begun to talk seriously of the need of having "a more fixed and settled provision for the preaching and administering the gospel ordinances among them," and it was decided by the church that it was desirable presently to settle a minister, if the right man could be found, and the parish committee were desired to consult the parish in the matter. Here is Mr. Appleton's record of July 30, 1783, which "was observed as a day of Fasting and Prayer by the church and congregation to seek of God divine direction and assistance in the important affair of procuring a more fixed and settled preaching and administration of the word and ordinances among us, considering the very advanced age and growing infirmities of me their aged pastor. The Rev. Mr. Eliot began with prayer: Rev. Mr. Cushing preached A. M., Rev. Mr. Jackson began with prayer: Rev. Mr. Clarke preached P. M."

At the general desire of the brethren of the church, "as well as in compliance with his own inclination and earnest wishes," the pastor called a meeting of the church for the purpose of choosing one to be his colleague in the ministerial office, if the church should see fit. When the meeting was held, the pastor was unable to attend, and Dea. Aaron Hill was moderator. A committee was appointed "to wait on the President of the University, and request him to pray with the brethren on the present occasion." The president complied with the request, and received the thanks of the brethren. This means, I suppose, that he came to the meeting and offered the opening prayer. It was voted by a large majority to proceed to the choice of a colleague pastor, and the Rev. Timothy Hilliard was chosen to that office. The parish concurred in this action, and Mr. Hilliard accepted the invitation. A council of the neighboring churches was called, and on the 27th of October, 1783, the pastor elect was installed. He preached on the occasion from Titus ii. 15: "Let no man despise thee." The Rev. Mr. Clarke of Lexington prayed before the charge, which was given by the Rev.

Dr. Cooper of Boston. The Rev. Mr. Cushing of Waltham gave the right hand of fellowship. "The greatest order, decency, and sobriety were observable through the whole. Soli Deo Gloria."

Mr. Appleton very soon gave the church-book into the care of his colleague, which was virtually relinquishing the staff which his decrepit hand could no longer hold. In the following February "he departed this life, in the ninety-first year of his age and sixty-seventh of his ministry." "1784, February 15. This day his funeral solemnity was attended. The body was carried to the meeting-house. Rev. Mr. Cushing of Waltham prayed. The surviving pastor of this church delivered a funeral address. A funeral anthem was sung, after which the procession advanced to the burying-place, and the body was committed to the tomb." A long Latin epitaph covers the stone upon his grave; but the last lines, which are in his own tongue, balance the rest: "They that be wise shall shine as the brightness of the firmament, and they that turn many to righteousness as the stars for ever and ever."

We have already noted some indications of the esteem in which the sixth pastor of this church was held. He was possessed of the learning of his time. He labored to instruct his people. His preaching was with great plainness and simplicity. "He frequently borrowed similitudes from familiar, sometimes from vulgar, objects; but his application of these was so pertinent, and his utterance and his air were so solemn, as to suppress levity and silence criticism." He expounded the whole New Testament, the Book of Isaiah, and other parts of the Bible. His aim in this was to promote practical piety. He made use of such events as were engaging the attention of the people, that he might lead them to serious thoughts. He was vigilant and careful in his parochial administration. "So great," says Dr. Holmes, "was the ascendency which he gained over his people, by his discretion and moderation, by his condescension and benevolence, by his fidelity and piety, that, while he lived, they regarded his counsels as oracular; and, since his death, they mention not his name but with profound regard and veneration." He was venerable for his age, but more for his piety. "His religion, like his whole character, was patriarchal. In his dress, in his manners, in his conversation, in his ministry, he may be classed with the Puritan ministers, of revered memory, who first came to New England." He was a popular man, and his church was "respectable for wealth, influence, and numbers." He had great weight of character, and made himself felt through the province. His praise was in all the churches. Ecclesiastical councils sought his advice. He was a wise counsellor, and strove for the peace and order of the churches. His portrait, by Copley, which hangs in the College, represents him, very fittingly, as holding in his hand a volume of Dr. Watts, entitled "Orthodoxy and Charity."

Dr. Appleton's manuscripts were burned in the fire in Boston in 1794; but a goodly number of his sermons are in print, and also a work published in 1728 and entitled, "The Wisdom of God in the Redemption of Man." He left a legacy of £40 for the benefit of the poor of the church, and one of £26, Massachusetts currency, to the College for a scholarship, in addition to £30 previously given by him. Dr. Appleton was married about the year 1720 to Margaret, daughter of the Rev. Henry Gibbs of Watertown. Dr. Sprague's "Annals of the American Pulpit" furnish this incident. "It is a current tradition in the family, that, while he was wooing the lady, he happened to call one day soon after a rival suitor had made his way to her father's house, leaving his horse fastened near the gate. The Cambridge minister, on his arrival, tied his own steed to the fence, and coolly unloosed the other, and with a smart stroke of his whip sent him off down the street. He then went into the house, and told his rival that he had just seen a horse running away at full speed, and asked if it was his. Whereupon the owner rushed out after his stray beast, leaving Dr. Appleton in possession of the field. He made the most of his opportunity, offered himself, and was accepted." They had twelve children. One son was a merchant in Boston, and a zealous patriot during the Revolution, and for many years held the office of Commissioner of Loans. Two daughters married clergymen.

There are some other events which fall into this period, which should have a mention here. After Mr. Appleton had been invited to the pastorate, a committee was appointed by the town to consider the expediency of raising the meeting-house, so that an upper tier of galleries could be put in. The College agreed to bear one-seventh part of the expense of this alteration, on condition that certain parts of the house should be reserved for the use of the scholars. I do not find any account of the work, and presume that the project was abandoned. In 1746 the parish proposed to repair the meeting-house, and the College again agreed to pay a portion of the cost. There was a difference of opinion regarding the amount of work which should be done, and the extensive repairs contemplated were abandoned; but it would appear that the immediate want was met by making the roof tight, and mending the windows, doors, and seats. It is probable that some thought the time was not distant when a new house would be needed, and that it would be poor economy to spend much money on the old one. In 1753 the inhabitants voted to build a new meeting-house upon some part of the hill on which the house was then standing. The Corporation of the College agreed to pay one seventh part of the cost of the new house, upon certain conditions. The students were to have the improvement of the whole front gallery, and one of the best pews was to be set apart for the president. A petition was to be sent to the General Court, asking such help in the affair as should seem meet to their wisdom and goodness. The College afterwards agreed to add £20 to the previous subscription. There was a protracted negotiation to arrange matters between the parish and the College, but on November 17, 1756, the house was raised, and Divine service was first performed in it July 24, 1757. This fourth house remained until 1833. "In this edifice," writes President Quincy, "all the public Commencements and solemn inaugurations, during more than seventy years, were celebrated; and no building in Massachusetts can compare with it in the number of distinguished men who at different times have been assembled within its walls." During the investment of Boston in 1775, when Washington had his army here, he worshipped with his companions-in-arms in that church. In 1779 the delegates from the different towns of Massachusetts met in that church, and framed the Constitution of the State. When Lafayette was here, in

MEETING-HOUSE, ERECTED IN 1756.

1824, upon his "triumphal visit," the address of welcome was given to him within those consecrated walls. A large stone from the foundation, one which very likely had served the preceding houses, has been built into the wall of the church we are now completing, and is inscribed with the date "1756."

In 1749–50, a committee was appointed by the parish "to treat with the governors of the College, in order to their being assisting of said Precinct in the support of Mr. Appleton." Here are appropriations for schools; a law that if any dog is found in the meeting-house on the Lord's Day, in time of public worship, the owner shall be fined; officers are appointed to preserve order; provision is made for the care of the "French Neutrals"; the court-house is to be rebuilt, as far as possible from the materials of the meeting-house about to be taken down. In 1761 an Episcopal church was opened here, at the desire, says the historian, " of five or six gentlemen, each of whose incomes was judged to be adequate to the maintenance of a domestic chaplain. A missionary was appointed to the care of the church by the English 'Society for Propagating the Gospel in Foreign Parts.'" In 1764 the College suffered a severe loss by the burning of Harvard Hall, which contained the library, the philosophical apparatus, and various objects of interest. "In one stormy winter's night, the scanty but precious accumulations of a hundred and twenty-six years" were lost. But the friends of the cherished college, if cast down, were not destroyed, and immediate measures were taken to erect a new building, and replace what had been lost, as far as it could be done. In 1780 the church-members on the south side of the river made known their desire to be dismissed and formed into a distinct church, and a new church was organized there on the 23d of February, 1783. It was in Dr. Appleton's pastorate that Whitefield was exciting the country with his marvellous preaching. He came to Cambridge in 1740 to see and to preach, and made a sad report of the lack of discipline, the low state of religion, and the reading of bad books. " I chose to preach from those words: 'We are not as many who corrupt the word of God'; and in the conclusion of my sermon I made a close application to tutors and students." The Faculty of the College published a pamphlet bearing their testimony "against the Reverend Mr. George Whitefield and his conduct." Mr. Whitefield replied, modifying some things which he had said, expressing his good will to the College, asking forgiveness if he had done any wrong, and offering forgiveness to those who had wronged him. Among the donors of a late date we find his name, and the acknowledgment of his journal and a collection of books, and also of his influence by which he procured a large number of valuable books from several parts of Great Britain. The career of Whitefield in this country, and certainly in Cambridge, must have elicited the eager interest of the church; and we may be certain that the liberal and prudent pastor stood for the defence of the College, and showed himself always the friend of moderation and order, of zeal with knowledge, and of that work which stands the tests of this world and the judgment of another. There were blessed results of the wide and deep movement of that time. Tutor Flynt wrote in his diary, "Many students appeared to be in a great concern as to their souls, first moved by Mr. Whitefield's preaching, and after by Mr. Tennent's and others, and by Mr. Appleton, who was more close and affecting in his preaching after Mr. Whitefield's being here."

But the great events of this period, so far as this land and the world were concerned, were the Declaration of Independence by these colonies and the realization of independence through the struggles and sufferings of a long contest. The spirit which dared and achieved the end ruled here. The brief records of the town ring with the cries of men bent on liberty, — men who knew their rights and meant to possess them, and were willing to endure for the generations to come. England changed her sovereigns; three Georges ruled. In France Louis XV. finished his reign, and was succeeded by his well-meaning, but irresolute and ill-fated grandson. These changes did not mean so much for the world as the rise of this free Republic, whose destiny is more glorious than its history, if the patriotic devotion of the fathers shall be the cherished heritage of the children.

It remains to say a few words more of our own history. The death of Dr. Appleton left Mr. Hilliard the sole pastor of the church. Mr. Hilliard was the son of a worthy farmer and deacon of Kensington, N. H., and was born in the year 1746. In his youth he showed an unusual facility in acquiring knowledge, and an amiable and cheerful disposition. He graduated here with high honor in 1764. While in college he made such advances in the various branches of useful learning as laid the foundation for that eminence in his profession to which he afterward attained. In 1768 he was appointed chaplain of Castle William. After a few months' service there, he was elected a tutor in this College, and for two years and a half discharged the duties of that office with fidelity. He was invited to settle in the ministry at Barnstable, and was ordained there April 10, 1771. He remained there for twelve years, winning the affection of his people and the esteem of all who knew him. The strong sea-air proved injurious to his health, and he resigned his parish. On recovering his health, he resumed his professional labors, and, after preaching here for a short time, was invited to become the colleague of the venerable pastor, and soon became the sole pastor of this church, as we have already seen. He died on the Lord's Day morning, May 9, 1790, in the seventh year of his ministry here, and the forty-fourth year of his age. The records of his ministry contain nothing beyond the usual routine of parish work. There were one hundred and forty-five baptisms, and twenty-three persons were admitted to the church. The "committee to inspect the manners of professing Christians" seems to have been discontinued after Dr. Appleton's death. Care was taken of the funds belonging to the church, provision was made for the poor, and the late pastor's legacy was applied according to his wish. The church received new members, children were baptized, men and women were joined in marriage, and the grave claimed its own. Thus the work went on. The word of God was preached as aforetime, and men were called to obey the gospel, which "unfolds the glorious plan of redemption which was laid in the counsels of infinite wisdom and goodness before the foundation of the world." The years of the Revolution and those which immediately followed it were a dreary time for the churches, and for the interests of piety in the land. Many had been drawn away from the restraints of the law and the sanctuary, and exposed to the excitement and temptation of a soldier's life, often among the irreligious and unprincipled of other lands. With the war uppermost in the minds of the people, religion suffered a decline. Errors of belief and practice, corruptions of divers kinds, came in like a flood. The Sabbath lost its sacredness, the Bible its authority, the church its sanctity. The preacher had his task doubled. The pastor here felt the force of the conflict and the greatness of the issue. He put on the panoply of God for a warfare that was not carnal but spiritual, to win for men a liberty which was perfect and eternal. Amid the last echoes of the Revolution he preached the gospel of peace. And when a proclamation, nailed to the court-house door, offered pardon to the rebels, in the meeting-house he preached the forgiveness of sins.

Through all his ministry Mr. Hilliard was studious and earnest. Both the learned and unlearned were profited by his judicious, instructive, practical discourses. His sermons were of cost to him, and therefore were of worth to his hearers. The government of the University regarded him as "an excellent model for the youth under their care who were designed for the desk, and considered his introduction into this parish a most happy event." He excelled in public prayer, and was "tenderly attentive to the sick and afflicted." His whole temper was amiable, candid, liberal. While not ranking among what are called popular preachers, he had excellent pulpit talents, and his ministrations were highly acceptable to the churches. His reputation was increasing when he died. He had much influence in ecclesiastical councils and associations, and his brethren paid him a marked respect. He was watchful of the interests of the University, of which he was a son and an overseer.

The publications of Mr. Hilliard were five sermons, including a Dudleian Lecture. I copy a few sentences, that we may see how well his doctrinal views agreed with those held by this church from the beginning.

"It is observed that the Saxon word 'gospel' signifies WELCOME NEWS: it brings us the news of an Almighty Friend and compassionate Saviour, who came from heaven to deliver us from the condemning sentence of the Divine Law, and to restore us to the image and favor of our Maker. . . . . Amidst all the variety of sects and parties into which Christians have been divided, they have been generally agreed with respect to the capital and most important truths of religion. All Christians believe the existence and perfection of the one supreme God, the author and supporter of the universe, and his providential government of the world; they believe the advent of his best-beloved Son to redeem and save a perishing world; they own that salvation is by grace through faith; that a Divine influence on the mind is necessary to produce and cultivate a holy and heavenly temper; that Christ, having been delivered for our offences, was raised from the dead by the glory of the Father, 'was vested with' supreme dominion, and constituted the Judge of quick and dead; they believe the resurrection of the dead, and a future retribution according to the deeds done in the body."

In a sermon from the text, "But not as the offence so also is the free gift," he says: "The advantage here mentioned may consist in this, that all who die do not suffer this calamity merely for the sin of Adam, but oftentimes bring death upon themselves for their own sins; but all that are justified, and so freed from death, are thus exempted from it only by virtue of the blood of Christ."

Yet, while Mr. Hilliard held his own views firmly, he cherished a charitable spirit towards those who judged differently, and enjoined this upon others.

In person Mr. Hilliard was rather spare, of a medium height, with an intellectual and attractive countenance. His last illness was very short, and in it he was sustained by the truths he had preached, enjoying those consolations which he had given to others. He mentioned his people with affection, and with great satisfaction testified "that he had not shunned to declare to them the whole counsel of God, having kept nothing back through fear or any sinister view." Thus passed away the seventh minister of this church. He was buried, with those who had preceded him, in our sacred ground, "in the Christian hope of rising again to eternal life." His "bereaved, affectionate flock" erected a monument to his memory, and inscribed upon it the virtues with which he had adorned his life.

Here we pause, after the survey of more than a hundred years. We turn from these pages of our history, witnessing to the truthfulness of the word of promise and of hope in which our fathers trusted, and strengthening ourselves with the assurance which God grants to us, for our comfort and courage, "My covenant will I not break, nor alter the thing that is gone out of my lips."

LECTURE VII.

"REMEMBER ME, O LORD, WITH THE FAVOR THAT THOU BEAREST UNTO THY PEOPLE: O, VISIT ME WITH THY SALVATION; THAT I MAY SEE THE GOOD OF THY CHOSEN, THAT I MAY REJOICE IN THE GLADNESS OF THY NATION, THAT I MAY GLORY WITH THINE INHERITANCE." — Psalm cvi. 4, 5.

THE patriot Psalmist sought for himself the blessing with which God would visit his people. He identified himself with his people, both for confession and desire. It was enough for him to see the good of the chosen of God, and to rejoice in their gladness. I have placed this passage at the head of this discourse, because it forms the text of two sermons preached by the venerated man of God whose ministry we are now to review. They were first delivered in 1820, upon the twenty-eighth anniversary of his installation over this church, and were repeated in 1836, at the beginning of the third century since the formation of the church. The sermons set forth the peculiar privileges of the people of God, and the duties which attend those privileges. He accounted it a great honor to be numbered with those whom God had chosen, and a great advantage to share their experience. Yet the people of God to whom he ministered knew both the blessing of prosperity and the blessing of adversity. In the day of their prosperity he stood in his place, and prayed, "Remember me, O Lord, with the favor that thou bearest unto thy people"; and when the day of adversity had come, taking the same sermons to another sanctuary, he still prayed, "that I may see the good of thy chosen." It was glory enough for him to be as they were.

In the town of Woodstock, now in Connecticut, but at that time within the bounds of this State, on the 24th of December, 1763, was born the man who became the eighth pastor of this church, and who long filled the office with distinction and success. He preserved the renown of an illustrious line of ministers, and enhanced its praise by adding his own name. The father of Abiel Holmes was a practising physician. He served as captain during the war in Canada, and as a surgeon during the first half of our Revolutionary War. He died when his son had reached his sixteenth year. It is inferred that the early years of the son were marked by studious habits and a serious regard for religion. He entered Yale College in 1779, and graduated in 1783. It was a stormy period in his country's history, and New Haven shared in the stirring scenes of the time. But the young student improved his opportunities, and was considered one of the most accomplished scholars in his class. In his Sophomore year he united with the College church. In the year following his graduation he was in South Carolina. While there, the church and society at Midway, Georgia, learning that it was his intention to enter the ministry, invited him to preach to them for a year, and in August, 1783, he began his labors among them. This church and society had removed from Dorchester, in this State, about the year 1700, and first settled in South Carolina, at a place which they named Dorchester. Some fifty years later they removed to

Georgia, where, after an exciting experience, in which their meeting-house and almost all their dwellings and crops were burned by the British troops, the society was broken up and dispersed. On the return of peace the people came back to their old home, and resumed their former ways. It was at this new beginning of their work that Mr. Holmes, then in the twenty-first year of his age, entered upon his labors with them. When he was about to return to the North, in the following year, he was earnestly solicited to obtain ordination, and then to return and resume his ministry. He consented to this, and was ordained in the College Chapel at New Haven on the 15th of September, 1785, being the day after Commencement. The services at his ordination were printed. The Rev. President Stiles was moderator of the council. The sermon was the regular Concio ad Clerum, and was delivered by the Rev. Levi Hart, of Preston, Conn., from St. Paul's words, " For do I now persuade men, or God ? Or do I seek to please men ? For if I yet pleased men, I should not be the servant of Christ." The sermon was entitled, " A Christian Minister described, and distinguished from a Pleaser of Men," and, as we read it to-day, has a prophetic tone. The act of consecration and the ordaining prayer were by President Stiles.

The work of the young minister was regarded as of great importance, inasmuch as he was not merely the pastor of a single flock, but was to labor in a region where it was hoped new churches would spring up around him, and the gospel make its way, through his influence, beyond the reach of his voice. He went to his people, but was obliged, by impaired health, to return the next year to the North, where he exchanged places for a year with Mr. Jedediah Morse, then a tutor in Yale College, after which he resumed his pastoral work. During his absence from his people he kept them on his heart, as a printed "Pastoral Letter," still preserved, bears witness. He continued with his church for about four years longer, when it was found that his health was unfavorably affected by a southern climate, and he resigned his charge and came to New England.

This church had been without a pastor since Mr. Hilliard's death in May, 1790. Mr. Holmes was employed to preach, with a view to his settlement. In October, 1791, he was called to the pastorate by the church, and the parish concurred in the choice. In his reply to the invitation, Mr. Holmes writes: "In respect to the office of which you have asked my acceptance, I can truly say that I consider it above my years and my improvements. But the singular candor with which you received me and my ministrations while I was with you, and the remarkable unanimity with which the transactions relative to my proposed settlement among you were conducted, silence my objection on this head." On the 25th of January, 1792, an Ecclesiastical Council met at the parsonage. President Willard was chosen moderator. After the usual examination, the council adjourned for dinner at Mr. Owen Warland's. After dinner, the brethren of the church received the pastor-elect as a member. Then the council, with the pastor-elect, preceded by the church and as many of the inhabitants of the parish as were present, proceeded to the meeting-house, where the installation services were performed. Rev. Mr. Jackson of Brookline offered prayer. Rev. Dr. James Dana of New Haven preached from our Lord's words, which contain the authority and limitation of his ministers, "My doctrine is not mine, but his that sent me." Rev. Mr. Clarke of Lexington offered the installing prayer, Rev. Mr. Cushing of Waltham gave the charge, Rev. Mr. Porter of Little Cambridge extended the right hand of fellowship, Rev. Dr. Howard of Boston offered the concluding prayer, and the pastor pronounced the benediction. The record closes in this way: "Throughout the whole process the greatest order, decency, and harmony were observable. Soli Deo Gloria." Mr. Holmes's first sermon after his installation was from the First Epistle of St. Peter, iv. 11. "If any man speak, let him speak as the oracle of God; if any man minister, let him do it as of the ability which God giveth: that God in all things may be glorified through Jesus Christ, to whom be praise and dominion for ever and ever. Amen." That was the key-note of his long ministry. He was duly impressed with the greatness of his work, and with the honor of the position which he was called to hold. In closing this sermon he said, "In a word, aided by Divine grace, he will endeavor to speak to you the words of eternal life with that seriousness and zeal which their singular importance requires. If, impressed with the weight of what he utters, he should at any time seem to forget the respect due to his auditory, still, if he keeps to the oracles of God, he hopes you will pardon him, duly considering that he is not mad, but speaks forth the words of truth and soberness. . . . . But I am again constrained to cry out, Who is sufficient for these things? The place in which I stand reminds me of my venerable predecessors in the ministry. Your fathers, where are they? And the prophets, do they live forever? . . . . Other men labored, and I am entered into their labors. Such an one as Paul the aged no longer addresses you from this pulpit, but a youth who would have esteemed it a singular honor, as a son with the father, to have served with him in the gospel. May the examples and counsels of your worthy pastors who have gone to rest be long kept in faithful remembrance among you; and may the recollection of their excellent characters excite your present minister to fidelity in the very arduous and important work to which he is renewedly devoted."

The records of the church during Mr. Holmes's ministry are in his own handwriting, which is only less plain than printing, and they exhibit the method and accuracy which marked all his life. From these and collateral sources we are able to write the story of his life. I shall follow in the main the chronological order, but there are some events which should be grouped.

Let us look for a moment at the surroundings. Cambridge in 1792 did not differ much from the town of 1800, when Mr. Holmes compiled its history. The bridge which we usually cross on our way to Boston was begun in the year of his settlement, and finished in the next year. He describes it as "a magnificent structure." "It is very handsomely constructed; and, when lighted by its two rows of lamps, extending a mile and a quarter, presents a vista which has a fine effect." This bridge had a perceptible influence on the business of the town. Houses and stores were built near the bridge, where a rapid progress of trade and commerce was expected. In 1790 the number of inhabitants in the town was 2,115. In ten years from that time there had been an increase of 330. The number of dwelling-houses in the town in 1798 was 301, of which one half were in the first parish. At the beginning of this century there were five houses of worship, — one used by the Congregational church in each of the three parishes, in the first parish also one for the Episcopalians, and, in the second, one for the Baptists. The University had five buildings. These were the second Harvard Hall, Massachusetts, Hollis, Holden Chapel, and College House, a wooden building of three stories, containing twelve rooms with studies, and standing outside the yard. The historian says, "There are now one hundred and ninety-one students in this ancient and very respectable seminary; and, for several preceding years, there have been upwards of two hundred. . . . . An extensive and beautiful common spreads to the northwest of the Colleges, and adds much to the pleasantness of this central part of the town." The county court-house, used also for a town-house, stood in Harvard Square. On the corner of Market Square stood the wooden jail. The grammar school-house was a little westward of the Episcopal Church. There were, besides this, six school-houses in town, two in each parish. The grounds of Thomas Brattle, Esq., once the property of the Rev. William Brattle, were greatly admired. "In no part of New England, probably, is horticulture carried to higher perfection than within his enclosure." On the road to Watertown were "several elegant seats" which attracted the attention of travellers. And the Washington elm, which guards our new church, stretched out its broad branches, hanging with historic memories. The meeting-house of this church and the first parish was the fourth house which they had occupied, and stood near the present site of Dane Hall. The parsonage was on a glebe of four acres now included in the College yard.

From this external survey we pass to the history of the church. The first matter in the regular records of this period is the report, made in 1792, of a "committee appointed to inquire into the state of the church stock, and of the fund appropriated to the poor of the church." It appears that the deacons had in their charge £356 19 s. 8½ d., which was nearly all invested, and drawing interest. One third part of the interest was to be paid to the parish treasurer, by vote of the church. In the account of the fund for the poor of the church, the deacons were charged with £82 7 s. 6½ d., which had been properly distributed among the poor, or remained on investment, except a very small balance. The deacons declared their agreement to the report of the committee. The church passed a vote thanking "Deacon Hill for his generous services in providing for the Communion and negotiating the funds of the church." This examination was repeated, year by year, and the vote of acknowledgment was regularly passed for several years, enlarged, however, by thanks "to the deacons in general for their services in behalf of the church." The last of these statements of the monetary affairs of the church was made in 1830, when the funds of the church had increased to $3,236.99, and the fund for the poor to $667.18.

The first statement made by the deacons is signed by Aaron Hill, Gideon Frost, and James Munro. In the same year Deacon Hill died, after a service of eighteen years in that office, and Captain John Walton was chosen to fill the vacancy. In a modest letter, expressing his surprise at the election, and his fear lest he could not fill the office with that propriety which it required, he confessed himself not entirely at his own disposal, and, heeding the call of duty, acceded to the wishes of the church. Deacon Walton died thirty-one years afterwards, in 1823. It will be best to bring together here the changes in this office during this pastorate. In 1803 Deacon Frost died, after a service of twenty years, and, in 1804, Mr. William Hilliard was chosen in his place. "The deacon-elect offered a modest excuse for declining the choice, on account of his early age; but, after due consideration, he accepted it, and signified his acceptance by assisting at the next Communion service." The pastor adds, in a note, "He is in his twenty-sixth year; is a son of my worthy predecessor in the ministry; and, though recently admitted into our church, has been several years a member of a church in Boston, and has had frequent communion with us." He remained in office until his death in 1836, a period of thirty-two years. Deacon Munro died in 1804, having been twenty-one years in office. In his place Mr. Josiah Moore was chosen. He filled the office for nine years, and died in 1814. His house stood upon the land now occupied by our new church. His place was not filled until 1818, when a meeting was held for that purpose. "After prayer by the pastor for the Divine direction and blessing, and the recital of the apostolical instruction and precedents on the subject, the brethren proceeded to bring in their written votes, and it appeared that the whole number of votes was ten, nine of which were for Brother James Munro. He was, accordingly, declared to be chosen a deacon of this church." The records proceed as follows: "Sept. 6. After the morning sermon (Lord's Day) the pastor, having admitted four members in full communion into the church, mentioned the election of Brother James Munro to the office of Deacon, and his acceptance. The deacon-elect, signifying his acceptance by taking his seat, this day, with the deacons, near the Communion-table, rose, on being addressed by the pastor, who briefly stated to him the duties of the office to which he was elected, exhorted him to fidelity, and announced him a deacon of this church. In the concluding prayer, immediately following, he was commended to the grace and blessing of God." Deacon Munro remained in office until his death in 1848. His term of office, therefore, like Deacon Hilliard's, extended through the difficult times which befell the church. To the character of these two men we have the testimony of Dr. Albro, who was the pastor at the time of their death, and who said of them, " In many respects dissimilar, they were alike in their love of the truth, in their zeal for the glory of Christ, and in their efforts and sacrifices for the welfare of the church. They were, as the Apostle says that deacons should be, honest, faithful, and good men, "not double-tongued, not greedy of filthy lucre, holding the mystery of the faith in a pure conscience." They "used the office of deacon well, and purchased for themselves a good degree, and great boldness in the faith which is in Jesus Christ."

In this connection I bring forward a few changes relating to the Communion. It had been the usage of this church to have the Lord's Supper administered once in eight weeks. This naturally produced inconvenience, because the particular days were not specified.

Accordingly, in 1797, at the suggestion of the pastor, the church decided to have the Communion on the first Lord's Day of every other month, beginning with January. That arrangement remains to this day. In September, 1818, there is this entry: "It had been the usage of the church, at the Communion service, for the members to remain in their own pews. To lessen the time and to facilitate the duties of this service, on the suggestion of the deacons, the pastor recommended it to the communicants to seat themselves in the pews on the broad aisle. These pews were, accordingly, occupied at the Communion this day." In 1825 the time of the lecture preparatory to the Communion was changed to the evening; and it was voted "that the examination of the annual accounts of the church take place at the lecture previous to the first Sunday in March." It may seem a blending of sacred and secular things, but to the church all its doings should be sacred. At the same meeting it was voted that the Sabbath service from September to March should begin at half-past two o'clock, and during the rest of the year at half-past three. In 1826 "two of the tankards and two cups were recast, and two cups altered in such a manner as now made seven cups of a uniform shape and size. A new silver spoon and six Britannia-ware dishes, more adapted to the use for which they are designed, were also procured."

There are three cases of church discipline recorded in this pastorate. All were for offences demanding attention, and the proceedings were conducted in a kind and faithful temper. The first case was settled by the satisfactory confession of the offender, after the admonition of the pastor had brought him to penitence. The second resulted in excommunication, after persistent efforts to bring the offender to repentance and amendment. But four years afterwards, upon her contrition, and desire for forgiveness and readmission, she was restored to the fellowship and privileges of the church, and the pastor " exhorted the members to conduct toward her accordingly." The third instance was that of a man who had " renounced his Christian profession, ... and proved himself to be, not merely an apostate from the Christian church, but an enemy to the Christian religion." The faithful efforts of the church to reclaim him were ineffectual, and he was excommunicated.

But let us turn to pleasant things. In 1805 a committee, consisting of the pastor and two others, was appointed to consider the expediency of "procuring religious books for the use of the members of the church." The report recommended that a contribution should be made by the church for that purpose, and this was accepted. The committee was directed to prepare a list of suitable books. The report names some twenty volumes, beginning with " The Holy Bible," and including " Leslie's Short and Easy Method with Deists," " Baxter's Saint's Rest," " Doddridge's Rise and Progress of Religion," " Wilberforce on Christianity," and kindred works. The estimated cost of the books was $13.50. The deacons were desired to solicit donations of money, or of any of the books which had been named, to begin the library. There was a generous response. The library was accordingly established, and placed under the care of the church, which was annually to choose the librarian and a standing committee. The title of Library of the First Church was agreed upon. The pastor was chosen librarian. A catalogue was printed, embracing one hundred and nine books. An excellent work was thus begun, which it seems very desirable that the church should renew at the present time. A small expenditure in each year would establish a library which would prove of great usefulness.

This is the place to bring together a few other matters of a similar character. In the summer of 1815 a Sabbath school was opened at the meeting-house, with the design of promoting "the moral and religious improvement of children and youth." The school was taught during three summers by Miss Mary Munro and Miss Hannah Tenney. Then five other young ladies came to their assistance, and Mr. James D. Farnsworth, master of the grammar school, tendered his services for the instruction of the boys. "More than eighty children of both sexes received instruction at the Sabbath school. They were taught to read and to commit to memory select portions of the Bible, catechisms, hymns and prayers, and to answer Cummings's questions on the New Testament. Books and tracts were early provided for their use." In 1819 the pastor stated the object of the school to the congregation, "and a collection was afterward taken for purchasing small books to be distributed among the children, as an encouragement for punctual attendance, correct lessons, and good behavior." "In 1827 books and tracts were collected by subscription for a juvenile library." A board of trustees was chosen, with the pastor at the head. He was also chosen librarian. In July, 1831, seven trustees were elected, and Miss Mary Ann Sawyer became librarian. The trustees were authorized to make selections from the library to form a Sabbath School Library for the Shepard Congregational Society. We are now carried beyond the pastorate of Dr. Holmes. But it may be added that in 1832 it was voted that "Mr. Stephen Farwell, then superintendent in the Sabbath school, be appointed and requested to deliver the books selected for the use of the Sabbath school." Afterwards, in 1835, a Sabbath School Society was formed by members of the Shepard Congregational Society, "for the purpose of promoting more effectually Sabbath-school instruction," and both of the libraries for the young were transferred to its care, and were brought together under the name of Juvenile and Shepard Sabbath School Library. We have just celebrated the fifty-seventh anniversary of our Sabbath school. While enjoying the goodly measure of prosperity which is granted us, we should gratefully remember the work done by those into whose labors we have entered.

We come now to transactions affecting the connection between the church and the University. From the beginning they had held their Sabbath services together, and the relation had been in all respects an intimate one. In 1814 the Corporation and Overseers decided that it was best for the members of the University to hold religious services by themselves. The expected benefits of this were the better opportunity to give special appropriateness to the exercises and instructions of the sanctuary, and to bring into the Sabbath certain discourses which had been delivered on a week day. The approved practice of other universities encouraged the separate service. The completion of University Hall, which would contain a commodious chapel, favored the proposed change. It was designed to form a church, and to have the ordinances duly administered. Members of the College government with their families, and students, graduates and undergraduates, were to be the only stated communicants. A committee, including the reverend President, was appointed to notify the minister and congregation of the First Parish of the design, and "to express the sentiments of regard and fraternity felt by the members of the several College Boards, and the desire of Christian and friendly communion between the two societies." President Kirkland, as Chairman of the Committee, addressed a letter "to the pastor, the church and congregation in the First Parish in Cambridge," informing them of the proposed action, and describing very feelingly the pleasant associations of the past, and the sacrifice of personal feelings which was involved. "The ties of neighborhood and friendship, the sympathy and regard naturally produced by a communion in religious acts, the experience of edification and comfort in attendance upon your services, combine to make us wish to continue going to the house of God in company." The committee expressed the belief that the separation, though in some respects undesirable and painful, would, on being viewed in all its circumstances and bearings, receive approbation and good wishes. A conference to determine the future connection of the University and the parish was desired. It was also asked that such members of the University as should request dismission, in order to join the new church, should have their request granted; and that the pastor and delegates should be present at the formation of the church within the walls of the University. The church voted "that the reasons assigned for the proposed measure, so far as it respects this church, are entirely satisfactory; and that the church is ready to concur in the change." Five delegates were appointed to attend, with the pastor, at the formation of the new church, and the pastor was "requested to reciprocate the assurance of regard and fraternity so kindly expressed by the University towards us." The pastor replied to the communication of the President in a letter full of feeling, recalling the past, and the delightful intimacy which had been enjoyed, and which rendered the thought of a separation equally solemn and affecting. This is the close of the letter: "Allowing ourselves, however, to be influenced on this occasion by no other consideration than a regard to the best interests of the University, we cannot but acquiesce in a measure designed for its benefit. Our prayer to God is, that it may, in all respects, be of kindly and salutary influence, and particularly that it may conduce to the religious interests of the University, — a seminary consecrated 'To CHRIST AND THE CHURCH.' We are grateful for your benevolent petitions for us; and ask you to continue the prayers which you so affectionately offer for us and our children. May brotherly love continue. Short as is the distance, and small as will be the partition, between the places of our religious services, we indulge the pleasing persuasion that we shall be united in affection, and that the interchange of fraternal and Christian offices, as occasion shall invite or require, will be perpetuated. We gratefully acknowledge the regard uniformly shown us by the University, and the numerous acts and offices of kindness and fraternity we have experienced as individuals, and especially as a church and society. The remembrance of them will be always precious to us. Brethren, farewell. 'We bless you out of the house of the Lord.'" "The covenant subscribed by the members of the College church is dated, 'Harvard College, Nov. 6, 1814.'" It was signed by the President and fifteen others. Our church record closes by stating that, "On the morning of Lord's Day, 6th Nov. 1814, the church was organized at University Hall, in the presence and by the assistance of the pastor and delegates of the First Church in Cambridge."

In the following year the pastor informed the church of his recent discovery, among the collections of the late Rev. Thomas Prince, of a manuscript register in the handwriting of Rev. Jonathan Mitchel, containing a list of the members of the church under the following title: "The Church of Christ at Cambridge in New England. The names of all the members thereof that are in full communion; together with their children who were either baptized in this church, or (coming from other churches) who were in their minority at their parent's joyning, taken and registered, in the 11 month 1658." The church directed that this list, which has of late proved of great service in the preparation of our church Manual, should be bound up with the records, and that blank leaves should be left for the record of other papers. Another blank book was to be procured "for the preservation of the reports on the state of the church stock, etc., and other important papers suitable to be preserved with them; such as Acts of the Legislature relative to Parish and Ministry lands, the setting off of parishes within the town of Cambridge, etc., etc."

There are two or three other events of interest which should have a brief notice. In 1807 Dr. Holmes left the ancient house in which the ministers had so long resided, and removed to the house which is now standing in Holmes Place, and which has but recently passed from his family into the possession of the College. In 1807 a meeting-house was erected in that part of the town which was already the scene of large visions of commercial prosperity, and which, in anticipation of its coming importance, had been made a port of entry, and was designated as Cambridgeport. That part of the town had received the parochial care of the minister of the First Church, "who was wont in his visits to distribute catechisms and hymn-books, and to question the children upon religious doctrines and duties." The new meeting-house was a spacious structure of brick, and stood in a barren common near the northwest corner of the square now occupied by the Allston school-house. The sermon at its dedication was preached by Dr. Holmes. The church seems to have been organized in 1809. The first pastor was Rev. Thomas Brattle Gannett, who united with our church in 1810, and was dismissed and recommended to the new church in 1814. The sermon at his ordination, in 1814, was also preached by Dr. Holmes, and was from the text, "I am made all things to all men, that I might by all means save some." The historian of that church says of the sermon and the preacher, "It reads as placid as he looked. . . . . It is another instance of that now lost art of felicitously weaving in Scripture language with the texture of every sentence, and the expression of every thought, which gave such peculiar unction to the most common utterances of the older divines." That meeting-house was injured in a severe gale in 1833, and afterwards taken down. A large part of the material was used in the erection of another house on Austin Street, where the society still worships under the pastoral care of the Rev. George W. Briggs, D.D.

Among other relics of Dr. Holmes's ministry is a pamphlet entitled, "A Sermon delivered at the Episcopal Church in Cambridge, by the Request of the Wardens and Vestry, December 25, 1809, in Celebration of the Nativity of our Blessed Saviour. By Abiel Holmes, D.D., Minister of the First Church in Cambridge." The sermon was preached at a time when the Episcopal Church was for the most part supplied with lay-readers. The thanks of the society were presented to the preacher for "the learned and appropriate discourse," and he was requested to furnish a copy for the press.

I find in the records no signs of the war of 1812, unless it be in the small number of admissions to the church. In 1812 but two persons were received, one of whom was Edward Everett, and in 1813 but one person. In 1814 there were five admitted.

In connection with the service of song in the house of the Lord, it is of interest to find one of Dr. Holmes's sermons marked, "This day Watts's psalms and hymns introduced instead of Tate and Brady." It was preached on the afternoon of June 29, 1817. The text was, "Let the word of Christ dwell in you richly in all wisdom; teaching and admonishing one another in psalms and hymns and spiritual songs, singing with grace in your hearts to the Lord." The sermon teaches the spirit in which this service should be performed, and justifies the use of hymns in addition to the psalms. The grace of Christ and the joys of a Christian life might properly find expression in new songs, " in the plain language of the gospel," rather "than in the obscure diction of prophecy." The people were urged "with one heart, and, as far as practicable with harmony and propriety, with one voice, to unite in the songs of Zion." The preacher adds, "To the skilful performance of the choir we are much indebted for the order and harmony, the solemnity and effect, with which this part of Divine service is performed. The style of sacred music is, of late years, essentially improved; and the exclusion of light and unhallowed airs, so foreign to the solemnity of the subject and the place, is itself highly favorable to our improvement in piety and devotion, and, at the same time, more easily admits the union of a great proportion of the assembly in this common duty, — the social praise of Almighty God. Let us not, then, leave this interesting, improving, and delightful service to be performed wholly by others. Let none be listless, or indifferent to it. Let none regard it as a mere entertainment. Above all, let none either perform, or hear it performed, with levity. Let us all be supplied with books. Let those who can, with any propriety, bear a part in singing the high praises of God; and let the rest keep their eyes fixed on the psalm or hymn that is sung, and join with the understanding and affections in the sublime employment, and thus make melody, at least in their hearts, to the Lord. And here, my brethren, I would suggest to you the propriety of performing this part of the service, even when we do no more than perform it in heart, in a standing rather than in a sitting posture." In 1827 an organ was placed in the church; and this sermon was repeated on the 30th of September, with the insertion of these remarks: "The introduction of an organ, instead of diminishing, should increase the number of singers in the congregation. It is not, you will remember, intended as a substitute for the voice, but as an aid to it. It may be accompanied by those who are not thoroughly skilled in music, though great care should be taken not to violate either the time or the harmony. In the use of this instrument, it is hoped and believed great regard will be shown to the spiritual nature of the worship which it is intended to aid. It is not meant for our entertainment, but for our improvement; not simply to delight the ear, but to inspire the heart. It will not, I trust, be suffered to overpower the vocal music, of which it should be but an accompaniment. Let us have the distinct articulation of the human voice, that it may not give an uncertain sound, or be so merged in the sound of an instrument that the meaning cannot be understood. Let us remember, my brethren, that we are required to sing with the spirit and with the understanding."

"The First Evangelical Congregational Church in Cambridgeport" was gathered in 1827. The word "Evangelical" is the distinctive term in this name. For before that church was formed, the word had come to have a precise, and, to some extent, denominational significance. We are brought now upon the events which separated our church from the parish with which it had so long been connected. I should be glad if I might be spared the recital of these scenes. But they were real, and history must accept, not select, its facts. In regard to the points of this controversy there is a substantial agreement. Each party published a pamphlet, weaving into its narrative such comments as it chose. On the 20th of July, 1827, a memorial signed by sixty-three members of the parish was presented to the pastor, remonstrating with him for discontinuing professional exchanges with certain ministers, and recommending a return to his former custom. To understand the meaning of this, it is necessary to go back a little. As early as the year 1787, Unitarianism, which had already been adopted by many persons, became a "substantial reality" in Boston by the action of the society worshipping in King's Chapel, which set aside the English Liturgy it had been using, and adopted one prepared by its own minister, which carefully excluded all acknowledgment of the Trinity. For many years this remained the only confessedly Unitarian society of any note in New England. By what gradual progression the new belief extended itself, and of the methods of its advance, it is not my purpose to speak. That has already become written history. But by the time which we are now considering, a large part of the ministers of the churches in this immediate neighborhood had embraced the liberal principles of belief. It was about this time that this new belief became organized and "The Unitarian Association was formed." Manifestly here was a great change, and naturally it changed the relation of such ministers to those who adhered to the old belief. Freedom of professional intercourse became restricted, more and more restricted as one man after another declared himself in favor of the new views. There were men of all degrees of conviction and confession. Some were pronounced Unitarians, and from these men shaded away into such as could hardly be distinguished from the Orthodox. Religious belief and usage for a time were in solution, but coming steadily to take on a precise form. Now, the minister here recognized these changes among his neighbors, and governed himself accordingly. Hence some who had heretofore been invited to an exchange of pulpits with him no longer received such proposals. No single year drew the line of demarcation between the ministers and churches of the two parties in theology. It was a slower process by which men found their places. Therefore no single year marked the complete cutting off of ministerial exchanges among clergymen of the different parties. This came about by degrees, and was variously affected by the circumstances and judgment of individuals. But as in the course of events some of the previous exchanges ceased here, it came to be noticed by the people. This would have made no trouble if they had continued to hold the views which for two hundred years had been preached in the parish, and for a third of a century by this pastor. But a large majority of the legal voters in the affairs of the parish chose the more liberal side. They complained of the change in the pastor's practice, and asserted that he was changing the policy of the church, and deviating from the customs of his immediate predecessors, and departing from the views which had governed his own procedure and shaped his own preaching. They complained, also, that he introduced preachers whose teaching was irrational, and offensive to a majority of his parishioners, while he excluded others whom they desired to hear. It is probable that the preaching of some who were brought in for extra services did more to provoke the parish than the preaching of the pastor. Out of this state of things grew their memorial, in which the signers gratefully testified to the order, peace, and harmony with which the church and society had walked together, and expressed their fear lest there should arise disaffection and disunion in consequence of the pastor's action, and requested him "to exchange a reasonable proportion of the time with such respectable clergymen of liberal sentiments in this vicinity as had heretofore been admitted into his pulpit, and with others of similar character." The pastor replied, in dignified terms, that he thought an interview with him, before any paper had been drawn up, would have been more favorable to truth and peace. He said, further, to show that this ceasing of professional intercourse was not all with the orthodox ministers, that some liberal ministers were of the opinion that such exchanges as were proposed were not desirable. He added: "The subject is believed to be uniformly left to the discretion of the pastors, who are, or ought to be, the best judges of what is profitable for their hearers, and who are bound religiously to determine what is right and consistent for themselves." This was the beginning of a protracted controversy, which I have neither time nor heart to review. The whole discussion is in print. It was conducted with a large amount of earnest feeling on both sides. The effort of the parish was to secure the preaching of Unitarian ministers here for a portion of the time. This was to be brought about either by exchanges with such clergymen, or by the settlement of a colleague of liberal sentiments, or by the introduction of ministers of the liberal denomination at such times as would not interfere with the services already established. To neither of these measures would Dr. Holmes consent. He claimed that the original principles of the church had been maintained here with remarkable uniformity during its whole history, inclusive of his own ministry. From these principles he would not depart, neither could he consent that others should come in to undo the work which his predecessors and himself had accomplished. His ordination vows were upon him.

I have a document prepared by him, which he entitled "Religious Principles of the Ministers of Cambridge." By citations from their printed works, or their manuscripts, he traces the line of doctrine from Shepard to himself. He then adds, "Doctrines held and taught by the present pastor from the commencement of his ministry here to this time; collected from his discourses on the Anniversary of his Installation." The object is to show that there has been no change in doctrinal teaching, and that he is standing on the old foundation, and continuing the instruction for which he was called to this pastorate.

Through all this trial of his constancy the church stood by him, upholding him in his action, and expressing their decided approbation of the doctrines and duties uniformly inculcated by the pastor. They remonstrated in writing against the course which things had taken. "Let us not attempt to drive from us a man, by urging upon him a course of measures, which, should he submit to them, would render him a stranger among his brethren, not satisfy those who make the demand, and would leave him dishonored in his own eyes and in theirs." They made their plea for those not permitted to speak for themselves. "We also apprehend that, were the females of this parish allowed to come here and speak, a majority of them would entreat you to forbear; and we would hope that we shall not be regardless of their feelings, because they are not allowed the poor privilege of begging you to consider them." It became evident that the difficulty was not to be settled by discussion. The church and pastor on one side, and the parish on the other, were alike decided. The pastor would be master of his pulpit, admitting and excluding according to his own discretion. The parish would hear liberal preaching, and would not listen to certain preachers, Calvinists, who were invited by the pastor. For such differences as this Congregationalism, in the days of the Apostles, had made provision. In the multitude of counsellors wisdom was to be sought. Therefore, at length, the parish proposed to the pastor to unite in calling a mutual ecclesiastical council to advise in regard to the matter in controversy. There could be no objection to a council. But the church and a minority of the parish declared that the ancient usage in New England, and invariably in this parish, was for the church and parish to concur in questions touching the settlement of a minister, and in his removal if that should become necessary. It was proposed, therefore, that the council should be called by the church and parish in concurrence. But these memorials did not induce the parish to change its course.

The church insisted upon their right to participation in the calling of a mutual council, because Dr. Holmes was their minister, as well as the minister of the parish, and had been settled by them in concurrence with the parish, and because the proposed changes deeply affected their interests. The parish objected to the admission of the church, on the ground that, if admitted, "they would make all the resistance in their power to the attempts of the parish to remedy the evils of which they complained, and would give Dr. Holmes all their assistance and support in his opposition to the principles and wishes of the parish." This fear was certainly well grounded. The church were as firm in defence of the pastor as the parish in opposing him.

The pastor was asked to confer with the parish committee. He took time to consider his reply. The church sent him a memorial assuring him of their approval and support. Dr. Holmes replied to the parish, that he had been settled by the distinct and separate, yet concurrent, invitation of the church and the parish, and that he was not at liberty to overlook or to interfere with the equitable claims of the church; and that he would consent to a mutual ecclesiastical council, if regularly called, according to the usage of our churches, that is, by the church and parish together. The parish refused to have the church considered in the matter, placing their refusal upon the ground that the church had no complaint against the pastor or the parish. The pastor would not deny the church their right in a matter so greatly concerning their welfare. Again, there was no hope of agreement by discussion. The parish proceeded to call an *ex parte* council, which assembled in the old Court House on the 19th of May, 1829. It was composed of the representatives of six Unitarian churches. A copy of the complaint to be presented against him was given to the pastor before the meeting of the council. In a written communication to the ministers and delegates who had been called together Dr. Holmes denied the jurisdiction of a council called after this manner, and the remonstrance of the church and a minority of the parish was presented. These were of no avail. The council sent a committee to apprise Dr. Holmes of their readiness to receive any further information which he or the remonstrants should think proper to introduce. He received the committee kindly, and replied " that he had no further communication to make to this council." After hearing the complaint of the parish against the pastor, which embraced eight specifications, the substance of which has already been given, and listening to the evidence which was presented by the committee, and to the argument of the Hon. Samuel Hoar, counsel for the parish, this *ex parte* council " voted, That the First Parish in Cambridge have sufficient cause to terminate the contract subsisting between them and the Rev. Dr. Holmes as their minister, and this council recommend the measure as necessary to the existence and spiritual prosperity of the society." The parish accepted and confirmed this " result," and voted that the " Rev. Dr. Abiel Holmes be, and he hereby is, dismissed from his office of minister of the gospel and teacher of piety, religion, and morality in said parish, and that all connection between said Holmes as such minister, or teacher, and said parish, do and shall henceforth cease." But a grant of three months' salary was made " to said Holmes, on equitable principles, but not as legal right"; and he was to have the use and occupation of the real estate held by him as pastor of the parish " until the twenty-fifth day of January next, but no longer." In a communication of the 12th of June, the committee of the parish inform the discarded friend of thirty-eight years, that "they have employed a preacher to supply the pulpit in the meeting-house of the First Parish in Cambridge on the next ensuing Sabbath, that they will procure and employ a preacher or preachers for the succeeding Sabbaths, and that your services will not be required or authorized in the public religious services in the meeting-house in said parish hereafter." Dr. Holmes replied that he had entered his protest against the jurisdiction of the council, and added, "I now give notice to you, and, through you, to the inhabitants of the parish, that I still consider myself as the lawful minister of the parish, and hold myself ready to perform any and all the duties, in or out of the pulpit, which belong to my office as pastor of the First Church and Society in Cambridge." The closing communication of this long series was addressed by the parish committee to the pastor, and concludes in these words: "In answer to your said letter, said committee, in behalf of said parish, state to you that said council had jurisdiction of the complaint exhibited to said council against you; that said result is legal and valid; that said dismission from said office conforms to said result and to law; that your connection with said parish as their minister is legally dissolved; that you are not the minister or pastor of said parish, nor have you been such minister or pastor since said dismission; that as such minister or pastor you do not owe any such duties as aforesaid to said parish, and that said parish refuses to accept from you any service, or services, as such minister or pastor thereof. Hereafter you cannot occupy nor use the pulpit of the meeting-house of said parish, as it will be exclusively appropriated to such preacher or preachers as said parish shall employ to supply it."

I make no comments upon this termination of thirty-eight years of affectionate intercourse in cares and pleasures, in worship and work. But the pastor, thus thrust out by his own people, was not without comfort. He had the testimony of a good conscience, and he knew that he had kept faith with the illustrious line of ministers to which he belonged, and he had peace with God. In one of the sermons upon the anniversary of his installation, preached a few months before his dismission, and while the controversy was at its height, he used this language: "I acknowledge that the precept of the gospel, 'If it be possible, as much as lieth in you, live peaceably with all men,' is alike binding upon us, the ministers of Christ, as upon you who pertain to our charge. But whether it were possible for a minister to live peaceably with those who would constrain him to bring into the pulpit doctrines which he does not believe to be Scriptural, or to invite others to stand there and deliver them in his place; with those, who, in disregard of his pastoral responsibility, and of his right of private judgment and conscience, would have him do what he cannot do honestly, and what, if done, would, in his judgment, be of baneful tendency and influence, with respect both to the peace of the society and to the welfare of the church committed to his care, — whether it were possible to live peaceably with all men, were such things asked or expected of him, judge ye." Thus speaks the pastor in his own defence. He carried a manly, dignified, Christian spirit through the whole discussion. He was willing to give to others the liberty of conscience he asked for himself. He was the minister of Christ, set for the defence and furtherance of the gospel. It was his heart's desire to gratify his beloved people in all ways consistent with his vows, and with his duty to Christ and the church. He was not his own. What would the Lord have him to do? He testified that he had " devoutly and importunately sought Divine light and guidance." He spoke like an apostle: "If I seem to disregard the wishes or the taste of my hearers, it is because I am more desirous to save than to please them." In his reply to a letter asking a copy of these anniversary sermons for publication, Dr. Holmes writes, "The fulness of our assemblies, and their increased solemnity; the considerable accessions to the church; the degree of unanimity of the church in its memorial, and in its address to the pastor, are at once consolatory and encouraging."

There was but one course open to the church, and that was to withdraw from the parish. They desired to go out from the parish meeting-house, and to meet for worship in some other place, where they could enjoy the ministrations of their pastor. He acceded to their desire, and, crossing the street, as the founder of the church had crossed the sea, the pastor and church began Divine service in the old Court House, in the presence of "a full, attentive, and solemn assembly." On the last Sabbath which the church spent in the old meeting-house, Dr. Holmes preached from St. John's words, "I have no greater joy than to hear that my children walk in truth." Near the close he said, tenderly, "These, my beloved brethren, these, my dear children, — for such you will allow me to call you, — these are sources of the greatest joy to him who labors among you in word and doctrine. Fulfil ye therefore my joy. Be steadfast in faith and holy in life." The next Sabbath morning the church was in the Court House, when the pastor preached from the words of St. Peter, "Beloved, think it not strange concerning the fiery trial which is to try you, as though some strange thing happened unto you; but rejoice, inasmuch as ye are partakers of Christ's sufferings; that, when his glory shall be revealed, ye may be glad also with exceeding joy." The text was affectionately commended to the remembrance of "all who are in affliction, and especially to the church and the attendant worshippers constrained to assemble in this place."

"The whole number of members belonging to the church at that time was about ninety, full two thirds of whom followed the pastor and attended upon his ministry. The number of male members was twenty-one, fifteen of whom were the uniform friends and supporters of the pastor, and two only took an active part in the measures of the parish" for his dismission. "Of the whole number who usually worshipped in the meeting-house previous to the separation, about one half have withdrawn, and statedly worship with the church and its pastor." "Let all things be done decently and in order." The church and pastor proceeded to call an advisory council, which met on the 17th of June, 1829. Did they select the 17th of June from any feeling of its fitness to their condition and resolution arising from its historic associations? Ten churches were represented in the council. It was a grand assembly of men. William Greenough was moderator. There were Daniel Dana, Moses Stuart, Benjamin B. Wisner, and others worthy of such fellowship. The church and the pastor told their story. The substance of the result was in these words: "As Dr. Holmes is still, according to ecclesiastical usage, the pastor and minister of the first church and parish in Cambridge, and as the parish has by its votes excluded him from its pulpit, the council approve the course pursued by him in continuing to perform parochial duties wherever and to whomsoever he may have opportunity, and advise him and the church and other friends of truth 'not to forsake the assembling of themselves together'; but to maintain Divine worship and the celebration of Divine ordinances." The church approved this advice, and resolved to follow religiously the counsel given them.

As the church was separated from the First Parish, it was necessary to organize another society, to include others besides members of the church, and to be the parish with which the church should be connected. Such a society was formed, and the society unanimously voted that it should bear the name of "The Holmes Congregational Society." But the good man declined the proffered honor, and advised that the name of the first of his line should be chosen for that use. In accordance with his wish the new body took the title of "The Shepard Congregational Society." The pastor could not connect himself with this organization, because he did not consider himself legally and according to established usage dismissed from his pastoral connection with the First Parish. But the church agreed to unite with the new society to maintain "the worship and ordinances of the gospel, according to the established principles and usages of Congregational churches in this Commonwealth." This union was to last until the rights of the church and pastor should be again respected by the First Parish.

With the approval of the aged pastor, it was decided to associate a colleague with him, and Mr. Nehemiah Adams, Jr., was invited, and was ordained on the 17th of December, 1829. A lot of land for a new meeting-house was given by Miss Sarah Ann Dana, and funds were collected at home and abroad for the erection of the house. It is said that Dr. Holmes was the largest contributor to the building-fund for the new house. At six o'clock on the morning of the 5th of August, 1830, the ground was broken, with prayer and singing, and a brief address by the senior pastor. On the 21st of September the corner-stone was laid with fitting ceremonies. On that occasion an address was delivered by the Rev. Samuel Green, of Boston. This address is an index of the feeling of the church, and of the sentiment of those around them who held with them to the faith and order of the fathers, and many of whom had suffered in like manner. This speaker felt the greatness of the time and the significance of the service in which he bore a part. One sentence will illustrate the prevailing feeling: "We speak with freedom and boldness, as becometh the descendants of Puritans on Puritan ground." On the 23d of February, 1831, the house was dedicated to God, the Father, Son, and Holy Ghost. The sermon was preached by the senior pastor from the words of the Lord by Jeremiah: "Therefore hear, ye nations, and know, O congregation, what is among them." The sermon in the new house on the first Sabbath morning after the dedication was also by Dr. Holmes, and was from the words, "The Lord is in his holy temple." After the sermon the sacrament of the Lord's Supper was administered. That house, repeatedly enlarged and improved, has been the home of this church until this day.

After the separation the Rev. William Newell was called to the pastoral care of the parish, and he was ordained May 19, 1830. The old meeting-house continued to be used by the parish until December, 1833, when it was taken down. A new house had been erected nearly opposite, and this was dedicated December 12, 1833. That is the house still used by the First Parish, although it has been very much changed in its interior arrangements. Its ample walls have held most of the large assemblies in connection with the College, and from its doors year by year the graduating class has gone out to its work in the world.

Dr. Newell has remained until recently in the pastoral office here; and now, although released from official service, he dwells among his own people, crowning the labors of forty years by ministering to them still in their joy and grief with paternal kindness, blessing them with the ripe and abundant fruitage of his long, industrious, and beautiful life.

When this church celebrated the twenty-fifth anniversary of Dr. Albro's settlement, Dr. Newell was able to say, in all sincerity, that the personal relations of these neighboring ministers had always been pleasant and friendly. He was ready to manifest what he described as "the kindly feeling which I hope will always subsist, not only between your pastor and myself, but also between the societies with which we are connected; branches as they are of the same old stock, descended from the same old congregational family, looking back, amidst their honest differences of opinion, with common pride to a common ancestry."

Let his good words stand in this record at the place where the church and the parish took their different paths.

It would be pleasant to pause here. But history sets its own bounds. In February, 1831, the deacon of the

MEETING-HOUSE ERECTED BY THE FIRST PARISH IN 1833.

portion of the church which remained with the First Parish demanded of the deacons of the church the delivery of certain articles of church property, to wit, the church fund, the poor's fund, the Communion service and baptismal basin, the church records and papers, the library, and a few minor things. The demand was not obeyed, and in August a suit at law was begun. The church appointed a committee to take legal advice, and to defend the church in its rights, or, if found necessary, to surrender the property to the parish. They found that, by a decision of the Supreme Court of the Commonwealth, the church could not retain the property, and it was accordingly given up to the parish under the constraint of the law as it had been interpreted. The decision upon which this action was based was made in what is known as the Dedham case, and was given in 1820. The principle laid down by the court was this: "Where a majority of the members of a congregational church separate from the majority of the parish, the members who remain, although a minority, constitute the church in such parish, and retain the rights and property belonging thereto." The church was regarded as holding ordinary property in trust for the benefit of the parish, while to property of such a nature as to be a trust simply for church uses, as the Communion service, and to property which might be given expressly for the use of the poor of the church, the parish would have no claim. But, so far as property was concerned, under this decision, there was no church separate from a parish. Property, I say. For the court said, "That any number of the members of a church, who disagree with their brethren or with the minister or with the parish, may withdraw from fellowship with them, and act as a church in a religious point of view, having the ordinances administered and other religious offices performed, it is not necessary to deny; indeed, this would be a question proper for an ecclesiastical council to settle, if any should dispute their claim. But as to all civil purposes, the secession of a whole church from the parish would be an extinction of the church; and it is competent to the members of the parish to institute a new church, or to ingraft one upon the old stock if any of it should remain; and this new church would succeed to all the rights of the old in relation to the parish." This distinction between a church in law, as a holder of property, and a church ecclesiastically, was repeated when the church in Harvard College was cited as an instance of a church existing without any parish. The court replied, "We have before said that it was not intended to deny that there may be such churches in an ecclesiastical sense." In this case of ours about one third of the members of the church had remained with the parish. This decision pronounced that fraction the church so far, and only so far, as civil rights were concerned. The property was therefore delivered to them, as it must have been had but a single person remained; nay, if not a member had remained, the parish could have organized a new church, which would have been entitled to all the property hitherto enjoyed by the old. I beg that it may be noticed that, even under this remarkable decision, the ecclesiastical existence and rights of the church were not impaired by the separation of the church from the parish. But the ecclesiastical existence of a church is surely its real existence. Under this decision, if the object of a church is to hold property, then the part of a church, be it large or small or imaginary, which adheres to the parish is the old church. But if the object of a church is to maintain the worship of God and observe his ordinances, then the church is independent of the parish, and by its own action can remove to another building or another town, and still be the old church with the old name. Therefore, even under this decision which took away the property, this church of ours ecclesiastically, and for those purposes for which churches were instituted by the Lord and his Apostles, and for which this church was established by men who had exiled themselves, not for property, but for conscience' sake; not to hold lands, but to hold the faith, and enjoy it, and transmit it, — this church of the Puritans, this church of Christ, remains what it was in the days of Shepard, "The First Church in Cambridge." Such was the decision of the Supreme Court of Massachusetts; such was the decision of an ecclesiastical council; such has been the usage of Congregational churches from the beginning.

In regard to the decision of the Supreme Court, it is proper to say that to a great extent it failed to receive the approval of the public, and of many eminent jurists. The able author of the "Half-Century of the Unitarian Controversy," has frankly written, "We do not feel perfectly satisfied with the legal decision in two cases bearing upon the ownership of church property, though we admit that the issue raised was quite a perplexing one."

In our own case the decision was peculiarly hard. For "the church fund, for the recovery of which this suit was brought, was originally constituted by the donation of fifty pounds by a member of the church, and increased entirely by contributions of the church-members at the Lord's Supper. A part of the church plate was given to the church, and the rest was purchased with its own funds." The baptismal basin was the gift of the Rev. William Brattle, Pastor, "to the church of Christ in Cambridge, my dearly beloved flock." The money surrendered amounted to upwards of four thousand dollars.

But, whatever might have been the justice of the decision under which this property was given up, it must seem to us, who have succeeded the two parties in the controversy, and who look calmly upon the matter after the lapse of forty years, that the true course for old neighbors and fellow-worshippers was to make a fair division. The majority of the parish should have said to the minority, "Friends, it is plain that we cannot dwell together in peace; let us divide our goods, and separate." The majority of the church should have said to those of the church who agreed with the parish, "Brethren, we have come to hold different views and to desire different things; let us divide our goods, and separate." These are things of the past. The generation which moved in them has gone on to God, who knoweth the hearts of the children of men. We who have entered into their places in the old church and old parish dwell together in peace. There are honest differences of opinion, but we have no controversy. We are good neighbors, and join hands in many good works. Let the ancient strife be buried and forgotten, while we both strive to excel in love for God and in service for man. Not for purposes of controversy, but because they came in the course of our church history, have I recalled these painful events.

These were sad experiences for the church. It was sad to be loosed from the parish, to be exiled from the meeting-house, to give up the sacred vessels of the sacraments, and the silver and gold wherewith they had served God and relieved his poor. But they had themselves, and their minister, and their ancient faith. The eternal things were unseen and indestructible. They had courage and hope. They were ready to begin again. The senior pastor, it is believed, drew no salary after the separation. Christian friends in other places came to the aid of the impoverished church with generous gifts. The trials of that day were of great profit to the church. They were aroused to greater activity, to a closer fellowship, to a fresh study of the Scriptures, and to more diligent endeavors to make the truth felt in the blessedness of its power. This is a better church to-day for the severity of those trying times. In our ability to erect the sanctuary which we are soon to consecrate to God we have the visible sign of his favor which was with the fathers and has been continued to the children.

In their time of especial need He came to his people with large blessings. The preaching was "in demonstration of the Spirit and of power." The meetings for prayer were solemn and effective. The Lord watered the grass, even the mown grass. In the year following the separation thirty-one persons were received to the church, twenty-four of them upon profession of faith. In the next year twenty-three were added, all but two of whom came upon profession of faith. In a very short time the membership of the church was doubled. The Lord interposed for the comfort of the church, and prepared a table before them. After the Communion service had been given up, members of the church furnished their private plate for use at the Communion. But the junior pastor came into possession of the autobiography of Thomas Shepard, which was given in trust to him and his successors in the ministry of "The Shepard Congregational Society." To this book reference was made in a previous lecture. This book was printed, and with the proceeds of its sale was purchased the service from which the church now receives the body and blood of its Saviour and Lord. Thus do the hands of the first minister serve us still in holy things. We believe in the communion of saints on earth and in heaven, and in this sacrament is the happy symbol of it. Here is the book wherein that suffering, godly, now sainted man, wrote the story of his life, that his son might "learn to know and love the great and most high God, the God of his father." No man knoweth Thomas Shepard's grave, but this small, rude book, which his hands have handled and hallowed, holds his expression of his life. No chiselled inscription recites his praise, but the crooked letters which his fingers set in these closely written lines reveal his piety and affection; and the souls which cherish his memory keep tryst with him here, as at a shrine.

The pastoral work of Dr. Holmes drew towards its close. His continued and increasing debility unfitted him for the duties of the pastoral office, and he asked release. The church consented, and a council was called which confirmed the action. The council bore a noble testimony to the character and learning of the retiring pastor. He preached his farewell sermon on the 2d of October, 1831. He died on the 12th of June, 1837, in the seventy-fourth year of his age.

I have the manuscript of his farewell sermon. The text is from the First Epistle to the Thessalonians, iii. 8: "For now we live, if ye stand fast in the Lord." It is full of affectionate advice and entreaty and blessing; such a sermon as we should expect from such a man. I copy a few sentences addressed to the church: "To you, my dearly beloved of this church, I offer a parting benediction. The remembrance of the tokens and proofs of your affection and steadfastness in time past, especially in the time of our calamity, can never be obliterated. Danger did not intimidate, sufferings did not discourage you. When the storm was beating upon us, you stood firm under the open canopy of heaven to receive it. When the tide was rising and pressing hard upon us, you stood firm to meet it. When resistance would avail nothing, you stood still and saw the salvation of God. If it had not been the Lord who was on our side, now may we unitedly say, then the waters had overwhelmed us, the stream had gone over our souls. Our help is in the name of the Lord; to him be the glory. Let this house which we have built for the honor of his name be at once a monument of our gratitude and a temple for his praise." The impression was unspeakably touching and tender when, after the sermon, the 71st Psalm was given out by the aged man of God —

> "God of my childhood and my youth
>   The guide of all my days,
> I have declar'd thy heavenly truth,
>   And told thy wondrous ways.
>
> "Wilt thou forsake my hoary hairs,
>   And leave my fainting heart?
> Who shall sustain my sinking years,
>   If God, my strength, depart?

" Let me thy power and truth proclaim
 To the surviving age,
 And leave a savor of thy name
  When I shall quit the stage.

" The land of silence and of death
 Attends my next remove ;
 O, may these poor remains of breath
  Teach the wide world thy love ! "

The ministry of Dr. Holmes here was but a few months short of forty years. With a single exception, it was the longest which the church has known. For nearly the whole of the time he was the only pastor in this part of the town, and he stood at the centre of a large parish, making his influence felt in every direction. He preached the word with fidelity and diligence. He fulfilled the various offices of our holy religion. He instructed the children, and gave them books. He formed libraries for the use of the parish. He watched over the schools. He gave of his substance to the poor. He brought into the parish the aid of others whom he esteemed able to edify the people. He zealously followed every good work. He was a true friend to our College. During a portion of its earlier history the Society of Christian Brethren held its meetings at his house. He lived here, before the people, a life of purity and sanctity and usefulness, an Israelite without guile, a man full of the Holy Ghost and of faith. In the day of trial he showed the sustaining power of his principles and his piety, and he won the commendation of men, the increased affection of his own people, and the esteem of the churches. In temper Dr. Holmes was calm and quiet ; in manner, urbane and courteous. He cherished a large charity

He taught his own household what he practised himself, to be careful of the reputation of others, and not to take up a reproach against a neighbor. His preaching was quiet, but his sermons were pure in style, rich in the use of words, happy in the application of Scripture, and full of profitable thought. He was conservative and cautious, no declaimer, not much given to the discussion of the doctrines of theology, but engaged with the facts of religion and their application to real life. His old friend, Dr. Jenks, in a memorial sermon delivered here on the Sabbath after Dr. Holmes's death, very truly remarks, "That blending of moderation and modesty with firmness and decision of character, where decision and firmness are needed, constitute, if I mistake not, an enviable, or rather a desirable, distinction. Especially in these days .... we can hardly praise too highly the peaceful, laborious, faithful, and humble follower and minister of Jesus Christ, who is learned without vanity or dogmatism, pious without cant or fitfulness, and charitable without ostentation. And such, if I mistake not, was our beloved and lamented friend. Never in extremes or chargeable with extravagance, his deportment and character united, in no common degree, the gentleman, the scholar, and the Christian." When he was no longer the pastor of the church, he continued to cherish a warm interest in all that concerned it, and aided it as he was able. Some who were children in his day recall his kindly manner towards them, and like to tell how, as he walked the street with his well-remembered cane, he would pause at a group of school-children, and, with a pleasant question and a word of counsel, would draw from his capacious pocket a handful of confectionery, which he distributed among the expectant listeners. And they tell how he stood here before the pulpit a few weeks before his death, and gave a good book to each of the members of the Sabbath School as they passed before him.

Dr. Holmes left a large number of printed works, consisting chiefly of sermons preached on various occasions, at an ordination or a funeral, on a Fast or Thanksgiving Day. One was preached on the death of Washington; one to commend the counsel of Washington; one to celebrate the landing of the Pilgrims. He compiled and published the biography of President Stiles with great taste and judgment. He published a small "History of Cambridge," which is invaluable to any one interested in the ancient town. His largest work was "The Annals of America, from the discovery by Columbus in the year 1492 to the year 1826." This work reached a second edition, and was republished in England. "It is not only regarded as a standard work in this country, but has attracted the respectful attention of European critics." His early intercourse with President Stiles, whose daughter he married, fostered a literary taste, and not unlikely gave his mind a bent towards historical research. As an historian he was patient and accurate, and his books will live. In 1816 this "renowned antiquary" discovered in the Prince Library the third manuscript volume of Winthrop's Journal, which was deciphered and published. He was connected with a number of societies. From 1798 he was a most devoted friend of the Massachusetts Historical Society, and for more than twenty years its corresponding secretary. He was one of the founders of the Society for promoting Christian Knowledge, and of the American Education Society. He was a member of the American Academy of Arts and Sciences, one of the trustees of the Institution at Andover, and an Overseer of Harvard University. His degree of Doctor of Divinity was received from the University of Edinburgh about 1805, and he was made Doctor of Laws by Alleghany College in 1822. Through these years of this extended fame and influence he was performing the laborious duties of pastor in a large and important parish.

Here is his well-worn sermon-case, and fastened in it, as he left them, are two sermons, one a double sermon, preached in February, 1836, and the other in December, 1836. He closes the former, which was delivered on the two-hundredth anniversary of the organization of the church, with paternal counsel to the brethren of the church, to the dear children, and to those of the society who were not connected with the church. Then followed the benediction of peace. When he had addressed the church, he seems to have turned to him who for thirty years was to stand in his place, but who had then just entered upon his work. Both have passed on; but the written prayer remains. "May you, my brother, still live, sustained and animated by the steadfastness and vitality of the church under your pastoral care; live to see its increase in numbers and in graces, and, at a distant period, finish your course with joy, and the ministry which you have received of the Lord Jesus, and be ready to depart, and to give up your account with joy. Mine I must soon give up, for I have nearly finished my course. And what, next to the personal hope which is an anchor to our own souls, — what is our hope or joy or crown of rejoicing? Are not the church and dear people of our pastoral care, are not even ye, dearly beloved, in the presence of our Lord Jesus Christ at his coming?" He closed the latter sermon with these words: "Does any one ask, What have I to give on this day of Thanksgiving? I answer, there is one gift which every one in this assembly, old or young, rich or poor, may alike offer with the assurance that it will be accepted. It is the gift of himself. Who will refuse this to Him who is crowning your life with his goodness, and who is this day reminding you that while he giveth us richly all things to enjoy, he is, by the unspeakable gift of his son Jesus Christ, presenting us with the hope of life and immortality? I beseech you therefore, brethren, by the mercies of God, that ye present your bodies a living sacrifice, holy and acceptable to him, which is your reasonable service." Thus, being dead, he yet speaketh. Once again these walls hear the sound of his good words. Hear them, beloved, as spoken out of heaven.

He preached his last sermon here to his old people, on the 22d of January, 1837, and its subject was, "The vanity of life a reason for seeking a portion in heaven." An illness of a few weeks terminated his long and useful life. A severe paralytic shock a few days before his death rendered him almost helpless, and made his articulation very imperfect. But he was comforted with the faith he had preached to others, and rejoiced in the cheerful hope of immortal blessedness through the grace of Christ his Saviour. He died in charity with all men. To a friend who bent over him on the the last night in his life he gave indistinct utterance to his charity, and said that he wished his injuries written in sand. He died on Sunday morning, as the

REV. DR. HOLMES'S RESIDENCE FROM 1807.

bell which he had been wont to obey was calling the people to worship. He died, having the respect and affection of the community. The bells of the town were tolled on the day of his death, in recognition of his worth and in tribute to his memory. His second wife, the mother of his children, the daughter of the Hon. Oliver Wendell, long survived him, and received the affectionate homage of many hearts, both for her own excellence and for her association with him whose life she had shared and adorned.

He was first laid in the sacred field where all his predecessors had been buried, where they awaited the resurrection. But his remains were afterwards removed to Mount Auburn. There he lies, in the company of the great and good. But his church has graven his name upon the column which is sacred to the memory of her ministers who have gone to their reward, and which rises above the dust of him who last had rest from the duties of his office. The names of both will be read on the mural tablet which will make our new church more hallowed; and their initial letters in monogram, carved in stone, are at the sides of the main entrance to the sanctuary which they would have rejoiced to see. But their best memorial is in the work which survives them, in the affection which cherishes them, in the glory which encircles them. At the installation of Mr. Albro, this hymn, written by Dr. Holmes, was sung, to be repeated at the subsequent installation, and again at the dedication of the new church in 1872: —

> "Great God! thou heard'st our fathers' prayer,
>   When, o'er the ocean brought,
> They, with a patriarchal care,
>   A sanctuary sought.

"Hither thy guidance led their feet, —
  Here was their first abode :
And here, where now their children meet,
  They found a place for God.

"Thy flock, Immanuel, here was fed,
  In pastures green and fair,
Beside still waters gently led,
  And thine the shepherd's care.

"That care two hundred years attest ;
  Thy seal is still the same :
To every bosom be it pressed,
  Graved with thy precious name.

"Here may the church thy cause maintain,
  Thy truth with peace and love,
Till her last earth-born live again
  With the first-born above.

"O glorious change ! From conflict free,
  The church, — no danger nigh,
From militant on earth, shall be
  Triumphant in the sky."

LECTURE VIII.

"HE THAT GOETH FORTH AND WEEPETH, BEARING PRECIOUS SEED, SHALL DOUBTLESS COME AGAIN WITH REJOICING, BRINGING HIS SHEAVES WITH HIM." — Psalm cxxvi. 6.

IT is not the going forth and weeping which insure the return with rejoicing. For this consummation of the sorrow and toil it is essential that he who goes out shall carry precious seed. If the seed has in it a vitality which cannot be destroyed, and a worth which will reward any pains and waiting, then the rejoicing shall come. Those who have the tears may pass away before the full harvest gladdens their eyes; but the harvest shall come, and if one sow and another reap, the sower and the reaper shall rejoice together. There is a glorious fellowship in all good work. In pursuing the history of this ancient church, we have come to the time of the going forth and weeping. Those who were banished from the sanctuary which had been their home took with them precious seed. They kept the faith; they retained the promises. Cast down, they were not destroyed. With hope and courage they made a new field ready for seed and harvest. The rejoicing began before they entered on their rest, and in the midst of plenty we mention their names with gratitude and with thanksgiving to him who prospered them, and who withheld from them the fulness of the promise, "God having provided some better thing for us, that they without us should not be made perfect."

The ministry of Dr. Holmes and that of his successor were for a time united. The advanced years of the old pastor, and his peculiar relation to the First Parish, made it expedient that he should have an associate in his work. Accordingly, as we have seen, Mr. Nehemiah Adams, Jr., was invited to become his colleague. The church records contain an account of a meeting of the church held on the 20th of November, 1829, at the house of Mr. Jacob Bates. After prayer and consultation the church came to the decision which is set forth in the votes which follow: "Whereas the Rev. Dr. Holmes, the pastor of this church, has been excluded by a committee of the First Parish in Cambridge from the desk and the sanctuary where he has so long officiated, under a pretence that he is legally dismissed from office; and whereas a great majority of the church, retaining their affection for him and confidence in him, have withdrawn, and attended public worship under his ministrations in another place; whereas the said committee of the First Parish have also manifested a disposition to deprive us as a church of our just and immemorial rights, and there is now no prospect that the gospel as it appears to us revealed in the Scriptures, and as it was embraced by our fathers from the first planting of this church, will at present be preached in the house over which the First Parish have legal control; whereas it is in our view of the utmost importance that this gospel should be maintained within the boundaries of this parish, and a society by the name of the Shepard Congregational Society has been formed for the purpose of supporting the gospel here in its purity, with which society we as a church are respectfully invited to unite and co-operate according to the rights and usages of congregational churches; whereas our venerable pastor, holding as he does and must that he is not legally dismissed from office in the First Parish, cannot now consistently attach himself to the new society and become in form its minister, but another person has of late been employed with a view to settlement in the ministry, — in consideration of all the circumstances, and having consulted with the Rev. Dr. Holmes, our pastor, whose relation to us as a church we wish to hold sacred and inviolate, and finding that in present circumstances the choice of a colleague pastor meets with his entire approbation: therefore, voted, 1st, that until such time as our rights, with those of our pastor, shall be respected, and the privileges of the gospel ministry be enjoyed, as heretofore, in connection with the First Parish in Cambridge, we will, as a church, accede to the invitation of the said Shepard Congregational Society, and co-operate with it in maintaining the worship and ordinances of the gospel, according to the established principles and usages of Congregational churches in this Commonwealth. Voted, 2d, that in pursuance of the object, and subject to the several conditions expressed in the first vote, the church now unite, and call Mr. Nehemiah Adams, Jr., — who has been heard by us for several Sabbaths with high approbation, and in whom we have full confidence, — to the office of colleague pastor in this church in connection with the Rev. Dr. Holmes as senior pastor." It was further voted to communicate this decision to the Shepard Society and desire its concurrence, and also to inform Mr. Adams of the wish of the church and society, and, if he should accept the invitation, to take the necessary steps for his ordination. The committee consisted of Deacons Hilliard and Munro and Mr. Richard H. Dana. The salary offered to the pastor elect was eight hundred and fifty dollars for the first year, to be increased fifty dollars a year until the amount of one thousand dollars was reached. I am informed, however, that by private subscription the salary was at once established at the maximum sum named.

The invitation was accepted by Mr. Adams, and a council for his ordination met in the vestry of the Baptist church in Cambridgeport, which had been kindly offered for the services, on the 17th of December, 1829. Twenty-three churches were represented. It is interesting to read over the names of the ministers and delegates. Rev. John Codman, D.D., of Dorchester, was moderator, Rev. David Perry of Cambridgeport, scribe, and Rev. Lyman Gilbert of Newton, assistant scribe. Other members were Rev. William Jenks, D.D., from the Green Street Church, Boston; Rev. Lyman Beecher, D.D., from the Hanover Street Church; Rev. Benjamin B. Wisner, D.D., and Mr. Samuel H. Walley, from the Old South Church; Rev. Edward Beecher and Rev. Louis Dwight from Park Street Church; Professor Moses Stuart and Mr. Calvin E. Stowe from the church at the Theological Seminary in Andover; Rev. Ebenezer Burgess from Dedham; Rev. Samuel Stearns and Mr. Samuel H. Stearns from Bedford; Rev. Jonathan Homer, D.D., from Newton; Mr. Samuel M. E. Kettle, afterwards Rev. William M. Rogers, with Dr. Codman, from Dorchester; Rev. John P. Cleaveland and Deacon Nehemiah Adams from the Tabernacle Church in Salem; Rev. George W. Blagden from Brighton. The action of the previous advisory council was submitted by the church; and a remonstrance presented to the pastor elect by a committee of those members of the church who had adhered to the First Parish was read. After the customary examination in doctrine and character, the council voted to proceed with the ordination, which was performed in the Baptist Church. Rev. Mr. Cleaveland offered the introductory prayer, Professor Stuart preached the sermon, Dr. Jenks offered the ordaining prayer, Dr. Holmes gave the charge to the pastor, Mr. Beecher the right hand of fellowship, Dr. Burgess the address to the people, and Mr. Stearns offered the concluding prayer. On the 3d of January following, the committee for the settlement of the new pastor was instructed "to make the application contemplated in the resolutions of the council in answer to an address presented to them by the church and Shepard Society in Cambridge, and also for aid from any other sources which they may deem expedient." After the heavy pecuniary losses of the church in its separation from the parish, it was necessary to make an appeal for aid, and to this there was such response as enabled the church to sustain the Divine ordinances and pursue its Christian work. It was another beginning, and with some difficulties of which our predecessors of 1636 had little knowledge after they had once reached these western shores.

The sermons of Dr. Holmes at this period give an insight into the state and feeling of the people. There is a manuscript marked "June 7, 1829: in meetinghouse." There is another dated a week later, "June 14, 1829: A.M., Camb. Courthouse." The text of the former is in St. John's words: "I have no greater joy than to hear that my children walk in truth." The text of the latter is in St. Peter's words, "Beloved, think it not strange concerning the fiery trial which is to try you, as though some strange thing happened unto you; but rejoice, inasmuch as ye are partakers of Christ's sufferings; that, when his glory shall be revealed, ye may be glad also with exceeding joy." With that spirit the church took up its work anew. Two hundred years had wrought no change. There is a sermon marked "Dec. 20, 1829, A.M., 1st Sabbath after ordination of Mr. N. Adams." The text is, "Now if Timotheus come, see that he may be with you without fear; for he worketh the work of the Lord, as I also do." Towards the close the venerated pastor says, "The Lord this day gives you an ascension gift, a pastor who is of the same religious principles which we unitedly believe to be according to the gospel, and which we are solicitous to maintain for ourselves and to transmit to our descendants; a pastor who has witnessed a good confession before many witnesses, and whom we cordially commend to you, in the belief that he comes to you in the fulness of the blessing of the gospel of Christ. Receive him. Treat him with candor and equity; preserve unity and peace; and pay an attentive and serious regard to his ministry."

Thus, with the commendation and blessing of the aged pastor, his young associate entered upon his work. The services of the Sabbath were divided between the two pastors. The senior preached in the morning and the junior in the afternoon and evening. The services were well attended, especially in the evening, when persons not connected with the new society would come to hear preaching in a place devoted to other uses. The labors of the ministers were greatly blessed, for the years 1830, 1831, and 1832 show large additions to the church upon confession of faith. The loss of members was soon more than made good. Plainly, the Lord had a favor unto this band of disciples who had suffered much for his name. The services on the Sabbath were held in the Court House for nearly two years. When there were lectures there in the evening the people carried their own lamps, sometimes giving occasion to the by-standers whom they passed to throw out jests at their expense. Meetings for prayer were for a time held in private houses, and were finally established in the house at the northwest corner of Mount Auburn and Brighton Streets, in a large room fitted up for that purpose. As soon as the church and society were able, with the assistance of friends, to erect a meeting-house, this house was built. The ground was broken on the 5th of August, 1830, with religious services; the corner-stone was laid on the 21st of the following month; and on the 23d of February, 1831, the house was dedicated with a sermon by the senior pastor from Jeremiah vi. 18. I have spoken of some of these things before, but it has seemed proper to repeat them in this connection. This new house was greatly admired. Mr. Washington Allston furnished the plan, and the house was an object of especial pride to him. He liked to take strangers at evening to a particular spot, about a hundred rods southeast of the building, where he would repeat the familiar lines of Sir Walter Scott, —

"If thou wouldst view fair Melrose aright,
Go visit it by the pale moonlight,"

and bid his companions mark the simple beauty of this unassuming structure. The first sermon after the dedication was by the senior pastor, from the words, "The Lord is in his holy temple," and this was followed by the sacrament of the Lord's Supper.

In September, 1831, the increased feebleness of the senior pastor made it necessary that he should be released from the duties of the pastoral office. The church acceded to his request for dismission, and this action was duly ratified by an ecclesiastical council. Thus ended the official labors of a ministry of forty years. This is his farewell sermon. The text is, "For now we live, if ye stand fast in the Lord." A portion of this sermon I have repeated in a previous lecture.

For nearly three years after the resignation of Dr. Holmes, Mr. Adams remained the pastor of the church. But in February, 1834, he received an invitation to the pastoral care of the Essex Street Church and Society in Boston. He deemed it his duty to accept this call. With great reluctance the church complied with his request for dismission; and a council on the 14th of March approved the action, and he entered into the pastoral connection which, after thirty-eight years, he still retains. This is the only instance, in the long history of this church, in which a minister has left it to assume the care of another church. Mr. Adams's pastorate was four years and three months in duration. But it was a critical time in the life of the church, when a year was in importance of more than its wonted length. In labors he was abundant and abundantly successful. It is too early to make a summing up of his ministerial work. May it be long before that can be done, very long before his name can be inscribed upon the monument and tablet whereon the church will hand down his name and his ministry here to the generations to come! In the fulness of his years, the richness of his life, the mellowness of his character, the wisdom and piety and purity of his spirit, his presence

Meeting-House erected in 1830–31.

is a blessing in the end as in the beginning, and a yet greater benediction.

For thirteen months the church had no pastor. Dr. Holmes was still living, and was a father to his people. His counsel was freely given to the young, his sympathy to the old, his comfort to the sorrowing. The church could not be desolate so long as his voice could be heard from the pulpit, and the familiar way to his door opened before the people. "My beloved brethren," he said in one of his sermons, "my dear children, for such you will allow me to call you." But it was needful that the church should have another minister. In August, 1834, a call was extended to Mr. Oliver E. Daggett, now of New London, but he felt compelled, for personal reasons, to decline the invitation. After a time there came a stranger into the pulpit. He preached but a single Sabbath, when he was unanimously invited to the pastorate. It was believed that he was "peculiarly qualified for the ministry in this place," and there was "a general and ardent desire of his ministrations." He accepted the invitation, and on the 15th of April, 1835, he was installed. Twenty-five years afterwards he said, "I was received with a unanimity, affection, and cordiality which in the flight of years and the changes of the world have remained, I hope, as strong as at the beginning. I came to you, as Paul went to the Corinthians, in weakness, and in fear, and in much trembling, and you encouraged me by your sympathy, and bore up my heart by your affection and your prayers. . . . . I came to you, as the disciples were sent upon their first mission, without purse or scrip, and, like them, I can tell the Master to-day that in all these years you have permitted me to lack nothing."

The mention of the name of the Rev. John Adams Albro reminds us that we have come into the present time. So much has been publicly said by different persons regarding the tenth minister of this church, and his long service here, that I can do little more than repeat what is already in print. But a good man's life is a perennial source of benefaction, and it will be both pleasant and instructive to recall the character and work of one whose name and influence abide among us. It is by describing the man and his work that the history of the church during this period is best made known. For the life of the parish centred in him.

Mr. Albro was born in Newport, R. I., August 13, 1799. By the death of his father he was early left to the care of a Christian mother. His mother married again, and the son afterwards found a home with his grandmother. It was necessary that he should maintain himself, and, possessing the fine talent which proved of so great advantage to him in his future work, he prepared himself to be a teacher of music. But at about the age of eighteen he entered the Law School at Litchfield, Conn., to fit himself for the legal profession. In 1821 he finished his legal studies, and with flattering prospects entered upon the practice of his profession in Mansfield, Conn. He had not enrolled himself as a disciple of Christ, but he felt the power of the truth, and gave serious thought to his immortal interests. At length, in deep humility and contrition, and apprehending the mercy of God in Jesus Christ, he believed in his heart on the divine Saviour, and made confession of him with his mouth. He united with the First Church in Mansfield on the 6th of July, 1823. This change in himself and in his relations to God and to the world created a desire to become a minister of the gospel in which he had found light and life. After spending some two years in the practice of the law, he entered the Theological Seminary at Andover. He had not received a collegiate training, but he had studied with fidelity, so that he took good rank with his associates in Latin, Greek, and Hebrew, while he had also mastered the French and German languages. He is described as at that time " a bright, genial man; winning, not to say fascinating, in his manner and conversation, fond of poetry, reading Shakespeare finely and with much interest, perhaps more devoted then to general studies than to theology, and especially enjoying and excelling in music." His scholarship was held in so high esteem by his companions in study, that some of them obtained for him from Yale College the honorary degree of Master of Arts.

He graduated in 1827, and on the 27th of November in that year he was ordained at Middlesex Village in Chelmsford, Mass. That was in the troublous times, the very year in which the first steps were taken which led to the separation of our own church from the old parish. The young pastor was expected to pursue the same general system of exchanges which was demanded here, and, like Dr. Holmes, he said that he could not do it. There came a division, but all the members of the church, except two, sustained the pastor, and with him and a few of the society withdrew from the parish, and began religious services in a hall. It seems like reading the story of our own church over again. About two years after this division Mr. Albro was invited to the pastoral office by the Calvinistic Congregational Church in Fitchburg. He was installed there on the

9th of May, 1832. But the church was in a disturbed state on account of an old controversy which he had supposed to be ended, and the new relation was in many respects trying and difficult. Accordingly, after a ministry there of two years and a half, he retired from the position. He had made many friends, had exerted a lasting influence, and his words and spirit were long treasured up. His services were sought by several churches. A hearty invitation was extended to him to enter the place made vacant by the resignation of Mr. Adams, and on the 15th of April, 1835, he became the pastor of this church and society. This was the real beginning of his work, for it was the entrance on a pastorate of thirty years. We are now to review his ministry, within a single day of the anniversary of its beginning. It was a good ministry, such as one might well choose for himself; a time of regular, quiet, successful work, faithfully performed, and with large and permanent results. Yet they were not stirring years in our church history. Few large events come to the surface as we examine them. They were years of steady, honest work. If they are not the best for the historian, they were the best for the minister and the people.

The population of the town at the time of Mr. Albro's settlement was about six thousand. The church, although greatly enlarged, was still small in numbers, and of very limited pecuniary ability. The prevailing social spirit of the community was not friendly to the church or its teaching. Yet the place had its own attractions. Here was Harvard College, whose library was open to the minister whose scholarly habits fitted him to enjoy it. And there were many persons of culture with whom he could find companionship and sympathy. The long history of the church from the days of Shepard was enough to inspire the heart of a man who admired the Puritan character and rejoiced in its works. He proved himself of the true lineage when he made haste to spend his first Sabbath in England at Towcester, the birthplace of Thomas Shepard, where his feeling was far deeper than at Stratford-on-Avon.

Thus, in the thirty-sixth year of his age, this pastor began his work. It was the regular work of preaching the gospel and administering its holy offices. The chief event which broke the even tenor of the years was the visit of the pastor to Europe in 1852, when he was absent for six months, through the liberality of his people. The facilities for a foreign tour were not as great twenty years ago as they are now. But this traveller went with taste and learning which prepared him to appreciate all that he saw, and, as he passed from country to country, to store his mind with treasures which he could bring home. His whole life was enriched by the rest which comes with a sojourn among the scenes of a strange land, and his people found bread coming back upon the waters where they had cast the seed.

One other event of large significance was the celebration of the twenty-fifth anniversary of his installation. The origin of the commemoration was in the desire of the church and society to mark a point in their history which is seldom reached, but which had now been most happily attained. From the published account of the doings on that occasion we are able in some measure to reproduce it, and to gain from it some idea of the results of the long work. On Sunday, the true anniversary day, the pastor preached an appropriate discourse, in which he brought together the past and the present, and sought to enforce the lessons which the day should teach. On the following Wednesday evening a public commemorative service was held in this church. The present senior deacon of the church made the opening address of welcome, and introduced the services of the evening. After religious exercises, addresses were made by several representative gentlemen, and each said that which it became him to say. Mr. Zelotes Hosmer, who had long resided here, and who rendered inestimable service to the church, who has now rejoined in another world the pastor of whom he spoke, said, " Let us be thankful that for five-and-twenty years we have enjoyed the faithful preaching of God's word from a faithful teacher, and trust that here may be his place of rest ; and I am sure you will all join with me in the expression of the hope that his ministry may be long continued." The Royal Professor of Law spoke in behalf of the Shepard society, and claimed that the early legal training of this minister in some degree accounted for the truthfulness of his reasoning in the pulpit, and testified, after a hearing of more than twelve years, " I have never known him to confuse the minds of his auditors by the enunciation of an unsound legal principle, nor mislead them by a specious but erroneous legal argument." President Felton represented the University and himself also, and with an earnestness and radiance which those who knew him can even now find in his words, said out of his imperial soul, " I join as heartily in all the honors you are paying your excellent pastor as if I were a member of the society. . . . . Your pastor and myself have been on the most cordial terms for the quarter of a century that he has been settled over you. . . . . I trust his days may be prolonged in the land." His honored and beloved predecessor spoke as only he can speak, and with a rare appreciation of the feelings of the "solitary man" upon whom kind words were lavished. He added his generous tribute to the rest, and said of his old friend, "He has both knowledge and wisdom. He is a full man. He reminds me of a place in Italy where, if you dig a few inches and apply a torch, a flame springs up. I feel toward him as one seems to have done toward a public building which he stood to view, leaning his head upon his hand, and soliloquizing every now and then, with much variety of intonation and emphasis, as he judges of its architecture, 'It is right! it is right!'. . . . And now, my dear sir and brother, in the name of all the Congregational ministers everywhere who either know of this occasion or shall be made acquainted with it, I feel empowered to say, The brethren which are with me greet you." His old neighbor, who had become the President of Amherst College, wrote of the commemoration in a letter which was read, "If ministerial fidelity, unpretending piety, ability in preaching, wisdom in affairs, largeness of heart, and persistent devotion to his people, entitle a man to such a notice, it is certainly deserved in the present case." The Rev. Dr. Newell of the First Parish, in a letter written after the celebration, expressed his "respect for your able and faithful pastor, with whom, during the whole period of his ministry, my personal relations, notwithstanding our theological differences, have always been pleasant and friendly." He was sorry not to have had the opportunity of manifesting by his presence " the kindly feeling which," he says, " I hope will always subsist, not only between your pastor and myself, but also between the societies with which we are connected, — branches as they are of the same old stock, descended from the same old congregational family, looking back, amidst their honest differences of opinion, with common pride to a common ancestry." And what said the pastor for himself? " Certainly it has never been my desire or my object to be rewarded by a demonstration like this. And now that I see this gathering of my people and my friends to do me honor, I hardly know what to say. I sincerely thank the church and society for what they have done. I thank the brethren and gentlemen for the kindness with which they have spoken of me and of my labors. It is a comfort for me now to know that there has been such unanimity of opinion and feeling with regard to my work among those whom I so highly respect, that I have lived in so much harmony with my neighbors of different persuasions, that I can look over the past and see no deep root of bitterness in the field that I have endeavored to cultivate, and that there is no dark shadow lying between the beginning of my ministry here and this day." The occasion was improved by gifts bestowed upon the pastor, and when he had returned to his home he found substantial tokens of the grateful affection of his people, which he acknowledged in a pleasant note. He wrote: " So quietly and secretly were these gifts conveyed to my residence, that I should have been surprised if I had not long since learned not to feel surprise at any kind or generous act of my people."

While all this was said and done, the pastor kept his anniversary with deep humility, with sincere gratitude, and with the conviction that the years of his ministry had not been spent in vain. He said truly, in his sermon, that the recapitulation of the number of services which he had performed would exhibit neither the significance nor the value of his ministry. He believed that causes which attract little notice may yet "send their roots into eternity, and bear fruit which can be gathered only in another world." Oppressed with a sense of his own infirmity, he knew that good had resulted from his efforts, and he gave the glory to Him unto whom all praise is due. It was something to remember that the meeting-house had been three times enlarged to keep pace with the necessities of the people, and that it was better filled after the lapse of twenty-five years than at the beginning. It was cause for thankfulness that nearly four hundred members, over one half of them by confession of faith, had been added to the church. These were the outward and happy signs of larger and eternal benefits.

The underlying principles of this pastor's character were well defined, and the structure of a life was built upon them with patience and decision. He knew what he meant to do, and how he meant to do it. Of the estimation in which he was held by his own people and by his neighbors we have already had a generous expression. His life was a wide one. It might well be wide when the foundation was deep. During his long ministry his influence was manifold. There are many who can never forget the sacred hours spent with him in the study of the Greek Testament during their college course. We went once a week to his study, and bowed with him in prayer, then sat about his round table, while, with his well-worn Testament before him, and his ivory paper-knife in his hand, he opened to us the Scriptures. He would have us read a verse, would ask some question upon it, and then would expound it in his own inimitable way, with learning and piety and rare facility of illustration. We questioned him more than he questioned us. The exercise was almost an expository lecture. One who belonged to his class has said: " His principles of interpretation were the soundest; and after studying the New Testament subsequently with Professor Stuart, I could hardly ascribe, even to that master of Biblical interpretation, any superiority, as a teacher, to the Cambridge pastor." Another has written: " Many theologians refer to the principles of interpretation which he gave them as laying the foundation of their interest and success in Biblical studies." It was a happy circumstance, that, when he lay a dying, one of the physicians who attended upon him should be recognized as formerly a member of his Bible Class. The results of such instruction as he gave to an ever-changing company of those who were themselves to be teachers cannot be measured. In this we have one other method of his usefulness.

His labors were not restricted to his own parish. He rendered valuable service to the city as a member of the School Committee. When the Cambridge Cemetery was to be consecrated, he was selected to make the address. His address was marked by great appropriateness, by rare beauty of language, and by richness and fidelity of thought. In his more strictly professional work he was greatly esteemed. At all gatherings of the clergy his judgment carried great weight, and when upon Councils his advice was much relied upon. The words of Dr. Adams express the general feeling: "As a personal friend and witness, I must be allowed to say of him that he is a tower of strength in our ministerial associations and ecclesiastical affairs. We depend upon him for counsel; we listen to his large and well-considered experience; we feel safe to be guided by him; we always look that he will be on the side of sound principles and well-established order; and we are not disappointed."

His published works are not numerous, but they are of value. They consist chiefly of sermons preached on various special occasions. He prepared question-books upon different parts of the Holy Scriptures, and these have not been improved upon. He published other minor religious treatises. His largest work is the "Life of Thomas Shepard." This is far more than the biography of one man; it is a concise history of the movement which brought our fathers to these shores, and a plain exhibition of their principles, and a fine tribute to their memory. It is a work which should be in every house in the parish, and which, with Mr. Shepard's autobiography, should form a part of the household instruction.

> "Let children hear the mighty deeds
> Which God performed of old."

He was a faithful member of the board of managers of the Massachusetts Sabbath School Society, and long served on the Committee of Publication. He usually presided at the meetings of the committee, and "always enlivened them by his genial and keen criticisms, and made them instructive by his learning." It is a witness to the honor in which he was held that the degree of Doctor of Divinity was conferred upon him by Bowdoin College in 1848, and in 1851 by Harvard College.

He was a decided and intelligent friend and advocate of the faith and order of the New England Fathers. He believed in the Bible, and in the system of truth which our churches from the first had found in it. He believed in the ways by which that truth had been established here. In a discourse commemorative of the character of the Fathers of New England, he said, "Congregationalism, the congregationalism of our fathers, I mean, rests professedly, not partly upon the Bible and partly upon the devices of men, like the angel of the Apocalypse, who stood with one foot upon the land and the other upon the sea, but directly and solely upon the foundation of the Apostles and prophets, Jesus Christ himself being the chief corner-stone."

In his temper and habit Dr. Albro was conservative. He had no fondness for innovation. This was not merely because he did not like new things, but because he had confidence in the old. He saw that the grass withereth, and that the flower thereof falleth away, and he knew that the word of the Lord endureth forever. Therefore he kept to the word. The ways which had been tried, and had survived, he prudently believed to be the best. Hence he was found firm. He believed in the truth. He believed in the church, and its ministry, and its divine ordinances. He had confidence in the covenant, and taught parents to bring their children to God, as Shepard had written aforetime, accounting, with him, that "because God loveth us, he chooseth our seed to be of his church also." He believed that the truth plainly preached, enforced by the Holy Spirit, illustrated by the lives of men, was mighty for the overthrow of evil and the establishment of good. He labored for eternal results.

His preaching was Scriptural, logical, convincing. There was no display, no effort at mere excitement, no courting of applause. He taught the people. His manner in the pulpit was quiet and reverential. He spoke in a voice low, but clear and musical, and capable of varied expression. His sermons were upon small, detached sheets, which he laid aside one by one. He carefully excluded from his sermons an affluent imagination and skill in illustration which made his conversation rich and delightful. He was a rare talker, and those who knew him best in private had the largest enjoyment in his public services. He never exhibited himself, but when one sat by his side his life would shine out through his words, and irradiate them. There was less of this in his public discourse. He would know nothing then, and let people see nothing, but Jesus Christ and him crucified. There were "the ground, the reason, and the power of his ministry." It was given to him to sing and make melody with the lips as well as with the heart. He could lead the songs of the sanctuary by his own voice, and give to this choice part of the service the guidance of a refined taste and a sanctified spirit. It was with his approval that congregational singing was introduced here, and he entered into the new ways with great zeal.

He was a choice friend. With his large experience and wide observation, with his ready wit and cheerful heart, he was able to instruct the young and the old who gathered about him and listened to his words as the "very lovely song of one that hath a pleasant voice and can play well on an instrument." Yet he had but a modest opinion of himself and his attainments. In his sermon upon Washington Allston he applies to him the saying of Jeremy Taylor concerning the Countess of Carberry, a saying of which his own life afforded an illustration: "As if she knew nothing of it, she had a low opinion of herself; and, like a fair taper, she shined to all the room; yet round about her own station she cast a shadow and a cloud, and so shined to everybody but herself." But the brightness which this burning and shining light cast upon others has left his own heart and deed illumined. We think of him, and at every thought give thanks.

Dr. Adams said of him, "He is a good successor." May I add, in my turn, "He was a good man to succeed"? One soweth and another reapeth. The sowing had been good. The church over which he presided was stable, dignified, united, holding the truth in the love of it, with intelligence and firmness. The children of the church were baptized, with hardly an exception, and the principles of religion were carefully laid in their minds. The whole parish was in order, settled in good ways, appreciative of its minister and mindful of his interests, free from the strife and discord which too often intrude even into sacred things, willing to add a good record to the history in which it gloried, while cherishing a hope which reached far into futurity. This was the field which I found when I came to enter into his labors. There was nothing to undo. I gratefully acknowledge that the peace and success of these later years have been largely due to his influence. He was a good man for the reaper who should come after him. He stands in the history of this church as a Christian minister.

I have said little of the external affairs of the parish during Dr. Albro's ministry. The salary tendered to him at his settlement was eight hundred and fifty dollars for the first year, with an annual increase of fifty dollars until one thousand dollars should be reached. There was a pledge also to procure a suitable dwelling-house at an annual rent not exceeding two hundred dollars. In case his salary for the second and third years did not cover his expenses, he was to have a further grant, not exceeding fifty dollars a year. He was to have a vacation of two or three weeks in each year, if he required it. In the year following his installation, arrangements were made to erect a parsonage. Money was given and borrowed for this purpose, and the house in Holyoke Street was built which was thenceforth occupied by the pastor. The original meeting-house contained sixty-six pews, which were enough for that time. In 1840 ten pews were added. In 1844 the house was enlarged, and twenty more pews were provided. In 1852 the house was increased to its present dimensions, and there was room for one hundred and thirty pews on the floor. The number of members of the church at Dr. Albro's installation was one hundred and one; in 1852 there were two hundred and forty-four; in 1865, after many changes, there were nearly three hundred members. But, as has been already remarked, these figures by no means measure the result of his work.

On the twelfth day of March, 1865, the congregation assembled here were surprised by a letter from the pastor in which he asked release from his office. The thirtieth year of his ministry was drawing to a close. He had for some time contemplated this retirement when that point should be reached. He said that the great length of his service, and the changes which time had produced, admonished him that his official connection with this people should cease. He deemed it expedient for himself and for them. Possibly there were premonitions of the malady which at length ended his life. The church and society consented to his request with feelings of deep emotion, and adopted resolutions expressive of their high estimate of his labors, their conviction of his great usefulness, and their earnest desire for his continued welfare. The society voted him the use of the parsonage and of the pastor's pew for as long a time as he should choose to occupy them, and expressed the hope that the parsonage might be his permanent home during his residence in Cambridge. His farewell sermon was from the prophecy of Micah, "O my people, what have I done unto thee? And wherein have I wearied thee? Testify against me." And they answered him. In words and deeds, and with generous gifts, they testified their love for him who had done them good and given them rest.

The 15th of April, 1865, terminated the labors of this long ministry. But although released from the pastoral office, Dr. Albro continued to be the pastor in many important respects. He preached often from this pulpit, he administered the sacraments, he performed many of the works to which he and the people had been accustomed. At the time of an unusual religious interest he was requested to instruct the new converts, and to direct those who were beginning a new life, and when the time came for them to unite with the church, he received them, as he had received so many before them. We have heard after a long time the words of one of our honored ministers from the lines which his own hand had penned. Here is a manuscript which has for the second time come into this pulpit. It is a sermon preached by Dr. Albro on the first Sabbath in July, 1866, when a large number of young persons were received to the church upon their confession of faith. The text is in St. Paul's words to Timothy: "These things write I unto thee, that thou mayest know how thou oughtest to behave thyself in the house of God, which is the church of the living God, the pillar and ground of the truth." The preacher says, "For the sake of these young disciples — most of whom were born in the church — who have to-day publicly joined it as members, I will speak of the nature, the design, and the privileges of the church." After unfolding these points, he bade them learn how they ought to behave themselves in the church, with what love and faith and charity, with what delight, devotion, zeal, earnestness, fervency, they should enter into their new relations and discharge their duties. "Such a spirit and behavior," he said, "would surely make the church the glory of the land, the pillar and ground of the truth, in the eyes of all people. It would enjoy peculiar manifestations of the Saviour's presence and favor. Its influence upon all the interests of society would be visible and permanent. It would be the delightful home of the soul, and afford a foretaste of the blessedness of that New Jerusalem the glory of which was revealed in the vision of the prophet."

Dr. Albro had no desire for another settlement in the ministry. He could not have another people.

But he preached by invitation in neighboring churches. On the morning of the 16th of December, 1866, he officiated in the church at West Roxbury, in the illness of the pastor. His text was, "One thing thou lackest." He was to administer the Communion in the afternoon, and he designed to preach in the evening from the words, " And whatsoever ye do, do all in the name of the Lord Jesus, giving thanks to God and the Father by him." When near the close of his morning sermon, a deathlike pallor overspread his face. He laid his hand upon his breast, and then upon his head. He finished his discourse, but not with the words which had been written. He offered an impressive prayer, and blessed the people. He resumed his seat, and became insensible. He was removed to his temporary home at the house of a deacon of the church. He regained consciousness, and, when the first surprise was over, resumed his wonted calmness and peace. He was not disturbed by the anxiety of his physicians. "I have a natural wish to live," he said, "but I think I feel submissive, and glad to leave myself in God's hands." At a time of intense suffering he uttered his thoughts in broken words: "I am in the dark valley — it is n't dark, though — the passage is gentle — it is all very peaceful"; he added, "There is a great deal necessary to make such a passage peaceful, but He speaks, and it is done." When some one reminded him that he had borne his pains with much patience, he turned the words to one whom he loved better than himself: "Did n't He suffer patiently? As a sheep before her shearers is dumb, so he opened not his mouth." He said that he could express his state by saying, "Vanishing into bliss." Again, "Underneath are the everlasting arms. My work is all done. Christ is the way, the truth, and the life. Not only are angels from heaven around me, but you all seem to be angels." Thus peacefully, cheerfully, he went on his way. New friends ministered to his wants, and old friends lavished their attentions on him. And the rod and the staff of God were for his comfort. The end was quiet. With a smile upon his face, and words of kindness on his lips, his voice faltered, he paused in the midst of his sentence, and in the twinkling of an eye he was gone. The one thing which he lacked had come to him. He had gone on to give thanks to God and the Father by the Lord Jesus.

> "He gave his honors to the world again,
> His blessed part to heaven, and slept in peace."

The translation was on Thursday, the 20th of December. On the following Monday his venerated form was borne into this sanctuary where he had ministered so long. The house was draped in mourning. A large concourse of his friends was here to do honor to the man of God. His old church at Fitchburg sent representatives to show its sympathy. The triumphal songs of Christian faith were sung. His life-long friends and associates performed the last ministries of our religion. The slow procession wended its way to Mount Auburn. Clergymen of five denominations served as pall-bearers. With tears of sorrow and affection and hope the face was covered from the sight of men.

When it was ascertained that he had expressed a desire to be laid to rest in the Cambridge Cemetery, his remains were removed to a lot which had been given to the church and society "for the use of their respective pastors and their families." It was to be called "the Shepard lot." The place of his repose was marked by the people with the memorial marble, and at the centre of the lot was erected a monument of granite to the memory of all the deceased pastors of the church, and that bears his name. These are near the spot where he stood when he delivered the address at the consecration of the cemetery. His burial gives a deeper meaning to his words that day : "Willingly we commit our friends to this consecrated earth. Willingly we ourselves come to rest by the side of those who here wait for our early or tardy return." He called it " our future dwelling-place." "May we, who, entering this place as the living, will hereafter pass along these avenues as the dead, and all who follow us from generation to generation, be, and remain, in life and in death, the blessed of the Lord." On the 12th of November, 1870, when the stones had been set in their places, we went to dedicate them and the ground which had been hallowed anew. It was a stormy afternoon ; but a few persons met at the grave, and then at the keeper's lodge, where we spoke of those who had labored in this ministry and had entered upon their rest, and with prayer and hymn we honored their memory, and asked that their works might abide with us. We ought every year to visit that "court of peace," and consecrate ourselves for life and death.

A few months after Dr. Albro's death a very appreciative discourse in his memory was preached, at the request of the church and society, by the Rev. James H. Means of Dorchester. The name of your tenth minister is engraved at the entrance of our new sanctuary, and upon the mural tablet within, where it will be read till the stone shall crumble. His picture, with the calm, saintly, paternal face, is in the homes of most of the people, and the memorial volume in which the church has expressed its esteem for the good minister. His memory is green among us. His work remains. It is interwoven with the lives of many of you, for he baptized you and your children, he joined you in holy marriage, he received you to the communion of the church, he brought Divine solace into your sorrowing homes, and he buried your dead with sacred rites. He was worthy to be written in with the renowned line of ministers who had preceded him. He rejoices in the worship of the skies. We shall see him presently. Blessed are they who have heard his words while yet in the flesh, and have obeyed them unto eternal life.

With a few words more this history rests. In October, 1865, the minister of the South Parish in Augusta, Me., was invited to the pastoral care of this church and society. For reasons which commended themselves to those who had thus called him the invitation was declined. In December, 1866, the call was renewed. The months which had come and gone had brought the affairs of his parish into a better condition to be given into other hands, and this invitation was accepted. On the 24th of January, 1867, he was duly installed by an Ecclesiastical Council. The sermon was by Professor E. A. Park, from the words, " The poor have the gospel preached to them." The prayer of installation was by the Rev. D. R. Cady, the charge to the pastor by the Rev. Dr. Kirk, the right hand of fellowship by the Rev. John E. Todd, and the address to the people by the Rev. Dr. Adams. And thus your eleventh minister was introduced to his work as the immediate successor of one whose friendship and instruction he had enjoyed, and by the side of the College which to so many of us is Alma Mater. Let me place it on record here, that during these five years he has had no reason to question the propriety of the decision to come to you, or to doubt that it was the will of our common Lord. You have left him no room to regret his compliance with your desire. He counts it a high honor to be the minister of this ancient church, the reaper after so many illustrious sowers, the sower on the broad field where other reapers are to be when the Master has come and called for us. After a few months of beginning, in accordance with a previous agreement, through your liberality he was permitted to spend six months in foreign travel. Since his return the work has gone on steadily day by day, year by year. I offer no estimate of results. God has blessed us with large blessings. To him be the glory. In him be our confidence as we press forward.

These years have been marked with one work deserving to be mentioned among the greatest which have entered into our parish life. We have begun, and almost completed, a new house of worship, which will be the sixth home of the church. It has been planned with large views, and brought thus near its end with great harmony and good-will. This event marks an epoch in the life of the church. It is almost a new beginning of our work. If our hopes are in any measure fulfilled, we are about to add a glorious future to an honorable past. The lineage we boast, the annals we read, the faith we profess, the trust committed to our hands, demand of us a loyalty and heroism in which this church shall prove itself the body of Christ.

As I bring this history to a close, there is no space for comment. None is needed. It is our turn now. The past is secure; the future is what we make it. Let the past instruct us, the future inspire us, the present find us standing in our lot and quitting ourselves like men, as becomes the sons of our sires, the heirs of Puritans, the followers of those who suffered loss for the love of Christ, and in their poverty reared these walls which so long have sheltered us. Not as if I feared; you are doing well; the record of these days will read well when we are dust. It is a grand time to live in. Let every man, every child, do his part promptly, generously, cheerfully. Then we shall go up to our new and beautiful temple with songs of rejoicing, bearing our sheaves with us, and every one with his own sheaves. And with every stone our own, we will dedicate the house to God, our Father and our Saviour, and throw wide its gates, that the people may enter in and worship him. So let us pray, with our gold and silver in our open hands, with our hearts in sympathy with man, while we seek the glory of Christ and the church, "The Lord our God be with us, as he was with our fathers."

APPENDIX.

I.

MEETING-HOUSES.

THE first meeting-house here was built by the church under the care of Rev. Thomas Hooker and Rev. Samuel Stone. It stood very near the southwest corner of Water, now Dunster Street, and Spring, now Mount Auburn Street.

The second house, erected in 1650, the third erected in 1706, and the fourth erected in 1756, stood upon Watch-house Hill, very near the present site of Dane Hall. The fourth house was torn down in 1833, when the new house built by the First Parish was dedicated. There is a drawing of the fourth house preserved, which is inscribed, "Plan of ye meeting House, and draft of ye Pews." From this plan it appears that the frame of the building was oblong. There were three entrances, — one on the west side, through the tower, one on the east, and one on the south. The last two had outer porches. Within these was a gallery on the east, west, and south sides, supported on eight wooden columns. The centre aisle ran from the south entrance to the pulpit and the deacons' seats in front. On the right of the centre aisle were two long benches, and on the left four more. These were evidently for free sittings. Pew No. 1 was next to the pulpit at the preacher's right, and the numbers followed the wall pews around the house, reaching the pulpit again at the preacher's left. The names of the occupants of these wall pews are given as follows: E. Trowbridge, P. Tufts, Foxcroft, S. Kent, Mary Tufts, Richardson, R. Gardner, Bradish, E. Trowbridge for W. Fletcher, Richard Champney, Seth Hastings, J. Fessenden, S. Palmer, Jr., T. Warland, Appleton, Holyoke, Vassall, Phipps, Brattle, Minister, Winthrop, Sparhawke, Oliver, J. Morse, E. Stedman, Wigglesworth, Boardman, E. Ruggles, C. Dana, Sprague, E. Wyeth, S. Hastings, N. Kidder, H. College, J. Hastings, Widow S. Hastings. Following the numbers, the names are Hancock, S. Whittemore, S. Prentice, W. Manning, A. Hill, J. Hicks, I. Bradish, J. Watson, E. Manning, O. Warland, Mr. Marritt's heirs, H. Prentice, T. Sodon, M. Gill, S. Thatcher, E. Wyeth, C. Prentice, I. Watson, J. Read, W. Howe, P. Stearns, R. Dana, S. Danforth, J. Monis, Grant, E. Marritt, E. Stedman, Z. Bordman, W. Angier, J. Stratton, J. Dickson, Widow Fessenden, Inman.

The fifth house erected for the church was that which has just been left, at the corner of Mount Auburn and Holyoke Streets. The following account of this house and of the changes in it was prepared in 1852 by Deacon Stephen T. Farwell: —

"The corner-stone of the house of worship for the First Church and Shepard Congregational Society was laid on the twenty-first day of September, 1830. The house was dedicated on the 23d of February, 1831. As the house was originally finished, it contained sixty-six pews, which furnished ample accommodations for the congregation at that time. The society gradually increased in numbers, more room was needed, and in 1840, by removing a partition from under the choir gallery and rebuilding the pulpit, ten additional pews were obtained. These were sufficient to accommodate the increasing growth of the society for a few years only. In 1844 it was found necessary to enlarge our borders. Accordingly, the house was separated into two parts. The northerly part was removed the distance of sixteen feet, land having been purchased for the purpose of Harvard College. The space was then filled up, making an addition to the building equal to one fourth of its original length, and adding twenty new pews. This addition sufficed for the growing wants of the society until the present year, when it had become impossible to furnish pews to families who were desirous of connecting themselves with the congregation in public worship. It was therefore determined at a parish meeting held July 7, 1852, to enlarge the house by the addition of thirteen feet to its width, six and a half feet to each side; also by a similar addition to the front on each side of the tower, enlarging thereby the room in the vestibule, and giving two additional entrances to the same. The size of the house with this addition, exclusive of the tower, is eighty by sixty-three feet, giving ample room for one hundred and thirty pews on the floor. The chapel in the basement, obtained by this addition and by raising the building six and a half feet above its former foundation, is sixty by forty-eight feet. Preparatory to this enlargement a strip of land thirteen feet in width was purchased of F. C. Loring, Esq., on the westerly side of the society's lot, and the house was removed six and a half feet in that direction. It became necessary, therefore, to remove the leaden box which was deposited under the corner-stone of the original house. It is replaced again this twenty-first day of September, A. D. 1852; being first enclosed in another leaden box, with this brief sketch of the several enlargements of the original church edifice, together with a copy of 'Some passages in the History of the First Church in connection with the Shepard Congregational Society in Cambridge,' prepared by the present pastor, and printed in 1842; also a copy of his 'Life of Thomas Shepard,' the first pastor of this church, published in 1847.

"The number of church-members who followed the pastor at the time of the separation of the church from the First

Parish, in 1829, was about sixty. At the installation of the present pastor, April 15, 1835, it was one hundred and one. The present number is two hundred and forty-four.

OFFICERS OF THE CHURCH.

Pastor.
JOHN A. ALBRO.

Deacons.
STEPHEN T. FARWELL,   CHARLES W. HOMER.
ZELOTES HOSMER, *Clerk.*

OFFICERS OF THE PARISH.

Clerk and Treasurer.
JACOB H. BATES.

Prudential Committee.
WILLIAM SAUNDERS,   WILLIAM BATES,
JONAS WYETH, 2d,   ZELOTES HOSMER,
WILLIAM A. SAUNDERS.

Building Committee.
WILLIAM A. SAUNDERS,   WILLIAM SAUNDERS,
GARDINER G. HUBBARD,   ISRAEL P. DUNHAM.

Architect.
A. R. ESTEY."

The last services in this church were held on the 19th of May, 1872. In the morning the pastor preached from Ezra iii. 12. In the evening a public meeting was held, when addresses were delivered by Hon. Charles Theodore Russell, Hon. Emory Washburn, Hon. Charles H. Saunders, Hon. Horatio G. Parker, Rev. William L. Ropes, George S. Saunders, Esq., and the Pastor. The chapel of the church is still used by the Sabbath School and for the social religious services of the church. But the chapel of the new house will soon be completed.

The sixth meeting-house was dedicated on Wednesday evening, May 22, 1872. It stands on the corner of Garden and Mason Streets. At the dedication the invocation was by the Rev. George R. Leavitt, pastor of the Pilgrim Church, Cambridgeport; the reading of the Scriptures by the Rev. David O. Mears, pastor of the North Avenue Congregational Church; the prayer before the sermon by the Rev. Andrew P. Peabody, D. D., of Harvard College; the sermon by the pastor from Psalms xcvi. 6: "Strength and beauty are in his sanctuary"; the prayer of dedication was by the Rev. Nehemiah Adams, D. D., the ninth pastor of the church. The music was appropriate, and included the singing of the following hymns: —

HYMN,

Written by the Rev. ABIEL HOLMES, D. D., and sung at the Installation of the Rev. JOHN A. ALBRO, D. D., and of the Rev. A. MCKENZIE.

Great God! thou heard'st our Fathers' prayer,
    When, o'er the ocean brought,
They with a patriarchal care
    A Sanctuary sought.

Hither thy guidance led their feet,
    Here was their first abode;
And here, where now their children meet,
    They found a place for God.

[Thy flock, Immanuel, here was fed,
    In pastures green and fair;
Beside still waters gently led,
    And thine the Shepherd's care.

That care two hundred years attest;
    Thy seal is still the same;
To every bosom be it pressed,
    Graved with thy precious name.]

Here may the Church thy cause maintain,
    Thy truth with peace and love,
Till her last earth-born live again
    With the first-born above.

O glorious change! From conflict free,
    The Church, no danger nigh,
From militant on earth shall be
    Triumphant in the sky.

HYMN OF DEDICATION,

BY MISS CHARLOTTE F. BATES.

Thou, whom the heavens cannot contain,
   Art willing yet to make thy home
Where Love makes ready for thy reign,
   And looks and longs for thee to come.

[As this fair temple make the heart,
   New, strong, and undefiled for thee;
Then may we, soul and sin apart,
   The King in all his beauty see.]

Before the cross, this holy hour,
   The house, the heart, we consecrate; —
Give every will a fruitful power,
   God's perfect plan to consummate.

Blow, Breath of the Almighty Strength!
   God's order nerve our souls to bring
From gross confusion, till at length
   The top-stone bid the builders sing.

[Let regal learning here bend low;
   With Christward face like Mary sit,
Till on her brow the Master throw
   A light the ages shall transmit.

With all these dawning hopes of ours,
   We dedicate our sacred past.
These memories, tender as the flowers,
   Will yet this massive stone outlast.]

Abide here, Father, till the day
   When thy great Church shall rest in thee;
Till heaven and earth shall pass away,
   Abide here, Blessed Trinity!

The Report of the Building Committee, containing a description of the new house, is here subjoined: —

REPORT.

On the 5th of August, 1870, ground was broken for the foundation of this building; appropriate religious services were held, and many interesting circumstances relating to the building of the meeting-house we have just left, and the worthy labors of many connected therewith, both living and dead, were kindly remembered.

Our work went on; the foundation walls were built and covered until the spring of 1871. On Saturday, the 29th of April, 1871, the corner-stone of this edifice was laid, when appropriate services were held, conducted by the Pastor, Rev. A. P. Peabody, D. D., Rev. C. W. Anable, D.D., Rev. Kinsley Twining, Rev. David O. Mears, Prof. H. E. Parker, of Dartmouth College, and Rev. Mr. Jackson.

RECORD OF DEPOSITS IN THE CORNER-STONE.

The leaden box unopened from the corner-stone of the church building on the corner of Holyoke and Mt. Auburn Streets.

A copy of the Church Manual of 1842.

Names of Members, 1861 and 1871.

Continuation of the Historical Sketch of the Church.

An account of the Sabbath School.

Statement of the Building Committee.

Names of the Officers of the Church and Parish, Architect, Contractor, etc., viz. : —

Pastor.
ALEXANDER MCKENZIE.

Deacons.

| Stephen T. Farwell, | Charles T. Russell, |
| Charles W. Homer, | George S. Saunders. |

Architect.
A. C. Martin.

Building Committee.

William A. Saunders,
James P. Melledge,
Joel Parker,
John L. Sands,
Ephraim P. Whitman,
Asa Gray,
Stephen T. Farwell,
Nathaniel N. Stickney.

Prudential Committee.

William A. Saunders,
Horatio G. Parker,
John L. Sands,
Charles W. Munroe,
Nathaniel N. Stickney.

Treasurer.

Francis Flint.

Sexton and Collector.

Benjamin F. Wyeth.

Contractors.

Thomas A. Graham,
A. L. Danforth,
Stephen Holmes,
Carew and Welch,
J. F. and F. L. Gilman,
James W. Bell,
T. B. Wentworth.

PAMPHLETS, as follows: —

Catalogue of Harvard College.

Catalogue of Andover Theological Seminary.

Mayor's Address to the City Government of Cambridge, 1871, with the Reports of the Departments to the City Council.

Services at the Dedication of the Soldiers' Monument, July 13, 1870.

Services at the Dedication of the Monument to the Men of Cambridge who fell on the 19th of April, 1775. Nov. 3, 1870.

Services in Commemoration of the Twenty-fifth Anniversary of the Settlement of Rev. J. A. Albro, D. D., and his Sermon on the Occasion. 1860.

APPENDIX.

Memorial Services in connection with the death of Rev. J. A. Albro, D. D. December, 1866.

Introductory Sermon by Rev. A. McKenzie. 1867.

Manuscript Sermon by the late Rev. Abiel Holmes, D. D., delivered the second Sabbath after his Installation in 1792.

A book entitled "The Free Gift," by Rev. Nehemiah Adams, D. D

PICTURES OF CHURCHES AND OTHER BUILDINGS.

Of First Parish Church, Rev. William Newell, D. D., Pastor.
" Christ Church, Rev. Nicholas Hoppin, D. D., Rector.
" Baptist Church, Rev. C. W. Anable, D. D., Pastor.
" St. John's Chapel, Rev. J. S. Stone, D. D., Rector.
" North Avenue Church, Rev. David O. Mears, Pastor.
" The Old Meeting-House built in 1756, on the site of Dane Law School building; removed in 1833. (In excavating for the moving of the Law School building in 1871, the corner foundation-stone of the old structure was found, and placed in the north wall of this building, with date inscribed, 1756.)

Of several of the College buildings, and a photograph from a drawing of the new Church building.

PAPERS.

A copy of the Boston Daily Advertiser, of April 29, 1871.
"   "   Boston Post,   "   "   "
"   "   Boston Journal,   "   "   "
"   "   Boston Transcript,   "   28,   "
"   "   Boston Traveller,   "   28,   "
"   "   Congregationalist,   "   27,   "
"   "   Cambridge Chronicle,   "   29,   "
"   "   Cambridge Press,   "   29,   "
"   "   Cambridge Sanitary Report.
"   "   Order of Exercises at the laying of the Corner-stone.

Before describing the building, we will pause and gratefully recognize the kindly favor of our Heavenly Father from the very commencement of the work until this moment. Favored in the season, in the promptness and faithfulness with which all the departments of labor and materials have been supplied, with few mistakes to amend, and, more than all, no accident to life or limb to record, may we not, as the result of these favoring providences, rightfully rejoice that we are permitted to assemble in this beautiful, substantial, and convenient church building? May it ever remain an ornament to our city, an honor to this interesting and historic locality, and by the blessing of God be a permanent memorial and worthy tribute to the ancient faith and record of the Fathers, the impress of whose labors and piety is indelible in the institutions of religion, good learning, and government around us.

It has been our purpose to erect a commodious, substantial building, in good architectural taste, adapted to the present wants of the parish, and we hope also for generations to come to be used for the simple forms of Congregational worship.

We are indebted to Mr. Martin, the architect, for the design and plan. He has given much time and thought to the work, and has been successful in the outlines and general grouping so essential to architectural effect.

The plan, in its general form, is that of a cross, with nave, side and central aisles, and north and south transepts.

The extreme interior length of the nave, from front to rear, is 120 feet. It terminates in the rear in an octagonal apse.

The width of the nave is 34 feet; it is separated from the side aisles by columns and semicircular arches which support the roof.

The breadth of nave and side aisles together makes the

body of the church 60 feet wide. The length across the transepts from north to south is 92 feet.

The ceiling of nave and transepts is of octagonal form, and finishes 46 feet in clear height from the floor.

Two galleries are constructed with convenient stairways within the audience room, one across the front, and the other across the north transept, for the organ and choir.

The building is supplied with 245 pews, affording 1,200 sittings.

The pews, doors, and finish throughout are of black-walnut.

Above the ceiling are large ventilating ducts carefully constructed to afford thorough ventilation.

In the rear are convenient rooms for the pastor, Sabbath-school library, etc., etc.

A vestibule on Mason Street gives access both to the church and the chapel to be built hereafter.

The principal entrance to the church is by a bold doorway on Garden Street. There are four other entrances on Mason Street. Two will connect with the chapel from the south transept, and with the tower by an arcade of eight arches supported by columns.

The tower and spire on the east corner will be 170 feet high, and will be distinctly seen from all the streets diverging from the Common.

The material of which we have built from the foundation to the tip of the spire is a durable slate, obtained within a short distance of this place; it will be found to have a warm, rich tint, and was highly recommended by persons whose opinion we may safely accept.

For the corners and such other parts as are subject to great pressure we were fortunate in securing a red granite, in color and texture like the Scotch, a material which has been but little used in this country. This harmonizes pleasantly with the stone used in the walls.

For other dressings, such as belts, doorways, windows, columns, and capitals, the red and light-colored Pictou stone has been used.

The architect says in his description:—

"The general character of the whole construction is determined by the use of the 'Round Arch.' It is employed for window and door heads, and for the arcades on Mason Street.

"It appears in the interior for the support of the roof and in the motive for all the ornament.

"No modern building can or should be a strict copy of the old, but if it be needful to specify the style of architecture to which the design of the church belongs, it will be found most closely to resemble the earliest of the so-called Gothic, in which the round or full centred arch has the same controlling influence as the pointed arch in the later style.

"The English call it Norman, but the true historic name is Romanesque, which marks its descent from the old Roman Basilicas, the churches in which the early Christians first worshipped."

The estimated cost reported and authorized by the society for building for occupancy, exclusive of but 30 feet of the tower, the chapel and land, was $70,000. This work has been done for about $2,500 less.

The entire cost when tower and spire are completed, and chapel built, with the land, will be $110,000.

The organ, adapted to the architecture of the building, was made by Messrs. E. and G. G. Hook & Hastings.

It has two manuals and a pedal of two octaves and two notes.

Compass of manuals, from C^o to A^3, 58 notes.

Compass of pedal, from C to D^o, 27 notes.

The case is of walnut with silvered pipes having gilded mouths; there are 31 stops; 1,705 pipes; 7 pedal movements. Cost, $5,000.

APPENDIX.

On the north and south walls are inserted two stone tablets, one giving the historical events of *Newtown* and of the church from the beginning; the other devoted to the memory of the ministers, with their names and dates of service.

ON THE NORTH WALL.

The Lord our God be with us as He was with our Fathers.

The Settlement of this Town was begun A. D. 1631.
The first Meeting-House was built A. D. 1632.
Rev. Thomas Hooker and Rev. Samuel Stone were ordained Ministers here Oct. 11, 1633;
They removed with their people to found Hartford, Conn., A. D. 1636.
This Church was formed February 1st, A. D. 1636.
The Cambridge Platform was adopted A. D. 1648.
The Church united with the Shepard Congregational Society A. D. 1829.
This House was dedicated A. D. 1872.

ON THE SOUTH WALL.

To the Memory of the Ministers of this Church.

Thomas Shepard,	A. D. 1636 – 1649.
Jonathan Mitchel,	A. D. 1650 – 1668.
Urian Oakes,	A. D. 1671 – 1681.
Nathaniel Gookin,	A. D. 1682 – 1692.
William Brattle,	A. D. 1696 – 1717.
Nathaniel Appleton,	A. D. 1717 – 1784.
Timothy Hilliard,	A. D. 1783 – 1790.
Abiel Holmes,	A. D. 1792 – 1831.
	A. D. 1829 – 1834.
John A. Albro,	A. D. 1835 – 1865.
	A. D. 1867 –

The beautiful "Memorial Window" in the south transept was made in London, by celebrated artists, and is pronounced admirable in design and execution.

For this we are indebted to the liberality of one of the families of this parish, from whom also we have received important suggestions, particularly as to the peculiar glass used in the other windows of the building.

The pulpit is the result of the labors of "little workers," the children, guided by those who are ever ready to respond to the calls of duty and good service. The font is also the children's gift.

The other furnishings of the church were supplied by the foresight, industry, and liberality of the ladies of the parish.

In short, in each department of labor necessary to complete the undertaking, we have found the right service cheerfully offered at the right time.

It only remains for your committee, therefore, to surrender this edifice for dedication to the worship of Almighty God and the promotion of his kingdom. May it also be a memorial offering to the long succession of faithful ministers, beginning with him whose honored name the society bears, — THOMAS SHEPARD.

For the Committee,
WILLIAM A. SAUNDERS.

NOTE. — The glass is English, called "Cathedral," and is the same as that used in the early churches of England.

The old method of manufacturing the glass has been lost, and the way of reproducing its effect has but recently been discovered. The glass is just coming into use in this country.

The plan of renting the pews in this house upon a permanent lease was adopted after full consideration, and has the approval of the parish. The pews have been rented with great readiness, and the financial success of the enterprise seems already secured.

Pictures of the fourth, fifth, and sixth meeting-houses are to be found in the preceding pages, with a picture of the house erected by the First Parish after the separation.

II.

PARSONAGE.

A PICTURE of the old parsonage, with the house of Judge Dana in the distance, will also be found in its place. Concerning this parsonage the records tell us that "at a public meeting of the church and town to consider of supply for the ministry, it was agreed that there should be a house bought or built to entertain a minister." That was in 1669, the year after Mr. Mitchel's death. In the same year the parish sold for this purpose the church's farm of six hundred acres in Shawshine for £230 sterling. Soon after four acres of land were purchased in what is now the College yard, nearly opposite the end of Holyoke Street. In 1670 a house was erected thirty-six feet long and thirty wide. This house was "to remain the church's, and to be the dwelling-place of such a minister and officer as the Lord shall be pleased to supply us withal, during the time that he shall supply that place amongst us." In 1720 a new front was put upon the house. All the ministers after Mr. Mitchel resided in this house until 1807, when Dr. Holmes left it for the house still standing in Holmes Place, and more particularly associated with his name. The old parsonage house was subsequently taken down.

III.

OFFICERS OF THE CHURCH
FROM ITS FORMATION IN 1636.

PASTORS.

Rev. THOMAS SHEPARD, ordained February, 1636. Died August 25, 1649.

Rev. JONATHAN MITCHEL, ordained August 21, 1650. Died July 9, 1668.

Rev. URIAN OAKES, ordained November 8, 1671. Died July 25, 1681.

Rev. NATHANIEL GOOKIN, ordained November 15, 1682. Died August 7, 1692.

Rev. WILLIAM BRATTLE, ordained November 25, 1696. Died February 15, 1717.

Rev. NATHANIEL APPLETON, D. D., ordained October 9, 1717. Died February 9, 1784.

Rev. TIMOTHY HILLIARD, installed October 27, 1783. Died May 9, 1790.

Rev. ABIEL HOLMES, D. D., installed January 25, 1792. Dismissed September 26, 1831.

Rev. NEHEMIAH ADAMS, ordained December 17, 1829. Dismissed March 14, 1834.

Rev. JOHN A. ALBRO, D. D., installed April 15, 1835. Dismissed April 15, 1865.

Rev. ALEXANDER MCKENZIE, installed January 24, 1867.

RULING ELDERS.

[The following list comprises the names of those who are known to have been Ruling Elders of the church.]

EDMUND FROST. He came to New England in 1635, and was made a freeman in 1636. He died July 12, 1672.

RICHARD CHAMPNEY. He came to New England in 1635, and was made a freeman in 1636. He died November 26, 1669.

JONAS CLARK. He was made a freeman in 1647. Ordained Ruling Elder November 15, 1682. He died January 11, 1699, aged eighty years.

JOHN STONE. He came to New England in 1635, it is thought, and was made a freeman in 1665. Ordained Ruling Elder November 15, 1682. He died May 5, 1683, aged sixty-four years.

DEACONS.

[The following list comprises the names of those who are known to have been Deacons of the church.]

JOHN BRIDGE. Freeman 1635. Died 1665.

THOMAS MARRIOT. Freeman 1636. Died 1664.

THOMAS CHEESEHOLME. Freeman 1636. Died 1671.

GREGORY STONE. Freeman 1636. Died 1672.

NATHANIEL SPARROWHAWKE. Freeman 1639. Died 1647.

NATHANIEL SPARROWHAWKE. Freeman. Died January, 1687.

EDWARD COLLINS. Freeman 1640. Died 1689.

JOHN COOPER. Freeman 1642. Died 1691.

WALTER HASTING. Born 1631. Died 1705.

SAMUEL COOPER. Chosen March 22, 1705. Died 1718.

NATHANIEL HANCOCK. Chosen June 7, 1705. Died 1719.

SAMUEL KIDDER. Chosen January 22, 1718. Died 1724.

JOSEPH COOLIDGE. Chosen January 22, 1718. Died 1737.

NATHANIEL SPARROWHAWKE. Chosen August 5, 1724. Died 1734.

SAMUEL BOWMAN. Chosen August 5, 1724. Died before 1741.

SAMUEL SPARROWHAWKE. Chosen April 12, 1734. Died 1774.

John Bradish. Chosen May 5, 1738. Died 1741.

Samuel Whittemore. Chosen November 24, 1741. Died about 1783.

Henry Prentice. Chosen November 24, 1741. Resigned July 14, 1774.

Aaron Hill. Chosen July 14, 1774. Died 1792.

Stephen Sewall. Chosen May 18, 1777. Died 1804.

Gideon Frost. Chosen June 30, 1783. Died 1803.

James Munro. Chosen June 30, 1783. Died 1804.

John Walton. Chosen November 19, 1792. Died 1823.

William Hilliard. Chosen April 5, 1804. Died 1836.

Josiah Moore. Chosen January 4, 1805. Died 1814.

James Munro. Chosen August 2, 1818. Died 1848.

Stephen T. Farwell. Installed April 30, 1837. Died Oct. 20, 1872.

Charles W. Homer. Installed January 4, 1849.

Charles Theo. Russell. Installed July 2, 1869. Resigned September 15, 1871.

George S. Saunders. Installed July 2, 1869.

PRESENT OFFICERS OF THE CHURCH.

1872.

Pastor.

Rev. Alexander McKenzie.

Deacons.

Charles W. Homer,   George S. Saunders.

Clerk.

George S. Saunders.

Standing Committee.

The Standing Committee of the Church consists of the Pastor, Deacons, the Clerk, Superintendent of the Sabbath School (Francis Flint), and the following brethren: Charles W. Munroe, James A. Shedd.

IV.

CONFESSION OF FAITH, AND FORM OF ADMISSION.

THE CONFESSION OF FAITH of this church is in substance, and for the most part in language, taken from the "Confession of Faith owned and consented unto by the Elders and Messengers of the Churches assembled at Boston, May 12, 1680." The "Boston Confession" is the basis of the confessions of the Congregational churches of New England, and it expresses the doctrinal views of this church through its entire history.

FORM OF ADMISSION TO THE COMMUNION OF THE CHURCH. — ADOPTED 1872.

The candidates shall present themselves before the pulpit, where they shall be met by the minister, who shall repeat one or more of the following sentences of the Holy Scriptures, or such other sentences as he may choose: —

Come unto Me, all ye that labor and are heavy laden, and I will give you rest. Take my yoke upon you, and learn of Me; for I am meek and lowly in heart; and ye shall find rest unto your souls. For my yoke is easy, and my burden is light.

And the Spirit and the Bride say, Come. And let him that heareth say, Come. And let him that is athirst come. And whosoever will, let him take the water of life freely.

Whosoever therefore shall confess Me before men, him will I confess also before my Father which is in heaven.

The minister shall then address the candidates as follows, and shall recite the Creed of the church for their assent: —

Dearly Beloved, — You have presented yourselves in this holy place to make confession of the Lord Jesus Christ, and to enter into covenant with his Church. We trust that you know the solemnity and the blessedness of this time, and we are confident that He which hath begun a good work in you will perform it until the day of Jesus Christ.

WE BELIEVE in one living and true GOD; creator, preserver, and ruler of all things: glorious in holiness, plenteous in mercy and truth.

In the FATHER ALMIGHTY: Lord and giver of life; who is to be supremely loved and perfectly obeyed; whose commandment is holy and just and good.

And in JESUS CHRIST, HIS SON, OUR LORD; who was in the beginning with God and was God; who for us men, and for our salvation, came down from heaven and was made man. He was crucified, dead, and buried. He arose from the dead and ascended into heaven, and sitteth on the right hand of the FATHER. He shall come again with glory to judge both the quick and the dead; when every one shall receive the things done in his body, according to that he hath done, whether it be good or bad. Of His kingdom there shall be no end.

And we BELIEVE in the HOLY GHOST, the COMFORTER; by whom the Scriptures were given; who renews and sanctifies the heart; by whose power we are kept unto immortal life. Who, with the FATHER and the SON, together ONE GOD, is to be worshipped and glorified, world without end.

Before ALMIGHTY GOD our HEAVENLY FATHER we humbly acknowledge our guiltiness, casting ourselves upon his infinite goodness and mercy.

We BELIEVE in the forgiveness of sins through our Lord and Saviour Jesus Christ, whose name we confess, whose

Word we receive, in whose mediation alone we steadfastly trust.

We BELIEVE in one Church, on earth and in heaven: in one Baptism: in one Communion in the body and blood of Christ; and we look for the Resurrection of the dead, and the Life of the world to come. Amen.

You who have now made this Confession do acknowledge the Lord Jehovah — the FATHER, the SON, and the HOLY GHOST — to be your God; to HIM you devote your supreme affection; to his service you consecrate your life; and naming yourselves with the name of Christ, you avow your purpose to glorify him in your body and in your spirit, which are his.

Baptism will here be administered to those who have not before been baptized, with these words, —

A. B., I baptize thee, in the name of the FATHER, and of the SON, and of the HOLY GHOST. Amen.

To the other candidates the minister shall say, —

You who were baptized in childhood do now gratefully accept that as your baptism, while you confirm the covenant which then was made for you.

The members of the Church shall here rise, and the minister shall continue : —

Because you make this Confession, we, the members of this church, affectionately welcome you to fellowship with us in all duties and blessings, rejoicing with you in the joy of the Lord, and praying for you with assurance and longing, that when the Chief Shepherd shall appear, ye may receive a crown of glory that fadeth not away.

Here the Church, with those who have just made confession, and those who have been received from other churches, shall repeat this covenant, saying : —

We who are now brought together and united into one Church, under the Lord Jesus Christ, our Head, in such sort as becometh all those whom he hath redeemed and sanctified to himself, do here solemnly and religiously, as in his most holy presence, promise and bind ourselves to walk in all our ways according to the rule of the Gospel, and in all sincere conformity to his holy ordinances, and in mutual love and respect each to other, so near as God shall give us grace.

<blockquote>Here the minister shall take the new members by the hand in token of fellowship with Christ and the Church, repeating some appropriate sentence of Scripture. He shall then address them in these words:—</blockquote>

Now, therefore, Beloved in the Lord, ye are no more strangers and foreigners, but fellow-citizens with the saints, and of the household of God; and are built upon the foundation of the Apostles and Prophets, Jesus Christ himself being the chief Corner-stone. For this cause —

<blockquote>[Here all will take the customary attitude of prayer]</blockquote>

we bow our knees unto the Father of our Lord Jesus Christ, of whom the whole family in heaven and earth is named, that he would grant you, according to the riches of his glory, to be strengthened with might by his Spirit in the inner man; that Christ may dwell in your hearts by faith; that ye, being rooted and grounded in love, may be able to comprehend with all saints, what is the breadth, and length, and depth, and height, and to know the love of Christ which passeth knowledge, that ye might be filled with all the fulness of God.

Now unto Him that is able to do exceeding abundantly above all that we ask or think, according to the power that worketh in us, unto Him be glory in the Church by Christ Jesus throughout all ages, world without end. Amen.

V.

MEMBERSHIP.

AS the early records are imperfect, it is impossible to ascertain the number of those who have been connected with the church since its formation. It is estimated that it is not very far from three thousand.

The records show that the number of admissions during the pastorate

of Dr. Holmes was	221
of Dr. Holmes and Mr. Adams	57
of Mr. Adams	26
of Dr. Albro	423
During the interim after Dr. Albro's pastorate	38
During the pastorate of Mr. McKenzie is	178

The present membership of the church is about four hundred. A new Manual of the Church has been printed during the present year, giving the names of the officers and members from the beginning, so far as they are known.

VI.

THE following statement of the decision of the Supreme Court of Massachusetts in the case by which the property rights of this church were practically determined, and of the contrast with that decision of one recently made by the Supreme Court of the United States, has been prepared for this work by members of the Suffolk Bar.

This statement should be read in connection with Lecture VII.

BAKER AND ANOTHER vs. FALES.

In the case of Baker and another against Fales, reported in the sixteenth volume of Massachusetts Reports, p. 488, the following were the facts: In 1641, John Phillips aliened and sold to the *church* in Dedham, forever, three acres of land. In the same year, Joseph Kingsbury, upon consideration, granted to the *church* in Dedham, and to the use of the same forever, three acres of land. In January, 1642, the proprietors voted that forty acres at the least, or sixty acres at the most, should be set apart, in an intended division, for public use, viz., for the *town*, the *church*, and a *free school*. In 1655 or 1656, there was granted to the *church* in Dedham, and to their successors forever, in the dividend near Medfield, one hundred and fifty acres of land. In 1659, there was a similar grant of twenty-four acres of upland in Natick dividend. In the two last grants, there was no designation of any trust or use.

In 1660, at a meeting of the inhabitants of the town, there was a grant to the *church* in Dedham, and to the use thereof forever, of certain common rights and cow rights, for the use and accommodation of a teaching church officer. There were several other grants from the proprietors to the *church* in Dedham and their successors in office.

These lands had been sold, and the proceeds invested in bonds and other securities.

The question was, who was the owner of these bonds and securities and certain records and documents, all of which were admitted to be the property of the first church in Dedham.

It was admitted that the first parish and first church in Dedham continued and associated together, in the support and maintenance of public worship, until November, 1818.

when the Rev. Alvan Lamson was settled and ordained as the minister of the first parish, that a majority of the church did not concur with the majority of the parish in giving a call to Mr. Lamson, or in his settlement and ordination.

It appeared from the records of the church, that in 1792 the church directed the trustees of the church fund to appropriate one year's interest thereof to the payment of the then minister's salary, and in 1819 the parish requested the church to pay and allow the sum of $600, towards Mr. Lamson's salary. At another meeting of the parish, the same year, it was voted to unite with the church to obtain the property of the church, to indemnify the deacons therein, and to put Mr. Lamson in possession of the parsonage house.

Those members of the ancient church who adhered to Mr. Lamson after his ordination, had continued associated and connected with the first parish, and had continued to act as a church, and to have the ordinances of the gospel administered to them by Mr. Lamson.

The defendant was a deacon of the church previously to Mr. Lamson's settlement; after which settlement he was removed, and the plaintiffs were elected to that office by the church who united with the parish in the settlement of Mr. Lamson.

The defendants contended that the majority of the members of the church, who objected to the settlement of Mr. Lamson, must be considered as the successors of the ancient church in Dedham; and proved that, after the settlement of Mr. Lamson, the majority of the members of the church, with the defendant, then one of the deacons of said church, met and worshipped with some of the parish at another house, and did not after that time attend public worship at the meeting-house. But the Christian ordinances were administered to them, and they held church meetings, and claimed to be the successors of the first church in Dedham.

They did not attend worship at Mr. Lamson's meeting-house when the meeting was notified from the pulpit at which the plaintiffs were chosen Deacons; and this was known when the meeting was notified.

The church in Dedham had always had exclusive control and management of the property and the funds raised from the sales of land before mentioned.

The members of the church who united with the parish in the settlement of Mr. Lamson never formed or were gathered into a new church.

The court said: If the plaintiffs are not the deacons of the first church in Dedham, they are not entitled to the possession of the property; if they are such deacons, then, as the articles are agreed to belong for certain purposes to the proper representatives of that church, the plaintiffs are constituted by law the proper persons to sue for and have the custody of them.

The court premised that all the securities in question arose from the sales of land granted to the church in Dedham, and that the records and documents in question related to that property and the proceedings of that church. The right to the securities must depend upon the construction to be given to the grants of land of which the securities are the proceeds.

Upon these facts the court held, —

That, as to all the grants, the church, however composed at the time, was intended by the grantors to be the mere trustees, to hold the grants for the purpose of supporting out of the proceeds a pastor or minister.

That when the donation is to the church, no trust or use being expressed, and no other implied from the nature of the property, the parish must be the *cestui que trust*, or the party for whose benefit the trust is made.

That the grants of land to the church in Dedham were intended to vest the property in that body for the purpose of the public worship of God; and that the members of the church acquired no legal estate or personal interest therein.

That the grants of the old proprietors gave an equitable fee simple to whosoever shall be found to be the *cestui que trusts*, and the want of a grantee in trust has been supplied by the statute of 1754, which constitutes the deacons of the churches the trustees in all such cases.

That upon the ground that, at the time the grants were made, there was a body of men in Dedham known by the name of the *Dedham Church;* distinct from the *society* of Christians usually worshipping together in that town; the church was intended to take nothing in the lands granted but estates in trust; and that as the particular trusts intended must have been the providing for the public worship of God in Dedham, the inhabitants at large of that town, as parishioners or members of the religious society, were the proper *cestui que trusts*.

That the land granted was for the beneficial use of the assembly of Christians in Dedham, which was no other than the inhabitants of that town who constituted the religious society, within which the church was established, and therefore these inhabitants were the *cestui que trusts*, and the equitable title was vested in them, as long as they continued to constitute the assembly denominated the church in the grants.

That, though since the grants were made parishes have been set off in the town, and other churches have been established within these parishes, a residuum has always been left, which, by the statutes of the government and the decisions of the courts, have thus become the first parish, and have lawfully succeeded to all the rights vested in the inhabitants of the town, of a parochial nature, which have not been parted with in some legal form.

That in 1754, the legislature, having found much property had been given to churches, with the intention that the same should be held in perpetual succession, constituted the deacons a corporation with the power of holding the property for the purpose of executing therewith the will of the donors.

We are now brought, says the court, to the question whether the plaintiffs have proved themselves to be the deacons of the *same church* to which the grants were originally made, for the trusts before mentioned?

Having stated the facts as follows, viz. : —

Until the invitation given to Mr. Lamson, the present officiating minister in the first parish in Dedham, the church and congregation appear to have acted in unison, and the funds held by the church, arising from the grants of land which have been considered, have been from time to time applied, as needed, to the support of the minister, and to defray other charges relating to public worship. On the dismission of Rev. Mr. Bates from the pastoral charge of the church and congregation in Dedham, at his own request, the unhappy dissension arose which has terminated in a dismemberment of the society and a litigation about the property. Mr. Lamson was elected by the parish, at a regular parish meeting, to be the successor of Mr. Bates. The church refused to concur in the choice, a majority of this body disapproving of his religious tenets, or for other causes. The parish, with *the minority of the church*, invited a respectable council, consisting of the ministers of several churches and delegates, who advised to the ordination of Mr. Lamson over the parish, and who accordingly ordained him, notwithstanding the remonstrance of a majority of the church, who finally seceded from the parish, and never since the ordination of Mr. Lamson have attended public worship there, but have in another place, within the territorial limits of the parish, attended public worship, and had the ordinances administered to them as a church.

After the ordination of Mr. Lamson, a church meeting was called, at which the members who acted with the parish attended, and they voted to remove from office the former deacons, who seceded with the majority of the old church, and elected the plaintiffs in their stead.

The members who seceded claimed still to be the first church in Dedham, and the successors of the church to which the property was given in trust; the defendant claimed to be the deacon of that church, and as such claimed a right to hold the property.

The court held, —

That, in whatever light ecclesiastical councils or persons might consider the question, the body which is to be considered the *first church in Dedham* must be the *church* of the *first parish* in that town, as to all questions of property which depend upon that relation.

That if a church may subsist unconnected with any congregational society, it has no legal qualities, and more especially cannot exercise any control over property which it may have held in trust for the society with which it had been formerly connected.

That, as to all civil purposes, the secession of a whole church from the parish would be an extinction of the church; and it is competent to the members of the parish to institute a new church, or to engraft one upon the old stock, if any of it should remain; and this new church would succeed to all the rights of the old, in relation to the parish.

That the only circumstance which gives a church any *legal* character is its connection with some regularly constituted society; and those who withdraw from the society cease to be members of that particular church, and the remaining members continue to be the identical church.

That where members enough of a church connected with a parish are left to execute the objects for which a church is gathered, choose deacons, etc., no legal change has taken place, the body remains, and the secession of a majority of the members would have no other effect than a temporary absence would have upon a meeting which has been regularly summoned.

That the members of the church who withdrew from the parish ceased to be the first church in Dedham, and that all the rights and duties of that body, relative to property intrusted to it, devolved upon those members who remained with and adhered to the parish.

The court then takes up the question, whether the plaintiffs were duly chosen *deacons* of the church which remained with the parish, and so became entitled to the possession of the property, as the trustees under the statute of 1754.

This question was thought to depend upon the validity of the settlement and ordination of Mr. Lamson; and the court held, —

That the parish had the constitutional right to elect and contract with their minister, exclusively of any concurrence or control of the church.

That the nonconcurrence of the church in the choice of the minister, and in the invitation of the ordaining council, in no degree impaired the constitutional right of the parish to choose the minister.

That the council ordained Mr. Lamson over the parish only, but by virtue of that act, founded upon the choice of the people, he became not only the minister of the parish, but of the church still remaining there, notwithstanding the secession of a majority of the members.

That Mr. Lamson thus became the minister of the first parish in Dedham, and of the church subsisting therein, and he had a right to call church meetings, and do all other acts pertaining to a settled and ordained minister of the gospel.

That the church had a right to choose deacons, and no legal objection is found to exist against their right to maintain the action.

It is not too much to say that the opinion in Baker *vs.* Fales has not commended itself to the judgment of the legal profession in its positions or its reasoning, while it is entirely at variance with such ecclesiastical authorities as are recognized by the Congregational churches of this Commonwealth. Whether the decision would now be made, or will be hereafter adhered to as law, we will not say. A recent opinion of the Supreme Court of the United States, in the case of Watson *vs.* Jones, reported in the 12 Wallace Reports, p. 679, seems to establish conclusions inconsistent with those in Baker *vs.* Fales.

In Watson *vs.* Jones the question litigated was, which of two bodies in Louisville, Ky., each claiming to be the " Third or Walnut Street Presbyterian Church," was such church. The question in Baker *vs.* Fales was, which of the two bodies, each claiming to be the " First Church in Dedham," was such church. The decision of the Supreme Court of Massachusetts in the latter case has been given in the foregoing abstracts.

In the former, the Supreme Court of the United States say: "The questions which have come before the civil courts concerning the right to property held by ecclesiastical bodies, may, so far as we have been able to examine them, be profitably classified under three general heads, which, of course, do not include cases governed by considerations applicable to a church established and supported by law as the religion of the State."

" The second is when the property is held by a religious congregation, which, by the nature of its organization, is strictly independent of other ecclesiastical associations, and, so far as church government is concerned, owes no fealty or obligation to any higher authority." — p. 727.

This describes simply a congregational church.

In regard to it the court use the following very sensible and significant language : —

"The second class of cases which we have described has reference to the case of a church of a strictly congregational or independent organization, governed solely within itself, either by a majority of its members, or by such other local organism as it may have instituted for the purpose of ecclesiastical government; and to property held by such a church, either by way of purchase or donation, with no other specific trust attached to it in the hands of the church than that it is for the use of that congregation as a religious society.

"In such cases, where there is a schism which leads to a separation into distinct and conflicting bodies, the rights of such bodies to the use of the property must be determined by the ordinary principles which govern voluntary associations. If the principle of government in such cases is that the majority rules, then the numerical majority of members must control the right to the use of the property. If there be within the congregation officers in whom are vested the powers of such control, then those who adhere to the acknowledged organism by which the body is governed, are entitled to the use of the property. The minority, in choosing to separate themselves into a distinct body, and refusing to recognize the authority of the governing body, can claim no rights in the property from the fact that they had once been members of the church or congregation. This ruling admits of no inquiry into the existing religious opinions of those who comprise the legal or regular organization; for if such was permitted, a very small minority, without any officers of the church among them, might be found to be the only faithful supporters of the religious dogmas of the founders of the church. There being no such trust imposed upon the property when purchased or given, the court will not imply one for the purpose of expelling from its use those who by regular succession and order constitute the church, because they may have changed in some respect their views of religious truth.

"Of the cases in which this doctrine is applied, no better representative can be found than that of Shannon *vs.* Frost, 3 B. Monro, 253, where the principle is ably supported by the learned Chief Justice of the Court of Appeals of Kentucky.

"The case of Smith *vs.* Nelson, 18 Vermont, 511, asserts this doctrine in a case where a legacy was left to the Associate Congregation of Ryegate, the interest whereof was to be annually paid to their minister forever. In that case, though the Ryegate congregation was one of a number of Presbyterian churches connected with the general Presbyterian body at large, the court held that the only inquiry was whether the society still exists, and whether they have a minister chosen and appointed by the majority, and regularly ordained over the society, agreeably to the usage of that denomination. And though we may be of opinion that the doctrine of that case needs modification, so far as it discusses the relation of the Ryegate congregation to the other judicatories of the body to which it belongs, it certainly lays down the principle correctly, if that congregation was to be treated as an independent one."

This decision, or rather its reasoning, restores to the Congregational church that independence and autonomy which are its characteristics, and which the decision in Baker *vs.* Fales entirely destroyed.

It can hardly be doubted which of these decisions is most in harmony with the universally recognized nature and character of Congregational churches, and the better exponent of the views and theory of their supporters.

The decision in Baker *vs.* Fales allows a church, whose fundamental and distinctive principle is *independency of all external control*, no existence independent of the control of another and distinct body, to wit, the society, or parish, of which no one of its members is necessarily a member. An independent Congregational church that has not within itself the power to determine, by its own vote, its own identity and continuance, or which by any system, justly construed, is so connected with another distinct body as to be incapable by independent action of preserving its own identity and purity, is an anomaly. Such is the only Congregational church under the reasoning in Baker *vs.* Fales. Such is *not* the Congregational church under the reasoning of the later case of Watson *vs.* Jones, or in the general understanding, determination, or usages of the Congregational churches of Massachusetts for two centuries. And such it is not, we think, will be the decision whenever a case presenting the point shall come up for adjudication in the Federal courts, or those of any State in which the case of Baker *vs.* Fales is not a binding authority.

In view of the reasoning in Watson *vs.* Jones, and other cases, it is not, perhaps, too much to hope that the courts of Massachusetts may consider the whole subject open for revision and reconsideration.

A few words in addition to the statements of law.

The decision of the United States Court in the case of Watson *vs.* Jones establishes the legal completeness of a Congregational church, independent of all connections. Congregationalism recognizes no ecclesiastical *authority* higher than the church itself. It is supreme in its own affairs. Upon this ground the First Church in Cambridge separated from the parish with which, for certain purposes, it had been connected, and with its minister established worship in another house. This action it was competent to take, and it remained the same church it had been since 1636.

Congregationalism has a system of advisory councils. Their decisions are recognized in the courts. In Cambridge, after the church had sundered its connection with the parish, an Ecclesiastical Council was duly called by the church. This Council confirmed the action of the church, and encouraged it in maintaining divine worship and the celebration of the ordinances of religion.

The bearing of the decision by the Supreme Court of the United States upon our own church case is clear. The highest ecclesiastical tribunals recognized among Congregational churches decided the position and rights of the church. And this decision is pronounced binding in law. The Supreme Court of Massachusetts substantially affirmed the same judgment, saving only in the matter of holding property. This exception is not made in the national court.

Let it be remembered, further, what was the intent of the donors of the funds which were taken from this church. The church fund was begun by a gift of £50 by a member of the church, and increased to more than $4,000 by the contributions of the church at the Lord's Supper.

The desire and purpose of the donors no one can doubt. If the funds were held by the church simply as a trustee for the benefit of the parish, even the majority of the church, worshipping wherever it might be, would be practically as competent to administer the trust as the minority of the church remaining in the old meeting-house. If any doubt were possible concerning the money, the design and expectation of those who gave the Communion and Baptismal Service are entirely plain.

The church was established for other purposes than to be the trustee of property. And these purposes have never been changed. Those who have persistently adhered to them surely have the right to declare themselves, in all respects, the successors of those who founded the church. The church has never lost or impaired its identity.

The original constitution of the church has not been amended. The same ends are sought by the same means. There is a continuity of principles which should have weight in deciding the questions upon which the church and council and the courts have given their judgment. The views advanced in Lecture VII. seem to be abundantly sustained, both on moral and legal grounds.

The "New York Evening Post," in commenting upon the decision in the United States Court, uses the following language: "This decision is henceforth established law in the United States. Had it been made a generation ago, the result of a large number of the disputes on church property, which have been settled by arbitration or otherwise, would have been different. But it is likely to be strictly adhered to hereafter by both civil and ecclesiastical tribunals. It is important to have a general rule on the subject, and yet any rule will, of course, seem to work hardship in some cases. The present decision is that to which the courts of this country have steadily tended, and probably could not have been different without making confusion."

INDEX.

Adams, John Quincy, 71.
Adams, Nehemiah, Jr., invited to become the colleague of Dr. Holmes, 218; his ordination, 220; names of the Council, 220; division of Sabbath services between the two pastors, 222; becomes pastor of the Essex Street Church and Society in Boston, 224; remarks on Dr. Albro, 231, 235; prayer of dedication, 253.
Albro, John Adams, early life, 226; settles in Chelmsford and Fitchburg, 227; installed as pastor, 228; visits Europe, 229; twenty-fifth anniversary of his installation, 229-233; instruction in the Greek Testament, 234; consecration of cemetery, 234; publishes a "Life of Thomas Shepard" and other works, 235; his connection with the Mass. Sabbath School Society and with the School Committee, 234, 235; receives the degree of D. D. from Bowdoin and Harvard Colleges, 236; his character and preaching, 237-239; his salary, 239; his resignation, 239; changes in the meeting-house and in the membership of the church during his ministry, 239; his farewell sermon, 240; services rendered the church and society after his dismission, 240, 241; his death, 243; his funeral, 243.
Allen, Rev. Mr., publishes a book with Thomas Shepard, 64.
Allston, Washington, 223, 238.
Ames, William, 89, 121.
Anabaptists, 103.
Antinomians, 53.
Appleton, Nathaniel, his ancestry, 145; his ordination, — additional town tax to defray the expenses of, — is elected a Fellow of the College, — the degree of Doctor of Divinity conferred upon him, 146; baptisms and admissions to the church during his ministry, 147; measures adopted "to reform the growing disorders," 149; the church lands, 150; the choice of a colleague pastor, 156; his death, 157; his character, 157; his legacies, 158; his publications, 158; anecdote of, 159; his children, 159.
Autobiography of Thomas Shepard, 12, 208.
Baker and another vs. Fales, 203, 272.
Baptism of children, 38, 78, 236; controversy with Henry Dunster, 102-110.
Bates, Charlotte F., hymn by, 254.
Bay Psalm Book, 43.
Belcher, Captain Andrew, 143.
Boradel, Margaret, 70.
Boston Confession, 33, 267.
Brattle, William, graduates at Harvard in 1680, — is chosen tutor, — his fidelity to the students, — receives the degree of Bachelor of Divinity, conferred for the first time, — Fellow of the Corporation and Treasurer of the College, 134; services at his ordination, 135; his salary, 138; donations, 139; gardening and weather record, 139, 140; additions to the church, 140; his charity and humility, 141; his bequest to the church, 142; Dr. Colman's testimony concerning him, 142; items from the town records during his ministry, 143; expenses of his funeral defrayed by the town, 144.
Brighton, church in, 161.
Brock, Rev. John, 89.
Building Committee of present church, report of, 255.
Burials, manner of, in 1641, 40.
Cambridge, the name, 60; first church in, 21, 24; noted men, 28; schools,

INDEX.

41; character of founders, 44; condition in 1647, 113; in 1792, 173; in 1835, 228; church in Cambridge village, 114; Cambridge Farms, petition to be set off, 132; church in northwest precinct, 152; church on south side of the river, 161; action at the Revolution, 153, 163.
Cambridge Farms, set off, 132.
Cambridge Platform, 32.
Cambridgeport, church in, 185; First Evangelical Church in, 188.
Cambridge village, new church organized in, 114.
Champney, Richard, 29, 265.
Charlestown, Covenant of First Church in, 32.
Chauncy, President, 109, 116, 119, 123.
Children, church - membership of, 78, 236.
Church discipline, 38, 147, 178; church plate, 178, 206, 208.
Clark, Jonas, 129, 131, 265.
College church, formation of, 181 - 184.
Collins, Edward, 30, 265.
Confessions, Shepard's book of, 28.
Congregational church. What, 31.
Committee to inspect manners of Christians, 149.
Confession of Faith and Form of Admission to the Communion of the Church, 1872, 267.
Contributions, taken every Sabbath afternoon, 38; mode of collecting, 39; different objects of, 130; by scholars, 130.
Corlet, Elijah, 30, 41, 45, 61, 115.
Cotton, Rev. John, 8, 10, 11, 18, 26, 27, 28, 52, 54, 57, 92, 95.
Covenant assented to by those who desired baptism for themselves, 136; by certain persons in order to their children's being baptized, 137; Covenant, Half-way, 111, 112.
Daggett, Oliver E., 225.
Dana, Miss Sarah Ann, gift of land, 201.
Danforth, Thomas, 30.
Darley, Sir Richard, 16, 51.
Day, Matthew, 29.
Day, Stephen, 42.
Deacons, 35, 265.
Decisions of Supreme Court of Massachusetts and United States, 203, 271.
Dedication of present church, 252.
Dignifying the meeting-house, 37.

Discipline, 38, 147, 178.
Downing, George, 118.
Dudley, Deputy-Governor, 6, 26.
Dunster, Henry, 30, 43, 45, 61, 102 - 110.
Dunton, John, 29.
Eaton, Nathaniel, 29, 60, 61.
Ecclesiastical Synod, first in America, 56.
Elders, 35.
Elders, ruling, 35, 264.
Eliot, John, 7, 43, 66, 89.
Eliot, John [Jr.], 115.
Endicott, Governor, 4.
Episcopal Church, 161, 186.
Everett, Edward, 186.
Families, inspection of, 125.
Familists, 53.
Farnsworth, James D., 180.
Farwell, Stephen T., 181, 250, 255, 256, 266.
Felton, President, 230.
First Church in Cambridge, organized, 21, 24; Covenant and Creed, 32; officers, 35; members in 1658, 116, — in 1829, 199, 251, — in 1835, 252, — in 1872, 271; lands, 150; stock and funds of, 175, 205; **mode of admission**, 153, 267; during and after the Revolution, 153, 163, 164; communion, 38, 177; plate, 178, 206, 208; library, 179; Sabbath school, 180; separates from first parish, 188; worships in Court House, 198; Ecclesiastical Council, 199; connected with Shepard Congregational Society, 200; relinquishes property, 203; meeting-houses, 249; officers from the beginning, 264; Confession of Faith and Form of Admission, 267; **membership**, 271.
First Evangelical Congregational Church organized at Cambridgeport, 188.
First Parish, surrender of church property to, 203 - 206; meeting-house of, 202.
Flint, Francis, 256, 266.
Flynt, Tutor, 162.
Form for the ordaining of a minister of the gospel, used when Mr. Brattle was ordained, 135.
Form of admission to the church adopted 1872, 267.
Frost, Gideon, 175, 176, 266.
Fuller, Samuel, 4.
Fuller, Thomas, 88.
Funerals, how conducted in 1641, 40.

Goffe, Whalley and, 118.
Gookin, Daniel, 30, 66, 114, 116, 129.
Gookin, Mrs. Hannah, 133, 143.
Gookin, Nathaniel, invited to assist President Oakes in the ministry, 128; ordained as pastor, 129; amount of Sabbath collections, — collections for the redemption of captives, — students' contribution, 130; reports of his sermons by Joseph Baxter and Benjamin Colman, — a Fellow of the College, — his death, — funeral charges, 131.
Gray, Asa, 256.
Green, Samuel, 29, 45, 67.
Green, Samuel, 201.
Half-way Covenant, 111, 112.
Hampden, John, 25.
Harlakenden, Richard, 18.
Harlakenden, Roger, 14, 19, 28, 30, 70.
Hartford, founded, 10.
Harvard College. Founded, 59; bequest of Harvard, 59; under N. Eaton, 60; overseers, 61; President Dunster, 30, 43, 45, 61, 102; Chauncy, 109, 116, 119, 123; Hoar, 89, 116, 123; Oakes, 89, 120, 128; Rogers, 89, 145; Leverett, 126, 143, 146; Mather, 116, 133, 135, 146; Wadsworth, 146; Langdon, 155; Willard, 171; Quincy, 124, 160; Felton, 230; in 1798, 174; church in, 181.
Harvard Hall, burning of, 161.
Harvard, John, 59.
Haynes, John, 26, 28.
Higginson, Francis, 4, 32, 48.
Hill, Aaron, 175, 250, 266.
Hilliard, Timothy, chosen as Mr. Appleton's colleague, — installed as pastor, 156; character of, 165; an overseer of the university, — his publications, extracts from, 166; description of his person, — his death, 167.
Hilliard, William, 176, 220, 266.
Hoar, Leonard, 89, 116, 123.
Holmes, Abiel, his early life, 169; his labors in Georgia, 170; is invited to become the successor of Mr. Hilliard, — his reply, — his installation, 171; his first sermon, 172; survey of the town at this time, 173; the church stock, 175; the deacons at this time and their successors, 175; time of observing the Lord's Supper changed, 177; church discipline, 178; church library established, 179; the sabbath school, — juvenile library, — library for the Shepard Congregational Society, 180; organization of the College Church, 181 - 184; dedication of a new meeting-house at Cambridgeport, — a church organized, 185; sermon in Episcopal church, 186; introduction of Watts's psalms and hymns, 186; organ introduced, 187; trouble with parish, 188; Unitarian Association formed, 189; the separation of the First Church and Parish, 188 - 200; Mr. Nehemiah Adams ordained as colleague pastor, 201; the transfer of the church property to the parish, 203 - 206; farewell sermon, — his death, 208; his ministry, 210; his publications, 212; his offices, 212; his last sermon, 214; his burial, 215; hymn of, 215; sermons in 1829, 221; his resignation, 224; his later care of the church, 225; hymn, 253.
Homer, Charles W., deacon, 252, 255, 266.
Hooker, Joanna, 70.
Hooker, Thomas, his history before coming to New England, 7; church organized in Newtown and he chosen pastor, 8; the meetinghouse, 9; removes with his congregation to Hartford, Conn, — is distinguished as a preacher and counsellor, — his death, 10.
Hosmer, Zelotes, 230, 252.
Hubbard, William, 88.
Hutchinson, Mrs. Ann, 10, 52 - 57, 131.
Hymn sung at the installation of Mr. Albro, written by Dr. Holmes, 215, 252.
Indians, provision for, 66; Daniel Gookin made superintendent of, 67.
Indian College, 66.
Jackson, John, 115.
Jenks, Dr., 211, 220, 221.
Johnson, Edward, 87; description of Cambridge in 1652, 113.
Johnson, Marmaduke, 29, 67.
Lafayette, 160.
Lands of the church, 150.
Langdon, President, 155.
Langhorne, Thomas, 36.
Laud, Bishop, 15, 16, 20, 25.
Lectures, 41.
Leverett, President, 126, 143, 146.

Manifesto Church, 141.
Manning, William, 121.
Marriage among Puritans, 39.
Marriot, Thomas, 27, 118, 265.
Martin, A. C., 255.
Massachusetts Sunday School Society, Dr. Albro's connection with, 235.
Mather, Cotton, 43, 88, 94, 102, 123, 126, 146.
Mather, Increase, 116, 133, 135, 146.
Mather, Samuel, 89.
McKenzie, Alexander, estimate of Dr. Albro's work, 238; invited to the pastorate and declines, 245; installed, 245, 253; visits Europe, 246; new church, 246; pastor, 255, 264.
Means, James H., sermon on Dr. Albro, 244.
Meeting-house, first, 8, 36, 69, 249; second, 70, 114, 249; gallery in, 125; third, 143, 159, 249; fourth, 154, 160, 201, 249; fifth, of parish, 202; fifth, of church, 201, 223, 239, 250; sixth, 21, 246, 252, 262.
Melledge, James P., 256.
Minister, salary of, 39, 125, 130, 138, 154, 220, 239; donations to, 125, 139, 152.
Mitchel, Jonathan, his early life, 90; his regard for Shepard, — is made a Fellow of the College, 91; the church in Hartford invites him to become their pastor, — Mr. Shepard and others induce him to become the minister of this church, — his ordination, 92; his regard for education, 94; his preaching, 95; he marries the widow of Mr. Shepard, 95; his death, 96; epitaph by "J. S.," 97; extract from sketch of his life in the Magnalia, 99; his views of doctrine, 101; his trial with President Dunster, 102; his influence in the synod held in Boston in 1662, 111; his reputation, 112; in influence, 116.
Mitchel, Mistress, 119, 123, 132.
Mitchenson, Ruth, 71.
Monis, Judah, 137, 250.
Moore, Josiah, 176, 266.
Morse, Jedediah, 171.
Munro, James, 175, 266.
Munro, James, 176, 177, 220, 266.
Munro, Miss Mary, 180.
Munroe, Charles W., 256, 266.
Newell, Rev. William, D. D., 116, 201, 202, 231, 257.

Newtown, founded, 6; church in, 8; name changed, 60.
Oakes, Urian, born in England and brought to this country in his childhood, 120; graduates at Harvard College in 1649, — publishes an almanac for 1650, — preaches his first sermon at Roxbury, — returns to England, — is invited to become pastor here, 121; after repeated delays he arrives, 122; is ordained, — the church observes a day of public thanksgiving, — the minister resides in the new parsonage, — ordination expenses, — he is made a Freeman, — preaches the annual election sermon in 1673, 123; becomes President of the College, 124; Mr. Nathaniel Gookin chosen to assist in pastoral duties, 125; Mr. Oakes's death, 126, 128; his elegy on the death of Thomas Shepard of Charlestown, 127.
Officers of the church, 35.
Officers of the church from its formation in 1636 to 1872, 264-266.
Oliver, Dr. John, 143.
Organ introduced, 187.
Parker, Horatio G., 252, 256.
Parker, Joel (Royall Prof.), 230, 256.
Parsonage erected, 120, 239, 263.
Pastors, 35, 364.
Pelham, Herbert, 30.
Peters, Hugh, 26, 118.
Peirce, Benjamin, 105.
Phillips, Samuel, 89.
Pierce, William, 42.
Pierson, Abraham, 116.
Plymouth, first church in New England at, 3.
Population of Cambridge in 1647, 113, — in 1790, 173, — in 1835, 228.
Prayer meetings, 223.
Preston, Dr., 13.
Prince, Thomas, 184.
Prophesying, 38.
Prout, Mr., 122.
Puritans, who they were, 3; first form a Congregational church, 6; usages of, 31-46.
Quincy, President, 124, 160.
Robinson, John, 89.
Rogers, John, 89.
Rogers, President, 145.
Ruling elders, 35, 264.
Russell, Charles Theo., 255, 266.
Sabbath, views of English reformers, 79; of Shepard, 79.

INDEX.   289

Sabbath school, instituted, 180; Francis Flint, superintendent, 266.
Salary of minister, 39, 125, 130, 138, 154, 220, 239.
Salem, organization of church at, 3.
Sands, John L., 256.
Saunders, George S., deacon and clerk, 255, 266.
Saunders, William A., 256, 262.
Savage, Habijah, 131.
Sawyer, Miss Mary Ann, 180.
Schools in Cambridge, 29, 30, 41, 61, 115.
Scrooby, church founded in the village of, — crosses the seas, and at Plymouth becomes the first church in New England, 3.
Shedd, James A., 266.
Shepard Congregational Society organized, 200.
Shepard, Jeremiah, 88.
Shepard, Jeremy, 29.
Shepard, Joanna, 70.
Shepard, John, 20.
Shepard, Margaret, 18, 51, 52.
Shepard, Samuel, 29, 88.
Shepard, Samuel, 60, 68.
Shepard, Thomas, birth and early life, 12; enters Emmanuel College, 13; appointed a lecturer and receives deacon's orders in the English church, 14; is forbidden by the Bishop of London to exercise any ministerial functions in his diocese, 15; goes to Buttercrambe, 16; his marriage, — goes to Heddon, 17; sails for New England, 18; installed as pastor in Cambridge, 21; his salary, 39, 68; death of his wife, — her character, 50; the troubles with Mrs. Hutchinson, 52; an ecclesiastical synod held at the meeting-house in Dunster Street, 56; connection with Harvard College, 59; his interest in its prosperity, 61; discussion with English brethren, 64; his doctrinal belief, 74; his views on the church-membership of children, 78, — on the Sabbath, 79, — on heaven, 81; his preaching, 82; his influence, 85; his sons, 88; his will, 71; his death, 71.

Shepard, Thomas, 2d, 88, 116, 126, 127.
Shepard, Thomas, 3d, 88.
Shepard, William, 12.
Sherman, John, 97.
Singing, how conducted in 1640, 42, — in 1817, 186.
Skelton, Samuel, 4.
Society of Christian Brethren, meet at the house of Dr. Holmes, 210.
Sparhawke, Esther, 37.
Sternhold and Hopkins's version of the Psalms, 42, 43.
Stickney, Nathaniel N., 256.
Stiles, President, 170, 212.
Stoddard, Solomon, 116.
Store, John, 129, 265.
Stone, Samuel, 8, 10, 15, 18, 26.
Stoughton, William, 116, 120.
Stowe, Calvin E., 220.
Strafford, 25.
Synod, the first in America, meets here, 56; of 1648, 64.
Taylor, John, 122.
Taylor, Samuel H., 63.
Tauteville, Margaret, 51.
Teacher, 35.
Tenney, Miss Hannah, 180.
Tithing-man, 37.
Unitarianism, 189.
Unitarian Association formed, 189.
Vane, Henry, 24, 26, 55, 56, 118.
Wadsworth, President, 146.
Walton, John, 175.
Warland, Owen, 171.
Washington, 154, 160.
Weld, 16, 18.
Wendell, Jacob, 152.
Wendell, Oliver, 215.
Whalley and Goffe, 118.
Whitefield, George, 162.
Whitman, Ephraim P., 256.
Wigglesworth, Michael, 116.
Willard, President, 171.
Willard, Samuel, 116, 135.
Williams, Roger, 28.
Willoughby, Francis, 97.
Wilson, John, 26, 55, 56.
Winship, Edward, 29.
Winship, Joanna, 29.
Winthrop, John, 6, 24, 26, 55, 56.
Wiswall, Elder, 115.
Wyeth, Benjamin F., 256.

Cambridge: Printed by Welch, Bigelow, and Company.

www.ingramcontent.com/pod-product-compliance
Lightning Source LLC
Chambersburg PA
CBHW022103230426
43672CB00008B/1265